江苏"道德发展智库"成果
江苏"2011计划""公民道德与社会风尚协同创新中心"成果
"道德国情与道德哲学前沿"江苏高校优秀创新团队成果

"古典今读《道德经》及四书"研讨会议,
承古典精华基金及圆玄学院汤伟奇主席鼎力资助,
弘扬文教,谨致谢忱。

古典今读（第三辑）

《论语》英文篇

THE FORM ON NEW INTERPRETATION OF CLASSICS:
THE ENGLISH VERSION OF *LUNYU*

杜祖贻 姚新中 樊 浩 主编
尹 洁 蒋天蝉 执行主编

中国社会科学出版社

图书在版编目(CIP)数据

古典今读.第3辑,《论语》英文篇/杜祖贻等主编.—北京:
中国社会科学出版社,2017.8
ISBN 978-7-5203-0157-2

Ⅰ.①古… Ⅱ.①杜… Ⅲ.①儒家②《论语》—英文
Ⅳ.①B222.21

中国版本图书馆 CIP 数据核字(2017)第 074532 号

出 版 人　赵剑英
责任编辑　张　林
特约编辑　文一鸥
责任校对　许　敏
责任印制　戴　宽

出　　版　中国社会科学出版社
社　　址　北京鼓楼西大街甲 158 号
邮　　编　100720
网　　址　http://www.csspw.cn
发 行 部　010-84083685
门 市 部　010-84029450
经　　销　新华书店及其他书店

印刷装订　北京君升印刷有限公司
版　　次　2017 年 8 月第 1 版
印　　次　2017 年 8 月第 1 次印刷

开　　本　710×1000　1/16
印　　张　20.25
插　　页　2
字　　数　316 千字
定　　价　88.00 元

序　一

习古典文献瑰宝，建现代文化大国

杜祖贻

"古典今读名家论坛道德经论语合集"付梓之时，正是国家领导人宣布重建中华文化大国之日，这是何等使人高兴的事。本书的出版，也就是作者们对这个期待已久的号召的响应。

自从改革开放，百废待举，全国上下，协力同心，进步一日千里。东南大学樊和平教授、伦敦大学姚新中教授及香港中文大学杜祖贻教授，应声气求，认为中华民族的的古典文艺，历千古而常今，既是中国文化的本体，也是世界文明的台柱，于是合作筹备"古典今读名家论坛学术会议"，提倡重新研习传统典籍的瑰宝，从而建立现代教育的根基：识古方可知今，继往始能开来，这是历史长流显示的道理。古典论坛的计划甫出，便得到各地学者的热烈响应和香港古典精华基金及圆玄学院的慷慨赞助，于是这个意义重大的学术年会遂告开始。

第一届会议于 2009 年 12 月在南京东南大学人文学院举行。由院长樊和平教授主持。大会的主题是老子《道德经》的原典。来自海内外发表论文或纲要的学者共 37 人，参加研讨的年青学员亦甚众。会议分节依次举行，计为经天纬地、经籍笺诂、经典纵横、经典释文、经传释词、经世致用及经义杂感七项。

第二届会议于 2010 年 10 月在英国伦敦大学国王学院举行，由中国研究中心主任姚新中教授主持。大会的主题是孔子《论语》的原典。这次会议的国际成分较多，出席的学者专家来自中国内地、台湾和香港,以及英、德、荷、美各地的学府,提交的论文或纲要 31 种。计分论语总论、语文诠释、伦理道德、政治社会、宇宙宗教等课题。

两届会议的过程热烈而融洽。由于主题明确集中,交流切磋的环境特别理想。参加的学者都带来其本人的力作,对《道德经》和《论语》的内容、思想、方法与意义,颇多创新阐发;会后再经修订,辑成此集。

《道德经》所蕴藏的洞察与睿智,堪称中外贤哲的先导。"无,万物之始……"的宇宙观和"一生二、二生三、三生万物……"的生物观,与两千多年后今天的科学天文学和进化论若合符节;道家的自然主义对中国的文学、医药、艺术、军事和科技深远的影响,固不待言。至于《论语》的人本哲学对中国的社会、政治、道德、伦理、心理和教育的整体融会,也是众所共知的。现将两届古典今读论坛所得的成绩,出版流播,弘扬国粹,为中华文化的复兴与文化大国的重建,共效绵力,这是作者和编辑们的共愿。

于此谨向香港圆玄学院和古典精华基金的赞助致谢。

2011 年 12 月于香港中文大学

序　二

古典第三"解"："和解"

樊　浩

如何解读古典，在当今中国已经成为学界和社会大众共同关注的问题。

无疑，古典是文本的一种，适用文本解读的理论与方法，但古典又是一种特殊的文本。一方面，古典之为古典，在于它已经不是少数专家或知识精英的专利品，而是大众共飨的圣餐，不仅拥有广泛的解读主体，而且可能因人因时因地获得不同的意义赋予；另一方面，古典解读之于一般文本的特殊性在于，因为是创生它的那个民族的话语符号与精神血脉，对它的任何误读与谬解都可能引发文化异化。科学"解释"的严格性和精神"理解"的广泛包容与不断的意义接纳，构成古典的自我坚持与生命绵延的两个不可或缺的构造。古典之为古典，不是因为它与生俱来的永垂不朽，而是接受与解读中与时俱进的生命赋予，无数的"今"构成古典之永恒生命与不易元色，在这个意义上，对于古典的任何解读，都是"今"读，也只能是"今"读，重要的是，必须在商谈对话中"今"读。现代解释学对传统解释学的重大推进，是在"含义"的"解释"之外提供了"第二解"，即"意义"的"理解"；当代多元文化背景下对于古典这一特殊文本的解读，应该也必须进行现代解释学的新推进，探索"解释"与"理解"的"二解"，以及多元主体的"诸解"达致共和的"第三解"，即"和解"。发展了的伽达默尔的"精神科学"，是古典"第三者"的可能哲学形态。

一 "解释"与"理解"的"二'解'纠结"

诚如一般文本一样，古典解读总处于"解释"与"理解"的纠结之中。

1960 年，伽达默尔出版《真理与方法》，提出文本解读或诠释学的一个具有标志意义的概念："精神科学"，试图颠覆科学主义与理性主义的现代性传统。他在导言的开卷便提出现代诠释学的一个基本立论："理解本文和解释本文不仅是科学深为关切的事情，而且也显然属于人类的整个世界经验。"[①] 这部现代诠释学的代表作被认为展现了西方人文主义的现代复苏和走向 21 世纪的活力，它宣示："真理不能用科学方法来界定，而必须表现在历史、艺术与哲学的主体活动中。"这本书的问世引发了关于文本或本文解读的巨大争论，并在争论中形成两大立场：一是对科学方法论和理性主义的坚持，以及对"精神科学"可能引发的主观主义和相对主义的预警；二是解构主义和后现代主义对思想对话和整体重建的坚持，以及对现代性和一元主义的批判。[②]

现代诠释学的诞生背景注定了它几乎不可避免地陷入科学与人文的矛盾，这一矛盾的概念话语以及对文本解读的复杂影响，集中表现为"解释"与"理解"的"二解"纠结。

文本解读的纠结，展现为现代解释学的三组相对的概念。

"含义"与"意义"。美国解释学家赫施在《解释的有效性》中，提出了"含义"与"意味"即"意义"的区别问题，努力捍卫解释的客观主义精神。在他看来，"含义"是文本符号的本意，而"意义"则发生于解释读者与文本的关系之中。"含义存在于作者用一系列符号所要表达的事物中……而意义则是指含义与某个人、某个系统、某个情境

---

① ［德］汉斯·格奥尔格·伽达默尔：《真理与方法》，洪汉鼎译，上海译文出版社 1999 年版，第 17 页。

② 参见成中英主编《本体与诠释》，生活·读书·新知三联书店 2000 年版，第 1 页。

或某个完全任意的事物之间的关系。"① 在他看来，文本的"含义"是确定的，而"意义"则处于变动不居的历史演进中。"作者对其文本所作的新理解虽然改变了文本的意义，但却并没有改变文本的含义。"② "只有含义本身是不变的，才会有客观性存在。"③

"解释"与"理解"。"理解"是现代解释学的核心概念之一。"理解"与"解释"、"释义"的区分，是解释学由传统的考据学发展为现代解释学的重要理论推进。"理解"把握的不是文本的"含义"，而是"意义"。"理解""不仅仅意味着对作者意指含义的把握，而且也意味着对含义是如何与作者的世界或我们自身的世界相吻合的这个事实的把握"④。"理解"本质上是一种意义赋予，"解释"是一种认知，但对意义的把握同样属于真正的认识，伽达默尔认为，理解不仅先于解释，而且先于判断。正如狄尔泰所说："一切理解都包含着释义。"⑤

"自我理解"与"偏见"。利科尔有一个著名论断："文本是我们通过它来理解我们自己的中介。""理解就是在文本面前理解自我。它不是一个把我们有限的理解能力强加给文本的问题，而是一个把我们自己暴露在文本之上并从它那里得到一个放大了的自我。"⑥ 海德格尔和伽达默尔极力为"偏见"或"先见"的合法性辩护。他们认为，偏见是人在历史中的存在状态，历史中的人及其理性不可能摆脱偏见。海德格尔认为，任何理解的先决条件都由三方面的存在状态构成："一是'先有'（Vorhabe）。人必须存在于一个文化中，历史与文化先占有了我们，而不是我们先占有了历史与文化。这种存在在上的'先有'使我们有可能理解自己和文化；二是'先见'（Vorsicht）。'先见'是指我

---

① ［美］赫施：《解释的有效性》，王才译，生活·读书·新知三联书店 1991 年版，第 2 页。

② 同上书，第 3 页。

③ 转引自［美］D.C.霍埃《批评的循环》，兰金仁译，辽宁人民出版社 1987 年版，第 15 页。

④ ［美］赫施：《解释的有效性》，王才译，生活·读书·新知三联书店 1991 年版，第 164 页。

⑤ 转引自［美］D.C.霍埃《批评的循环》，兰金仁译，辽宁人民出版社 1987 年版，第 65 页。

⑥ ［法］保罗·利科尔：《解释学与人文科学》，河北人民出版社 1987 年版，第 146、147 页。

们思考任何问题所要利用的语言、观念及语言的方式；三是'先知'（Vorgriff）。'先知'是指我们在理解前已具有的观念、前提和假定等。"① 他将"先有"、"先知"、"先见"统称为"偏见"，认为它是历史赋予的，人无法进行选择，它们是历史与传统为个人提供的理解的存在背景，也是个人理解活动的起点。

现代解释学虽然学派众多，但以下四方面是给现代人的文本解读产生深刻影响的共通的理论元素。（1）对文本解读来说，最重要的不是字面"含义"，而是隐藏于文字语言背后、作为文本实质的"意义"。它既是文本的精髓所在，也是文本对现实最为深刻的影响所在。（2）"意义"不能通过"解释"获得，只能借助"理解"获得。"解释"只能了解文本的"含义"，"理解"才能把握文本的"意义"。（3）"理解"不只是达到真理的一种方法，而且是主体的存在方式，对整个人类的"自我理解"来说，它是历史的存在方式。理解者和历史本身对文本解读具有前提性意义，因而最基本的理解是主体的自我理解，自我理解是主体对人生、对自己的历史、对自己生存于其中的文化的自我理解。（4）正因为如此，"偏见"或"先见"，或者说"前理解"对于理解不仅是不可避免的，而且是必然的和合法的，因为主体不可能也不应当摆脱"偏见"或"先见"的影响。如果将以上基本要素加以整合，那么可能得出的结论是：解释学从根本上说就是"理解学"。

现代解释学对文本解读的深刻意义，不在于其理论本身，而且于它所进行的具有某种革命意义的转向，在于这一转向所体现的现代人、现代文明对文本解读的忠实和创新的双重诉求。很难有足够的证据说明伽达默尔所开辟的现代诠释学试图与科学主义、理性主义彻底告别，比较审慎的判断，也许是它试图矫正和超越解释的现代性，使之回归人文主义，建立文本解读的"精神科学"。对"含义"与"解释"的肯定，就是对于解释的客观性，对科学性和理性主义的某种的承认，其革命性在于，它凸显解读的主体性和历史情境，在对"理解"的建构中，不仅赋予文本以新的时代活力，也对解读过程中主体的创造性予以承认和鼓励。它对"含义"及其"解释"，以及由此体现的科学主义的诉求有

① 参见殷鼎《理解的命运》，生活·读书·新知三联书店1988年版，第254—255页。

限的承认，但将更大的热情和努力付诸主体与文本建构"理解"关系中的"意义"赋予和创造性的活力。但是，也正因为如此，不仅解释学，而且现代人的文本解读，似乎总是落入"含义"与"意义"的纠结之中。一方面，无论科学和理性的追求如何执著，人们无论如何无法证明文本"含义"的"解释"是否真的客观或达到真理，而且，由于任何文本都是在特定的历史情境中发生和建构的，不仅语言而且指谓都有其特殊的历史时空，因而即使把握了文本的"真义"，达到文本的解读的"真理"或所谓客观知识，也只是进行某种知识与理论的还原，在这种还原中，人们只是回到历史，而回到历史很可能只是流连于一个往昔的时空，而失去现时代的立足点，更难以开辟未来，这便是所谓的"泥古"。而更多的情况是，由于语言只是一种表达真理、呈现自我的符号，对于那些终极性的真理，语言往往无能为力，所谓"道可道，非常道；名可名，非常名。道不可道，名不可名"。而且，即便身处现实的语言环境，"含义"本身也并不总可把握，孔子在给学生授课时常说"吾欲无语"，学生对此不解，"夫子无语，小子何学焉？"于是，孔子总是以"天何言哉"启发。皇天无语，但油然作雨，沛然作风，对天的理解，只能在敬畏中体悟，而体悟便是"自我主体"的"意义""理解"。由此，对于文本的解读，至少对于人文社会科学的文本解读，科学与理性，不仅内在着之于终极真理的某种极限，而且本身就是一种局限甚至缺陷。然而，另一方面，如果没有对于文本"含义"的"解释"，如果缺失解释的基本客观性，文本事实上就成了"任人打扮的小姑娘"，成为主体"理解"和"意义"赋予的触发器，于是，在相对主义与主观主义的臆测中，不仅文本失去存在的真正意义，而且更重要的后果是，文本，尤其是经典文本所承载的历史创造和文明延续性都将遗失和断裂，必然的情形和要求是：每一代人、每一个人都另起炉灶，重新创造文明和历史。无疑，它不仅不可能，而且即便假设新一代人的创造性足够强大，主体也将是彻底失忆缺乏时间概念的"飘忽幽灵"。

要之，现代解释学抓住文本解读的核心问题，作出了创造性贡献，它发现并揭示，文本解读可能是一个二元方程，而不是传统解释学那样的一元方程。文本同时存在两个"解"；一是"解释"之"解"；一是"理解"之"解"。它留给我们的课题是：无论其理论如何精微和智慧，却总是难以摆脱并深深陷入"解释"和"理解"的"二解"纠结。

二 诸"解"共和："和解"

如何走出"二解纠结"？必须在"解释"和"理解"之上寻找新"解"。

一般说来，文本解读及其真理性问题，发生于第二种信息方式时代。马克·波斯特曾提出一种理论，认为人类文明发展的基础和标志，并不是马克思所说的生产方式，而是信息方式。迄今为止的人类文明经历了三种信息方式。口口交流的信息方式；以印刷术产生为标志的信息方式；当今的电子信息方式。第一种信息方式的特点是口口交流，在信息产生之初，交流的双方都在场，然后通过口口相传，信息得以扩展和交换。印刷术的产生标志着第二种信息方式的产生。在这种信息交换中，往往只是阅读者在场，而信息生产者则以特殊的方式即语言文本出场。这种固化了但又不对称的信息生产和交换方式，为文本的含义解释与意义理解留下广阔的空间，同时也为跨时空的信息交流提供可能，借此，现代人可以与两千多年前的孔子对话。第三种信息方式不仅改变了文本的存在形态，也根本改变了文本的性质，最明显的是，它使文本从一部分人或所谓知识分子的专利，成为大众产品，甚至成为工业产品。孔子处于第一种信息方式与第二种信息方式的转换点上。他的最大的也是后人不可超越的贡献，就是将第一种信息方式时代那些口口相传的文化，转化为文字记载或通过印刷相互交换的固化成果，从而在信息方式的革命性转换中承上启下，由此文本诞生了，文本解读的难题也随之出现。《诗经》、《春秋》等都是第二种信息方式的第一批革命性成就，它们是具有文明标志意义的文本。孔子自谕"述而不作"，但又说"温故知新"。直觉中似乎相互矛盾的这两个命题不仅传递了孔子面对他以前的那个人类孩提时代也是最为漫长的人类文明时代所锤炼的知识与学问的敬畏和谦恭，也以最为传统的话语中国式地表达了他所体悟的在自己亲自创造的文本中的解读矛盾。如果用现代解释学的话语表述，"述而不作"是"含义""解释"，"温故知新"则是"意义理解"。之于第一个方面，孔子"敏而好学"，"入太庙，每事问"，试图了解作为他那个时代最重要的历史文本和最大学问的"礼"的真义，孔子向老子问礼这个令后来儒家在道家面前被动的史实就是最典型的说明。但之于第二个方面，"温故而知新"这一中国解释学的古老教训至少包含两个内在精微差异的意义结构。第一个结构的重心是"温故"，鼓励人们"传而时习之"，弄懂文本的含义；第二个结构的重心是"知新"，其逻辑是"知新必须问故"，或者说"温故为了知新"，但无论如何，以知新为取向的温故已经突破"含义"，诉诸"意义"追求甚至"意义"创造。不过，如果将"温故而知新"作为中国传统解释学的古典命题，那么，在孔子那里，文本中的两个可能的"解"，即"解释"与"理解"是乐观而紧张地合为一体的。但是，即便对于"礼"，二"解"的统一是如此的大学问，以致孔子必须用一生的努力去追求，"十有五而有志于学，三十而立，四十而不惑，五十而知天命，六十而耳顺，七十而从心所欲不逾矩"。这个生命历程的解释学路径是：三十以前追求礼的含义，此后理解礼的意义，至七十才达到二"解"统一的自由境界。

如果假定解释和获得文本的含义和真义是可能的，那么一个努力便必不可少：进行文本话语的历史还原，即将文本还原到原初的历史、文化和话语情境中。于是，对于历史知识的确切把握，文化传统的追溯与理解能力便成为解释可靠性的基本条件，而文本形成的特殊的话语背景，似乎又因话语的特定情境而赋予文本以某种偶然性和不可公度性，进而使任何可能的解释都具有相对性。这一难题往往使诸多文本的解释成为聚讼对象。最典型的就是中国传统伦理中对于妇女的态度。孔子曾说"唯女子与小人难养也"。此句几成孔子歧视妇女的铁证。但在考证中也发生很大分歧。一种解释是，此句是孔子见南后被南后狐假虎威的特定语境下的有感而发；另一种解释是，这里的"女子"特指"妾"而非泛指；而新的发现是，此句是对春秋时代女性生活放荡，常见异思迁弃夫私奔的不良风尚的批评。但无论如何，说孔子此句将包括母亲在内的天下所有妇女骂倒似乎难以成立。因此，在难以形成统一的解释而且很可能产生文本冤案的情况下，贯通性的"理解"便特别需要了。另一个公案是，宋代竖贞节牌坊，宣扬"饿死事小，失节事大"，压制妇女人性。但有学者做过仔细考证，发现宋代贞节牌坊并不多，更重要的是，在宋代"悍妇"、"虐夫"的现象普遍，成语"河东狮吼"就出自宋代，最典型的就是文学家沈括长期受夫人虐待，常被夫人张氏揪胡须打得血肉模糊，当时对妇女的道德要求实际是对这一社会现象的纠偏，真正对妇女的禁锢是清代恶性发展的结果。无论这些考证是否属实，但它至少可以说明，在很多情况下，"含义"解释难以获得确切的知识或真理是事实，因为，历史还原、文化理解、话语情境，同样具有相对性甚至主观性。

文本尤其是古典文本的解读，一般有两种可能的情况：一是同质文化的解读；一是异质文化的解读。学术史表明，即便同一文化内部严格意义上的解读，其真理性也不仅有其限度，而且有很大的局限。最典型的是两汉经学。两汉经学试图对先秦尤其是儒家经典进行严格的解读，然而它不仅遭遇古文经与今文经两大内部分歧，而且经学发展的结果，是对思想和学术活力的严重禁锢。中国学术史上不乏解读古典的大师，王弼对《老子》的注疏，朱熹对《四书》的集注，不仅被奉为经典，而且成为学术典范甚至科举的标准答案。然而，不难发现，这些解释本身已经是一种再创造，其中最杰出的部分无不体现解释者本身的"前理解"。已有定论的是，朱熹的《四书集注》已经融会了道家与佛家的思想精粹，事实上已经是以《四书》为本文的再创造。或者说，不是严格意义上的"含义""解释"，而是"理解"的作品。

来自异质文化的解读更为特殊，因为它不仅包含解释主体迥然不同的"前理解"，而且遭遇人文社会科学理论移植的难题。本土化与国际化是人文社会科学的一个悖论。正如杜祖贻先生所言："根据过去的经验，移植和借用西学是已成的事实，借用所产生的效果不理想也是事实。于是怎样使源出西方的社会科学本土化便成为学者们所关切的问题。可是，这问题虽经多年的辩论，至今仍未越出学术观念的探讨和个人意见表达的范围。"[①] 事实上，即使在西方，也存在诸多学术传统，因而也形成解释与理解的同一性。美国学者威廉·韩思曾以西方哲学为例，指出它的两大分支：一是作为西方哲学主干的英语国家的传统；一

---

① 杜祖贻主编：《西方社会科学理论的移植与应用》，香港中文大学出版社1993年版，第33页。

是繁衍于欧洲大陆的大陆哲学传统，如德国、法国哲学。在欧美传统中，前者是"我们"，后者是"他们"。其不同特点是："他们经常使用刻意求新的语言，令许多英语哲学家感到极其费解、支吾晦涩，甚至不知所云，我们则试图使语言达到力所能及的高度明晰；他们更注重创造性，而我们更注重为论点提供明确的正当证据；最后，他们的传统明显地分成领袖和追随者，作为领袖的个人倾心于创造完整和富于革新性的思想体系，而我们的传统则力求设法提出各种各样相对独立的具体问题。"最令"我们"不服的是：大陆哲学家所代表的传统之实质价值与他们个人的名望之间名实难符。① 这些情况说明，无论我们认为在解释与理解、含义与意义，以及不同传统和同一传统内部的不同分枝之间存在多么深刻的分歧，无论它们如何格格不入，多元并存不仅是事实，不仅具有合法性，而且具有合理性和必然性。

以上分析引出的结论是：文本的解读并非只有一个"解"，也并非只有现代解释学所说的"解释"和"理解"，而是多"解"。文本尤其那些已经作为人类文明共同财富的古典文本，其"解"往往存在于两大基本关系中。一个是解读者与文本之间的对话关系；另一个也是特别重要的一个是解读者与解读者之间的主体际的对话关系。后一种关系可以产生超出主体与文本对话关系总和的"解"，因为不同主体，尤其是不同文化背景的解读主体之间的对话必定产生出新的"理解"。因此，文本解读是一个商谈过程。既是主体与文本之间的商谈，也是诸解读主体之间的商谈。由于文本解读尤其是那些作为传统表征的古典文本的解读，根本目的是透过解读，建构共识，凝结和巩固社会的文化同一性，使传统成为可能，也使合法性成为可能，因而诸多解读之间的商谈便不仅具有过程意义，而且具有深刻的目的意义。一些重要的解读共识形成的过程，就是合法建构的过程。所以，文本解读的求"解"，并不像现代解释学所说的那样，只是"理解"和"解释"的非此即彼，也不只有传统诠释学的"解释"和现代诠释学"理解"的二解，而是诸"解"的多元共和。也许人们已经习惯于用民主的逻辑进行文本解读的

---

① ［美］威廉·韩思：《伦理学：美国治学法》，孟悦译，社会科学文献出版社1994年版，第4页。

判断，诉诸社会或学者的认同度，然而不仅民主作为一种政治形态是否可以移植于学术与文化生活应当被质疑，且即使在政治生活中，民主是否是一种最好的形式，也值得反思。因为在民主之外，还有一种社会同一性的政治形式，这就是"共和"。相对于民主，共和不是数量的暴力，而是基于包容的相互承认。多"解"共和并不是相对主义，也不会由于解读的主观性导致文本的虚无，恰恰是文本生命力的多元展开，是多元主体在"温故知新"的文本解读中的对话、共识与创造。

诸解共和形成文本之解的第三种形态："和解"。"和解"不是相对主义，不是调和折中，而是超越"解释"与"理解"之上、具有最大包容性、基于相互承认的文本"第三解"，或"解"的第三种形态。"致中和，天地位焉，万物育焉。"① 当然，作为一种解读形态，它以主体与文本之间的和解，以解读的多元主体之间的和解，以"解释"与"理解"之间的和解，也以作为"解释"与"理解"哲学基础科学主义与人文主义之间的和解为条件和基本内容。在这个意义上，作为第三解的"和解"，既是一种当代文本解读形态，也应当成为一种当代学术气象和学术气派。

三 "和解"之"精神科学"

古典今读的难题在于：如何"出入文本"，在"解释"与"理解"、本原性的"含义"与建构性的"意义"之间保持合理的平衡？

这一难题展开为三个课题：其一，如何尊重文本的客观性，追求对文本的准确把握？否则，如果"一千个人心中有一千个哈姆雷特"，文本就成为"任人打扮的小姑娘"，于是，训诂、字义疏证、文化还原等便是不可缺或的基本方法，此为"入文本"；其二，如何由"温故"而"知新"，赋予文本以时代"意义"和生生不息的生命活力，否则文本便只是文化"遗存"，而不是活的传统，于是创造性的"理解"便成为必须，此为"出文本"；其三，如何透过"解释"和"理解"，达成文

---

① 《中庸》第一章。

本诠释的基本共识或同一性，包括跨文化解读的同一性，从而使古典成为文明合法性的建构性力量。三大课题的意义一言以蔽之：使古典成为传统。因为，传统之为传统，必须同时具备三个条件：历史上发生的、一以贯之的、在现实生活中发挥作用的。"入文本"尊重并还原古典的历史发生；"出文本"激活古典，使之成为交融于人的生命与生活的活传统；而解读共识与同一性的形成，其意义绝不只是知识的获取，精髓是在温故知新、推陈出新中使古典"一以贯之"并生生不息。因此，古典便承载着一般文本解读更多的文化与文明使命。古典应当"古读"，但又必须也只能"今读"。也许，本于"古读"，归于"今读"，是古典解读的特殊规律。

伽达默尔试图建立"精神科学"，以探讨诠释学对于真理的"理解"问题。他认为，"精神科学"与"自然科学"的不同在于，它不是一般的智力活动，而要求一种"机敏感"，并与独特的心理条件联在一起。"精神科学的推论方式是一种无意识的判断。因此精神科学的归纳程序与独特的心理条件联在一起，它要求有一种机敏感，并且又需要其他一些精神能力，如丰富的记忆和对权威的承认，反之，自然道学家的自觉推论则完全依赖于他自身的智力使用。"[1] 精神科学中的所谓"科学"就在于它的"机敏"，这种机敏因抵制对现代科学概念的顺应而成为一个哲学难题。他曾反问："精神科学中合乎科学的东西，是否最终就在于这种机敏而不在于它的方法论呢？"[2] 由于对自然科学的抵制，"精神科学"成为一种真正的人道主义。"实际上，精神科学根本不会认为自己单纯从属于自然科学。精神科学在对德国古典文学精神遗产的继承中，更多的是发展了一种真正的人道主义。"[3] 伽达默尔的"精神科学"并不能简单地等同于人文科学。在德国古典哲学中，"精神"始终是与"自然"相对立的概念，在黑格尔哲学中，"精神"超越"自然"，成为人、历史与世界的主体与本质。

在"精神科学"中，同样存在"精神"与"科学"之间"乐观的

---

① ［德］汉斯·格奥尔格·伽达默尔：《真理与方法》，洪汉鼎译，上海译文出版社1999年版，第5—6页。

② 同上书，第9页。

③ 同上书，第10页。

紧张"，但这种"科学"完全不同于"自然科学"的理性，而是作为人道主义表现的"机敏"。伽达默尔将这种"精神科学"的人道主义归结为四个主导的概念。（1）教化。"在教化概念里最明显地使人感觉到的，乃是一种极其深刻的哲学转变。""精神科学也是随着教化一起产生的，因为精神的存在是与教化观念本质上联系在一起的。"① （2）共通感。共通感即共同的感觉，即情感、判断和推理中的一致意见，作为一种人文主义传统，精神科学认为，凡与共通感相矛盾的东西就不能是正确的。（3）判断力。在德国古典哲学中，判断力的概念与共通感的概念紧密结合，它规定"健全的人类理智"或"共同的理智"。（4）趣味。伽达默尔认为，"趣味概念描述一种真正的人性理想"。它是一种社会现象，而不是个人偏好。"趣味概念无疑也包含认知方式。人们能对自己本身和个人偏爱保持距离，正是好的趣味的标志。因此按其最特有的本质来说，趣味丝毫不是个人的东西，而是第一级的社会现象。"趣味不同于并且扬弃时尚的偶然性。"趣味概念包含着：我们即使在时尚中也掌握尺度，不盲目跟随时尚的变化要求，而是使用我们自己的判断。"②教化、共通感、判断力、趣味，构成诠释学，也是文本解读的"精神科学"的四元素，既是其"精神"，也是其"科学"之所在。

无论人们对伽达默尔的解释学是否认同或在何种程度上认同，我们确实需要一种关于古典解读的"精神科学"。这种"精神科学"中的"科学"概念，与"自然科学"的"科学概念"或狭义的科学不同，毋宁说它是回归康德以前的大科学或所谓广义科学的概念。如果将伽达默尔的四要素作为现代解释学的结构性元素，那么，古典解读所需要的"精神科学"便需要以下哲学前提。其一，关于"传统"的身份认同。古典与其他文本不同，它不仅本身就是传统的一部分，而且是传统最自觉的承载与标志，乃至本身就是传统的言说，兼具"传"与"统"的双重本性，因此，共通感、判断力，还有与之相对应的教化，以及

---

① ［德］汉斯·格奥尔格·伽达默尔：《真理与方法》，洪汉鼎译，上海译文出版社1999年版，第11、14页。

② 同上书，第44、46、48页。

“作为第一等级的社会性”的趣味就是“理解”古典的前提。显然，人们解读古典之前，已经对它心怀敬意，而不只是当作知识的对象，理由很简单，它是“我们”或“他们”的“传统”。其二，“精神对话”。古典解读本质上是一种精神对话，既是解读者与文本，或今与古之间的精神对话，也是诸解读者之间的精神对话，乃至是不同文明之间的精神对话。精神对话跨越“自然”的个别性，在“教化”的“哲学转变”中达到和建立共同感与“共同的理智”。其三，“文化理解”。“精神科学”解读古典的过程，本质上是文化理解的过程，是现代文化与传统文化、中国文化与外国文化，以及同一文化内部不同文化取向的主体之间在商谈对话中相互理解的过程。经过哲学改造，伽达默尔的“精神科学”，可以成为以“和解”为核心概念的当代诠释学的当代形态，或者说，是“和解”的解释学形态。

“古典今读”是诠释学的“精神科学”的话语形态之一，其要义是在文化理解中“精神地”贯通古今。“古典今读”意味着在今天的历史情境和话语背景下解读和理解古典，使古典成为今天的“活”传统；也意味着多样性的意义赋予在回归根源传统的过程中“共通感”和“共同理智”的形成，进而是新的社会合法性的造就；它从根本上表达和表现的是对古典的尊敬——不只是一种态度，也是对文本客观性的追求。因此，古典今读是一种基于精神对话与文化理解的诠释学，它在根本上是一个多元多次方程，不仅因解释主体的不同“前理解”有众多的意义赋予，而且古典文本中的任何问题都可能多“解”，最后的结果往往是经过充分商谈对话的“和解”。在古典今读中，和解既是过程，也是目的，因为它在多解共和中不仅形成关于古典解读的共识，而且建构行为与文化的社会合法性，于是，不仅是古典的“传”与“统”，而且古典的现代意义也获得诠释和承认。在这个意义上，古典今读也是古与今，以及不同解读主体之间的相互承认。古典今读首先意味着基于对古典客观性充分尊重的基础上的多元解读的包容，毕竟，“今读”已经昭示着对古典解读的“现理解”和“前理解”的承认，它构成古典诠释的“趣味”，当然，这种“趣味”并不是主观“心得”的某种时尚。但是，今天的古典解读不仅不应该像两汉经学那样玩古与泥古，也不可能像朱熹《四书集注》那样，终结古典的解读。历史已经证明，任何解读的标准答案最后终结的是学术与思想的创造性活力。古典今读期待"精神科学"的共通感和文化合法性，但展示和创造的恰恰是对话商谈的多解共和。

2008 年秋，我在与美国密西根大学杜祖贻教授交流时，谈及目前国内"国学热"中的种种问题，以及 19 世纪末他所发起的关于社会科学移植问题的讨论时，感到有必要也有责任进行关于古典解读的某种努力，于是确定以"古典今读"为主题（注："古典今读"的概念系杜先生提出），推动古典的积极传播与合理理解。这一动议得到英国伦敦国王学院中国研究中心主任姚新中教授的支持。于是，三人商定以东南大学、美国密西根大学、英国伦敦国王学院、香港中文大学（杜祖贻教授系该校讲座教授）四校学者合作的名义，共同发起"'古典今读'名家论坛"。计划的基本内容是：每年确定一本经典，在世界范围内邀请对于这一经典最有研究的学者参加会议，以多种形式对它进行研究和讨论。论坛以多学科、多文化交叉为目标，在广邀名家的同时，吸收一部分视角独特、思想敏锐的青年学者包括博士生、硕士生参加。研讨活动向学生全线开放。2009 年 12 月，在东南大学举行了第一次活动，主题是"《道德经》名家论坛"。大会发言在图书馆可容 600 多人的报告厅举行，学生广泛参与，大会之后学者就感兴趣的问题个别交流。第二次论坛于 2010 年 10 月在英国伦敦国王学院举行，主题是"《论语》名家论坛"，来自中国、美国、英国、比利时等国的诸多著名汉学家参加了会议。两次论坛，尤其是第二次论坛中关于解读力法的分歧乃至论争凸显，虽然因语言、时间等原因，交流难以充分和深入，但古与今、解释与理解的趣味迥异，表面无"果"，实际以"和解"而成其"正果"。两次论坛，积累了一些经验，更重要的是，这种尝试已经展示了它的魅力与意义，相信在不断改善中今后将会取得更多的收获。为记载两次论坛学者的成果，我们将与会学者的论文，包括部分与会青年学者和研究生的论文集册出版，以感谢同仁们的努力，也为今后的进一步研究提供文本。需要说明的是，第一次论坛中有数位学者到会作报告，因未及提交论文，灼见在文集中未能体现，实为遗憾，敬请谅恕。

CONTENTS

Morality and Re-interpretation of Belief

Wisdom and Modern Connotation

The Forum on New Interpretation of Classics:
the English version If *Lunyu*

Language and Text

The English-language Analects and Teaching Chinese Studies: Some Reflections on Lesser-known Twentieth Century Translations

T. H. Barrett SOAS(London)

The education system in our country, and no doubt to a greater or lesser degree in others, is failing to cope with the peaceful rise of China to resume the place of global importance that it once held in the somewhat narrower world of times past. The problem is not with the teaching of the Chinese language, but with finding the forms of education that manage to convey exactly what sort of a nation China is. Other nations can and sometimes still do orient themselves towards some past heritage, and fancy themselves the new Rome, or the new Byzantium, or the potential builders of the New Jerusalem. But these fancies are not here, at least, embodied in the educational system. Yet the new China is still in terms of rightful heritage quite simply the old China, and the education system anywhere Chinese has the right, or perhaps even the obligation, to convey that truth, with the result that anyone identifying themselves as Chinese senses some connection with a continuous heritage stretching back far into the past. This remains true even if participation in the global community continues to be a priority for all Chinese intellectuals. Even if they do not choose to draw upon their heritage at all (which does not seem to be exactly the case), the potential remains as a marker of difference from those who look to other heritages.

This is certainly very difficult for most English speakers to grasp. Our language may take us back to Shakespeare—though even his language defeats many schoolchildren today—but not much further, while our school history curriculum, at any rate in England, has given up even on its traditional task of covering the last millennium as a coherent unit, and if this trend is reversed, as seems possible, that still gives a much foreshortened view of history by Chinese standards. The idea of an ancient heritage at some far away point in the past is easy enough to convey, but thinking over a longer continuous span, ' from Plato to NATO', is something that seems far too challenging for schools and is usually deferred to the university level, if students are asked to engage with it at all. Besides, the only area where a truly ancient heritage remains meaningful—and then only to some—is probably in the sphere of religion, where the Judaeo-Christian tradition foregrounds texts as ancient as those that are available in Chinese. Hence there are possibilities of communication, and my friend, Professor Yao, has done much himself to explore the comparative approach to Chinese and early Judaeo-Christian thought. ①To the historian, however, the dissimilarities remain important, and very difficult to convey. For example, unless we happen to possess a good command of Hebrew and New Testament Greek, the Bible is always going to be something we approach in translation, within the short span of the history of modern English. By contrast, while it takes as much scholarship to read the Analects well, anyone Chinese will be able to find many phrases in the original that have remained part of the spoken language today.

And to the historian, it is not just then and now that is the problem: it is the years in between, when the Analects was always present to be re-read in a way that no one textual version of the Bible, not even the Vulgate, has been

①   Please see Xinzhong Yao's *Wisdom in Early Confucian and Israelite Traditions* (Aldershot: Ashgate, 2006), which would be a fine example of the sort of work that is possible in this field.

for so long and so widely. Obviously there are books now even in English on the history of the interpretation of *the Analects*, just as there are histories of Biblical interpretation. ①But they are works for scholars. And the basic problem in today's world is that a sense of how China draws its strength from depth in time is not something that just scholars need to know, but all men and women who wish to consider themselves educated. Thinking about this, after in the past trying to incorporate historical narratives of interpretation into my own specialized teaching, it seems to me that at least the history of the Analects in the English language itself is now lengthy enough to offer a few opportunities.

The full story of translating *the Analects* and British scholarship goes back at least to the efforts of Joshua Marshman (1768-1837) in the early nineteenth century, but any broader history of scholarship for present purposes concerns me less than the history of reading the Analects. This topic, too, I do not propose to cover in a comprehensive way, even while merely confining myself to the century before the present one, since in the last few years of the twentieth century a good number of worthwhile new renderings of Confucius have seen the light of day, and no doubt in due course it will become clear which of these show sufficient merit to be reprinted over the course of time. But if asked, as matters stand at the moment, to name the three most prominent translators of the Analects into English of the twentieth century from the point of view of readership rather than scholarship, I would have to list—and would not be alone in this country in listing—James Legge (1815 – 1895), Arthur Waley (1889 – 1966) and D. C. Lau (1921 – 2010). ②

The first might seem to be ruled out as a twentieth century translator,

---

① Notably John Makeham, *Transmitters and Creators: Chinese Commentators and Commentary on the Analects* (Cambridge, MA: Harvard University Press, 2003), though this very useful work does not aim to be comprehensive.

② Raymond Dawson, *The Analects* (Oxford: Oxford University Press, 1993), p. xxxiii, commends the same three predecessors that I have selected.

given the date of his death, but the printing of his version as part of a bilingual edition containing the original text has meant that he has been kept in print in East Asia, legally or illegally, for decades, and has therefore, especially since the expiry of the legal copyright of his translation, become a favourite source for those who wish to present *the Analects* or parts of it in an attractive format without the trouble of having to translate it themselves. This phenomenon admittedly is much worse in the case of *the Daode jing*, but it certainly does occur. ①Nothing like this refashioning has happened in the case of Arthur Waley's Analects, perhaps because of copyright barriers. But in any case he deserves a mention as the only figure so far whose literary talent has secured a listing of the Analects in general accounts of the history of English literature. ②His Confucius would no doubt have been printed more frequently in the late twentieth century were it not for the appearance in 1979 of the D. C. Lau version in the Penguin Classics series, based on a further four decades of modern scholarship. As recent obituaries for Professor Lau have stressed, too, few have been more concerned with shades of meaning in both Chinese and English than he, even if Arthur Waley, an inhabitant of the Bloomsbury environment more comfortably at home there than any mere academic, had more of a literary impact across his various publications. ③

So, the mainstream is easy enough to trace. What is more intriguing is the variety of illustrations of the theme of the strange individual destinies that

---

① A good example is James Legge, selected and edited by Peg Streep, with watercolours by Claudia Karabaic Sargent, *Confucius: The Wisdom* (Boston, New York Toronto and London: Bullfinch Press, 1995), the jacket of which bears the helpful notation for the potential purchaser ' A Spiritual Classic' and, for the bookseller, ' Inspiration/Gift'.

② As witness, for example, Dorothy Eagle, ed., *The Concise Dictionary of English Literature*, second ed., (Oxford: Oxford University Press, 1970), p. 603. Waley's *Analects* has, of course, been reprinted on occasion, e. g. by Vintage Books, New York, in 1961; it was also translated into Dutch in 1946: cf. Francis A, Johns, *A Bibliography of Arthur Waley*, Revised and Expanded edition (London: The Athone Press, 1988), pp. 52 – 3.

③ Two obituaries by native speakers of English that testify eloquently to Lau's precision in matters of translation, by Hugh Baker and Roger Ames, may be found in the *Journal of Chinese Studies* 51 (July, 2010), pp. 12 – 18.

befall books which emerge when we look beyond that mainstream to the
eddying side currents of British Analects scholarship. Here obscurity and
prominence, oblivion and acceptance, even within less than a century of
time, alternate in a much more complex way. Of course during the half
millennium or so of English literary history many books and writers have sunk
from sight and then been rediscovered. But by dwelling briefly on how
translations of an ancient Chinese text have fared in this respect over a
relatively short span of time might perhaps help us to consider how similar
processes of transmission and retrieval were played out over the more than five
times greater span of Chinese literary history.

The first example that I would like to introduce is that of a work plucked
from extreme obscurity after a quarter of a century to become in a new guise a
presentation of Confucius that achieved international renown, selling for over
two decades thereafter before seeing at least one further reprinting in the late
twentieth century, thanks in part (or so it would seem) to the very Confucian
virtue of filial piety. ① *The Analects* as translated by William Soothill (1861 –
1935) was first published some years before the start of his British academic
career as an Oxford professor, while he was still a missionary educator in East
Asia. His attempts at improving on James Legge's pioneering efforts included a
scholarly presentation of the original Chinese, since this was not a publishing
problem in Yokohama in 1910. But such a work, though now still available in
specialist libraries, was scarcely seeking a mass market and certainly does not
seem to have found one. Only after the translator's death in the nineteen
thirties did Oxford University Press look for an English version of Confucius to

---

①   According to the bibliography by Joel Sahleen in Bryan W. Van Norden, *Confucius and the
Analects: New Essays* (Oxford: Oxford University Press, 2002), p. 213, Soothill's translation was
republished by Dover in Mineola, NY, in 1995, but I have not seen this reprint. Sahleen's
bibliography, which runs to eighteen pages, lists *inter alia* most of the new translations of the late
twentieth century, often with references to relevant book reviews also. For useful discussions of *Analects*
translation, see the articles listed here by Durrant, Eoyang, Leslie and Taam; Anne Cheng also has an
important survey in *Revue Bibliographique de Sinologie*, n. s. XVII, (1999), pp. 471 – 479, that
Sahleen does not include.

include in their World's Classics series, and it seems that they turned for help therefore to one of Britain's best-known writers on China of that period, Lady Dorothy Hosie (1885 – 1959), widow of the China explorer Sir Alexander Hosie (1853 – 1925) and, as it happened, daughter of Professor Soothill. Her drastically modified version of her father's work contains no Chinese text but does include an introductory essay on Confucius, quite free from the burden of any academic annotation, from her own hand. ①As an educator, no doubt Soothill would have approved of his daughter's work; as a scholar, he may have blushed a little. It was, at any rate, only in 1993 that his university managed to replace his daughter's work with a decent substitute from one of its own teachers, someone who incidentally combined his sinology with a long and distinguished career as deviser of crossword puzzles for the New Statesman, Raymond Dawson (1923 – 2002).

My next example, from one of the most famous filial sons in British sinology, followed a slightly different course: from prominence to intriguing, even tasteful obscurity. The Wisdom of the East series initiated by Launcelot Cranmer-Byng (1872 – 1945) in a convenient format that has kept many of its volumes in print through the publisher John Murray for much of the twentieth century, dates back to the first decade of the century. For a version of Confucius highlighting most of his wisdom without baffling the English reader too much the series editor turned to Lionel Giles (1873 – 1958), son of the Cambridge professor of Chinese, Herbert Giles (1845 – 1935), who duly turned in a small book of translations from *the Analects*, arranged thematically rather than in the conventional order, in 1907. ②It may be

---

① I have consulted this work, William Edward Soothill, *The Analects, or The Conversations of Confucius with his Disciples and Certain Others* (London: Oxford University Press, 1937) in a printing of 1958 that lists six other printings up to that point since the first Oxford edition.

② Lionel Giles, *The Sayings of Confucius; A New Translation of the Greater Part of the Confucian Analects* (London: John Murray, 1907), pp. 10 – 13, 20 – 36, as John Minford (see below) recognises, takes to task Victorian translators (including Legge) more for their inaccurate comparisons of Confucianism and Christianity than on literary or philological grounds, but this in itself marked a major step forward in British *Analects* scholarship.

remarked in passing that such attempts at helping Confucius to express
himself by reordering his thoughts set something of a precedent for many later
translators and anthologists. ①Perhaps this reordering helped to keep John
Murray busy reprinting this version of *the Analects* from time to time until
after the Second World War. But it also seems to have attracted attention from
another quarter.

In 1933 the Limited Editions Club, a business based on a publishing
philosophy quite different from that which inspired either the World's Classics
or the Wisdom of the East series, included the Lionel Giles translation as the
forty-second of its titles, in the fourth series of its issues. The Club was
founded in 1929 by George Macy (1900 – 1956), and never produced more
than one thousand five hundred copies of any of its editions. ② For its luxury
version of the English Analects the Club resorted to the Commercial Press of
Shanghai, who—without mentioning the John Murray original in any way—
reproduced for the most part the contents of the 1907 work reincarnated in
traditional Chinese threaded binding, complete with a wooden box as a cover,
bearing the title in English and Chinese. Within the work itself no use seems
to have been made of the opportunity to use Chinese characters, so the
reasons for resorting to the Commercial Press, if not connected to copyright
questions, seems mainly to have been prompted by a somewhat whimsical
desire to produce a China-related title in a Chinese format. Giles does however
seem to have taken this opportunity to extend the scope of his translation and

---

① Apart from the editor of Legge mentioned above, one might mention Thomas Cleary, *The
Essential Confucius: The Heart of Confucius' Teachings in Authentic I Ching Order* (New York:
HarperCollins, 1992); I am not sure what ' authentic' means in this context. It cannot be denied that
some reordering illustrating the different layers of material in the *Analects* would be helpful, but one
fears that universal or even substantial agreement on the sort of analysis boldly demonstrated by E.
Bruce and Taeko Brooks, *The Original Analects* (New York: Columbia University Press, 1998), may
take some time to emerge.

② This information derives from http://www. majure. net/lechistory. htm, accessed 28
September 2010, Bill R. Majure, "A Brief History of the Limited Editions Club", which cites a
number of sources.

to add some other useful features to his earlier work. ①

Nothing stranger, surely, has happened to an English version of Confucius in the twentieth century. But we cannot even so be sure that nothing stranger will ever happen to a twentieth century English translation of *the Analects*, since we cannot be sure that the story of these translations has reached an end. The achievements of Lionel Giles, indeed, form a case in point. One would imagine that his scholarship would be by now well past its sell-by date, especially since he was the product not of a modern university education in Chinese Studies but of the amateur, largely self-taught period in British sinology that started before university degrees in Chinese were ever contemplated. Even so, his work has attracted the warmest praise from John Minford in the context of the Australia-based movement to reassess our studies of China known as the 'New Sinology'. ② Admittedly this reassessment is primarily designed to introduce to a new readership his translation of Sunzi, which is somewhat more carefully wrought than his digest of *the Analects* for a popular and easily affordable series, but the assessment he gives in his introduction of James Legge's approach to Confucius is never the less quoted by Minford with full approval. Is it possible that Lionel Giles on *the Analects* will be read with close attention again in the twenty-first century, leading to dusty copies of the John Murray volume, or even of the Commercial Press edition, being retrieved from library shelves once more?

---

① The title page to this edition, Lionel Giles, *The Analects of Confucius* (Shanghai: Printed for Members of the Limited Editions Club by the Commercial Press, 1933) removes the information, given in the original edition from John Murray, that the translation is only partial, and though I have not checked systematically, it may well be that the various added sayings incorporated by Giles into this version amount to a complete coverage of the original text. The title page is, moreover, followed by four illustrations: of Confucius, of two views of his temple, and of his tomb. The repagination of the original material has resulted in changes all the footnotes cross-referencing to other pages of the book, and Giles as a result seems to have used the opportunity to expand the number of the footnotes also. Very helpful marginal indications of the sources of the sayings by 'chapter and verse' within the *Analects* are added throughout.

② http://www. chinaheritagequarterly. org/articles. php? searchterm = 013 _ giles. inc&issue = 013, accessed 28 September, 2010: John Minford, "Lionel Giles: Sinology, Old and New", *China Heritage Quarterly* 13, March, 2008.

Stranger things have happened on this score, too, to twentieth century translators of Confucius into English, as may be seen from my final example. It is one of the most striking paradoxes of Analects translation during this period that the most famous reader and translator to use English, Ezra Pound (1885 – 1972), has been least widely appreciated. This is not in one sense surprising, since Pound's reading knowledge of Chinese developed over the years that he mulled over the sayings of Confucius from complete ignorance to a no better than rudimentary knowledge supported by a notoriously unhelpful dictionary, further complicated by notions concerning the Chinese script that have been entirely rejected by modern scholarship. Even more alarmingly, his British publisher, Peter Owen, has recently revealed in some reminiscences recorded in interview that when he first had dealings with the great man, he was "in the nuthouse". ① It would be wrong however to deduce from this that Pound's work is in any normal sense irrational, since as Peter Owen at least was well aware, the reasons for Pound's detention at the end of the Second World War were not straightforward: in fact, contemporary evidence suggests that he was saner about Confucianism than just about anything else at this point in his life. ②

In any case, the edition of the Analects put out by Peter Owen was the outcome of a long process, which had first seen published results as early as 1937 in Italy, at which stage Pound was working mainly with a copy of Legge's bilingual text, but which after his return to America involved him also in using a 1947 issue of R. H. Mathews, Mathew's Chinese-English Dictionary, for the versions of Confucius published in that country from 1950 onwards. ③ The Owens

---

① http://www.3ammagazine.com/3am/blazing-the-trail-an-interview-with-peter-owen/, accessed 28th September 2010: Steven Fowler, "Blazing the Trail: An interview with Peter Owen", 3: AM Magazine, Tuesday, November 24th, 2009.

② See the summary of his state of mind by Wendy Stallart Flory, on p. 149 of her study "Confucius Against Confusion: Ezra Pound and the Catholic Chaplain at Pisa", in Zhaoming Qian, ed., *Ezra Pound and China* (Ann Arbor: University of Michigan Press, 2003), pp. 145 – 162.

③ R. H. Mathews, *Mathew's Chinese-English Dictionary* (Cambridge, MA: Harvard University Press, 1943), as its preface makes clear, is but a somewhat revised and augmented version of a book that first appeared from a Chinese missionary press in 1931. For some information as to the sources used by Pound, see Flory, "Confucius Against Confusion", pp. 152 – 153.

edition of 1956 follows the latest American edition before that year in acknowledging Pound's use of this work by printing an additional note by Pound, not present in 1950. This note reveals that he checked his understanding not only against Legge (who is mentioned somewhat obliquely) but also against a French translation of 1840; otherwise Mathews is listed as a reference along with Ernest Fenellosa, The Chinese Written Character as a Medium for Poetry, which Pound had edited and published in 1936, and a couple of other works. ①While Mathews did a reasonable job for his day, considering the first edition appeared in 1931, when written Chinese was in transition from the pre-modern literary style to a more vernacular standard, it is a profoundly misleading jumble of ancient and modern meanings, and one can understand just why a past Professor of Chinese at Oxford University once seized a copy from a student and threw it out of the window. ② Fenellosa (1858 – 1908) as presented by Pound also embodies a great deal of wrong-headedness about the Chinese script, as many others have already remarked—though a reprinting of his edition that appeared in America bears on its cover the spirited response "Whether or not Pound proceeded on false premises remains an academic question. Let the pedants rave"—an invitation it is very difficult to resist. ③

And yet, despite all this, one of Europe's leading sinologists and a great authority especially on humour in the Analects, Christoph Harbsmeier, in reviewing a Norwegian translation of Confucius points out that occasionally

---

① See Ezra Pound, *Confucian Analects* (London: Peter Owen, 1956), pp. 5 – 6. The French translator is named as ' Pauthier', i. e, Pierre-Guillaume Pauthier (1801 – 1873), for the first edition of whose *Analects* see John Lust, *Western Books on China published up to* 1850 (London: Bamboo Books, 1987), p. 175, but I do not know what edition of Pauthier's translation Pound was using.

② The scholar concerned was not, to be clear, a professor at Oxford at the time. I did not witness this event, but I did once meet the owner of the dictionary, who confirmed the veracity of the anecdote.

③ For a good and entirely temperate recent summary that allows the reader to go on to explore the wider context of the ideas involved, see Haun Saussy, *Great Walls of Discourse and Other Adventures in Cultural China* (Cambridge, MA: Harvard University Press, 2001), pp. 38 – 44. My quotation is from the edition consulted by Saussy, namely Ernest Fenellosa, ed. Ezra Pound, *The Chinese Written Character as a Medium for Poetry*, (San Francisco: City Light Books, 1964), where the two sentences may be found on the back cover, together with a reference to the ridicule of sinologists such as George Kennedy, who is quoted as characterising the essay as "a small mass of confusion".

Pound is—albeit accidentally—philologically more precise even than the scrupulous D. C. Lau. He refers to Pound's version as a ' literary masterpiece' and commends in particular the appropriateness of its ' edgy, uncompromising prose' for the ' intellectual excitement and the abrupt poetry of Confucian diction' . ①Might it not be that in the unfolding story of *the Analects* in English, the comparatively neglected rendering by Ezra Pound could still have a part to play?

We cannot know for sure, and guessing the direction trends will take is, to repeat, no part of the exercise I am concerned with here. I am conscious, for example, that I have concentrated for obvious reasons very much on translations connected with the United Kingdom, whereas one day we may well find that the most important translation of Confucius is one produced for the benefit of persons of Chinese heritage familiar with the English language by members of the same widespread community. ②All I hope to have demonstrated by the foregoing discussion is merely that the notion of a steady, ordered sequence of gradually more accurate and readable translations that one might lazily tend to assume characterises the history in English of any famous foreign language text is no more exemplified by the Analects than by anything else. Even within a period of time during which written English style has not changed all that much, other factors have governed not simply the appearance but also the reappearance of different readings of Confucius. The examples I have given most obviously relate largely to commercial considerations within a modern print culture, though the tendency of scholars

---

① See his remarks in of *Copenhagen Papers in East and Southeast Asian Studies* 6 (1991), p. 114. He also refers to a comparison between Pound and Lau made by Stephen Durrant (cf. n. 7 above); Eugene Eoyang also compares Waley and Pound, so it would be unfair to describe Pound as completely neglected by sinologists.

② I have in mind John B. Khu, Vicente B. K. Khu, William B. S. Khu and Jose B. K. Khu, *The Confucian Bible, Book* 1: *Analects* (Manila: Granhill Corporation, 1991), a bilingual work including the original text and modern Chinese translation as well as English, collectively produced by a far-flung family based in the Philippines, that bears on its cover the alluring legend "What those with Chinese ties need to know but dare not ask! " (*sic*).

to recognise the merits of translators of earlier times when they have neither personal nor commercial grounds for recommending them is also in evidence here, I believe. Sinologists, it seems, cannot but develop a certain sense of a continuous tradition.

For, to come back to my initial statement of the problem, it is the simultaneous elasticity and coherence across both cultural space and cultural time of the Chinese tradition that marks it out from anything in the experience of most users of English. By cultural time I refer to the basic paradigms that are used to construe human history. The parody of China that developed in nineteenth century Western thought in order to construct new visions of exceptional Western modernity was of an immobile tradition, of eternal intellectual standstill. But it is clear that whatever patterns were read into the Chinese past in China itself, it was never seen as static or even monolithic. The problem was always to identify the unifying thread of continuity, of articulating coherence. This allowed for a constant process of reassessment, of the re-reading of texts such as *the Analects*, and of the revival of interpretations once discarded. I can understand why the notion of a renaissance, for so long (though not perhaps originally) deemed a Western monopoly, should now once more be extended to other places such as China also. ①But it seems to me that a renaissance requires that a tradition should become somehow estranged from itself, and that does not seem quite to have happened in China, despite some very dark moments. Instead, a much more diffuse and more continuous process of rediscovery appears to have operated albeit one naturally affected by overall historical circumstances, so that the

---

① Thus Jack Goody, *Renaissances: The One or the Many?* (Cambridge: Cambridge University Press, 2010), though in hesitating to ascribe a full measure of originality to him, I am bearing in mind that Oliver Goldsmith, in *The Citizen of the World*, Letter LXIII, writes "all mankind seemed to sleep, till nature gave the general call" and "in the year of the Christian era, 1400, the Emperor Yonglo arose to revive the learning of the East; while about the same time in Italy the Medicean family laboured in Italy to raise infant genius from the cradle"—the whole passage deserves more extended discussion.

intensity of the phenomenon might wax and wane, or vary in scope. ①

I am not sure if this very different quality of civilisation over time can be readily conveyed in English. It maybe that to appreciate the possibilities of such a span of culture one has to be able to read Classical Chinese and to dip in and out of the tradition over different centuries like educated East Asians of former times were able to do. But at least the foregoing discussion of *the Analects* in English has allowed me to indicate where the problem lies. Successfully solving the problem of how to educate the British and others about the facets of the Chinese historical experience that are quite unfamiliar to us is doubtless not something that can be achieved in half an hour. But someone somewhere had better start work on that project soon. Perhaps here will turn out to be the place.

---

① This I have argued in "China and the Redundancy of the Medieval", *The Medieval History Journal*, 1. 1 (1998), pp. 73 – 89.

Constructing Confucius Confronting Contingency in the *Lunyu* and the *Gongyang Zhuan*[①]

Joachim Gentz (Edinburgh)

I

In Chinese literature of the 3rd and 2nd centuries B. C. Confucius is represented in various ways. Nearly all of these representations serve the purpose of lending authority to specific arguments, which are developed to great parts independently from Confucius within the different texts. The arguments often conclude with a statement of Confucius summing up their point in an authoritative quote. Confucius quotes for the support of an own argument are also used in Chinese text exegesis that starts to blossom in early Han times. In all exegetical traditions to the classics Confucius occupies a central exegetical position. He is frequently quoted to justify basic exegetical approaches, interpretative strategies as well as specific and concrete exegetical moves. The differences and contradictions of the images of Confucius in the various texts are obvious. He is quoted as the central authority in the appendices to the Book of Changes as well as in many

---

① Draft prepared for the Forum on *the Analects*, King's College London, 22 – 23 October 2010. Please do not quote without permission of the author.

chapters of the ritual texts and also in the *Hanfeizi* and *Mengzi* a. s. f. in all cases lending authority to all the various arguments and theories.

Apart from this first field of constructions of Confucius which are embedded in an own line of argument for which the authority of Confucius is used in some way or the other we also find constructions of Confucius in collections like the Shuoyuan or the Xinxu. In these Confucius is quoted as one among other authorities. There is no specific and distinct construction of Confucius because these collections mainly quote earlier material with its own respective construction perspectives. The material of these collections contains different lines of argumentation in itself and is only vaguely ordered along certain thematic lines. The material concerning Confucius is scattered throughout these texts, which due to its fragmentary character often does not allow us to reconstruct the particular construction of Confucius.

Beside these collections there are collections which contain material concerning Confucius only, such as the *Lunyu*, the *Kongzi jiayu* and the *Kongcongzi*. The two latter works are not relevant for our investigation since their compilation is most likely of a late date (even if some of the material contained therein might be early). Like the collections Shuoyuan and Xinxu they contain Confucius-related material which has its origin in different textual and argumentative contexts thus representing different constructions of Confucius which are collected in a new order and exist only as fragments in these new compilations. We may assume that all of these collections create new specific constructions of Confucius through the order and selection of the compiled material. But all of these collections are of relatively late date and may be regarded as secondary material.

The *Lunyu*, however, differs from the other Confucius-related material in three points:

1. Although the formation of The *Lunyu* as a book may not be dated much earlier than late Early Han (approximately around 150 – 140 B. C.) as

Makeham has argued, [①]much of the material is very likely to be of early origin since we find quotations from it in books like *Mengzi*, *Xunzi* a. s. f. It is the first collection of material only concerned with the person and teaching of Confucius.

2. Despite countless efforts of an exegetical tradition of more than two thousand years to extract something like the one and only message of the book, the incessant and continual effort to find such a message and the different and contradictory claims of various exegetical approaches show that there is no clear-cut construction of Confucius in this book. We rather get a collection of completely different descriptions of actions, verbal sayings and definitions about different topics related to Confucius. Many of these single aspects can be found elaborated on in later texts and traditions[②]which often take single topics for the essential of the whole tradition denying all the other aspects. Both, the descriptions of Confucius and the nature of the contents of the *Lunyu* are disparate and heterogeneous to a degree that many attempts have been made to divide the book in different layers of tradition that seem to contain homogenous images of Confucius. [③]

3. The third point is a methodological one. In opposition to all the other texts which allude to Confucius in one or another way the *Lunyu* is the only early text in which Confucius is not depicted as the ultimate sage authority who knows an answer to all questions. Instead the Confucius of the *Lunyu* leaves questions open, opens new questions and although, and indeed just

---

[①]   John Makeham, "The Formation of *Lunyu* as a Book," in Monumenta Serica 44 (1996): 1 – 24.

[②]   See, for example, John Makeham, "Between Chen and Cai: Zhuangzi and the Analects", in: R. Ames (ed.), *Wandering at ease in the Zhuangzi*, New York: SUNY, 1998, pp. 75 – 100. A similar analysis of Confucius stories that appear across early Chinese texts has just been finished by Oliver Weingarten in his study: "Textual Representations of a Sage: Studies of Pre-Qin and Western Han Sources on Confucius (551 – 479 BCE)", unpubl. PhD, Cambridge 2009.

[③]   Two parts: shang/xia-Makeham, Formation, five blocks-van Zoeren (*Poetry and Personality*, 26), singlechapters-Suzuki Yoshikazu 铃木喜一 ("论语各章の年代决定试论," in: *Tokyo Shinagaku-ho* 15 [1969]: 77 – 88). See also Brooks & Brooks. *The Original Analects*. For an excellent presentation of this debate see the introduction in Weingarten, op. cit.

because of being a sage, he clearly embodies and hence points out ultimate limits of possible knowledge. To take this point a little more theoretical: Confucius in the *Lunyu* is depicted as someone who represents the fundamental attitude of confrontation of contingency (Kontingenzbegegnung)[1] . I would argue that in any other text Confucius stands for the opposite, for the coping with or the managing of contingency (Kontingenzbewältigung).[2] In a ilosophical sense this means that Confucius in the *Lunyu* doesn't represent a system of thought in which everything possibly may be answered in a necessary way[3] whereas in other early texts he does.

This last point is important for our further analysis. On the one hand I tried to argue that the *Lunyu* in opposition to many other texts which refer to Confucius has no clear-cut construction of a certain image of the personality or the teachings of Confucius. On the other hand I claim that the *Lunyu* contains a certain construction which is unique and not found in other early texts, besides perhaps the *Shijing*, but which corresponds to the absence of a clearcut construction that is: the construction of Confucius as someone who leaves certain questions open—not because he personally can't answer them but because of a fundamental methodological and epistemological problem— they cannot be answered. I proceed todemonstrate more clearly what I mean by confrontation of contingency and by leaving questions open.

The *Lunyu* expresses an often quoted attitude towards two, let's say-

---

① Cf. for this concept Kurt Wuchterl, Analyse und Kritik der religiösen Vernunft: Grundzüge einer paradigmenbezogenen Religionsphilosophie, Stuttgart, 1989, p. 14.

② Cf. for this concept Hermann Lübbe, "Kontingenzerfahrung und Kontingenzbewältigung", in: Gerhart von Graevenitz, Odo Marquard (eds.), *Kontingenz*, Munich, 1998, pp. 35 – 47.

③ Cf. *Lunyu* 9. 4: 子绝四：毋意，毋必，毋固，毋我 . Michael Nylan has shown in her first chapter of M. Nylan and Th. Wilson (eds.), *Lives of Confucius: Civilization's Greatest Sage through the Ages* (NY: Doubleday Religion 2010) that the biography of Confucius in the *Shiji* written by Sima Qian around 100 B. C. represents him as someone who is not successful, whose life is full of failures, despairs and missing answers. See also my unpubl. paper: "Can we Be in Time to Lead a Good Life? Discourses on the Human Ability to Lead a Good Life through Timely Action in Early Chinese Thought" given at the conference "The good life and conceptions of life in Greek and Chinese antiquity", Glasgow, June 2010.

invisible spheres: the sphere of the spirits and demons and the sphere of the past. The attitude towards these two spheres may be found summarized in two of the most famous quotations of the *Lunyu*:

1. (7. 20) "子不语怪,力,乱,神, Zi bu yu guai, li, luan, shen. The Master didn't talk of prodigies, forced matters, disorder or spirits. "

2. (7. 1) "子曰,述而不作,信而好古, Zi yue: shu er bu zuo, xin er hao gu. The Master said: I transmit but do not create; I am trustworthy in what I say and love antiquity. "

Both quotations express an attitude towards the unknown (either of the realm beyond the regular or of the past) which doesn't dare to talk about it in a speculative way. Throughout the *Lunyu* we find many statements which express in more detail an attitude of Confucius which is full of doubts, uncertainties and not-knowing [1]. We find many sayings in which Confucius is full of sorrow or despair[2], in which he admits that he doesn't know an answer and has no solution for certain fundamental questions[3]. Moreover, there are many clear statements about what Confucius did not talk about and what he did not teach[4]. This, in my view, reflects a specific construction of Confucius confronting contingency.

Although the topic of the necessity to be careful and prudent with one's words occurs frequently in the *Shangshu* and in old ritual chapters like the "Ziyi"-chapter of the *Liji* (in the Guodian version of which this topic is even more stressed than in the received version), this old topic differs from the one in the *Lunyu*. In *Shangshu* and other old texts we always find the opposition of speech and action, yan 言 and xing 行 . The necessity to be cautious in speech is always related to the danger of its consequences in concrete action. Speech is regarded in its effect being perceived as parallel to the effects of a normal action. This is the reason why a ruler has to be cautious in speech as

---

[1]   2. 17, 3. 11, 5. 8, 5. 19, 13. 3, 13. 4, 15. 1.

[2]   5. 10, 5. 11, 5. 27, 7. 3, 7. 5, 7. 25, 9. 9, 11. 2, 13. 21, 15. 13.

[3]   2. 17, 3. 11, 5. 8, 5. 19, 13. 3, 13. 4, 14. 41, 15. 1.

[4]   2. 18, 7. 27, 3. 21, 5. 13, 7. 1, 7. 21, 7. 23, 7. 24, 9. 1, 9. 7, 11. 12, 13. 3, 14. 6.

well as in action. In the parts of the *Lunyu* I referred to the necessity of careful words results from the specific attitude towards the unknown spheres as described above. The addressed subject is the gentleman, not the ruler.

Reading through the two main texts which throughout Confucian literature are quoted as the basic teaching material of Confucius, the *Shangshu* and the *Shijing*, we will find nearly no theoretical explanations of supernatural events. The *Shangshu* reports many calamities which are send down by Heaven but these calamities are always manmade like invasions, rebellions, usurpations a. s. f. We never find any natural calamity or anomaly as an answer to human conduct sent down by Heaven in order to punish or to warn like we often find this in later texts[1]. In the *Shijing* there is one eclipse of the sun which results from bad human conduct (Mao 193), apart from this we only find good harvest as an unspecific indication for good government and regular sacrifice. The discourse on supernatural events in the realm of nature is thus nearly absent in these two books which are said to form the basis of Confucius' teaching[2].

II

If we want to prove whether the attribution of this attitude towards the unknown to Confucius in The *Lunyu* is unique in the early literature we have to check other texts in which Confucius deals with the two spheres of the unknown towards which his *Lunyu*-attitude is directed: 1. the invisible supernatural realm of spirits and 2. the invisible world of the past.

1. In Guoyu (especially "*Luyu*") and *Hanfeizi* we find Confucius in the

---

[1]   Only exception being the passage in the Jin Teng chapter in which a storm is sent by Heaven, cf. Legge. *Shoo King*, p. 359f. .

[2]   Cf. Anazawa Tatsuo 穴泽辰雄, "Shi Sho ni okeru ten to jin 诗书における天と人," in: *Uno Tetsuto sensei hakuju shukuga kinen Tôyôgaku ronsô* 宇野哲人先生白寿祝贺纪念东洋学论丛, Tôkyô, 1974, pp. 63 – 82 or Miura Yoshiaki 三浦吉明, "Keisho yori mita ten no shisô: Shikyô, Shokyô wo chûshin ni 经书より見た天の思想: 诗经,书经中心に," in: *Shôkan Tôyôgaku* 集刊东洋学 34 (1975): 38 – 65. Both do not mention any disruption of the Heavenly order caused by man.

role of someone who is asked for explanations of natural calamities and anomalies which are taken to be based in supernatural institutions like spirits, ancestors or Heaven. Confucius answers the questions in all cases in a "rational" way never referring to spirits, ancestors or Heaven. Instead he always adduces natural grounds for the anomalies. Although Confucius seems not to speak about spirits and demons, he still talks about anomalies in a way which never leaves a question open but in each case gives a full "rational" explanation. We thus do not find the *Lunyu*—attitude of not knowing and leaving questions as unanswerable open. Rather, Confucius always knows an answer and I am able to explain every single question he is asked. The "Tian lun" chapter of the *Xunzi* provides the first systematic approach towards an explication of the unknown

Sphere of heaven. Unlike Confucius, Xunzi does talk a lot about a supernatural realm which he denies and gives many fundamental answers to questions Confucius would not have dared to talk about in the *Lunyu*. The same attitude may be found in texts like *Zuo zhuan* and *Lüshi Chunqiu*, both texts in which according to the different time of composition different approaches are taken to explain natural calamities and anomalies.

In contrast to the consciously intended gaps that Confucius leaves in respect to explanations of supernatural phenomena in the *Lunyu*, these other texts depict him only as the sage who knows, answers and judges and thus fills in all the gaps of lacking knowledge.

2. As to the second sphere, the invisible world of the past, our main source to seek for parallels of The *Lunyu*—attitude of Confucius in the early Confucius-traditions is the historiographical tradition of the *Chunqiu* commentaries which claim to transmit the oral teachings of the Master claimed to be the maker (zuo 作) of the *Chunqiu*. These commentaries are of particular interest for our question since the Chunqiu does not only contain records of historical actions of human protagonists but also contains reports on natural calamities and anomalies which may be regarded as events to be interpreted as belonging to the supernatural realm. We thus find a

combination of both aspects of the invisible and unknown world in this annalistic book. We therefore can pose a two fold question to the texts about their possible reflection 1. of the attitude towards supernatural events and 2. towards the past.

1. In the *Zuo zhuan* we find Confucius, like in most other early texts, without exception in the role of the sage who knows and judges. The *Zuo zhuan* contains many and diverse theories and explanations of natural calamities and anomalies, which become increasingly abstract and complex after duke Zhao. Yet, however, none of these theories is quoted as deriving from Confucius himself. Confucius is only concerned with moral judgements about historical

Precedents. Thus we can neither tell whether the author thought that Confucius believed in these theories nor whether he was conscious about himself believing in certain theories and Confucius restraining from it.

2. With regard to the second question concerning the attitude of Confucius towards the past, we don't learn much from the *Zuo zhuan* either. The *Zuo zhuan* tends to interpret certain formal deviations in the Chunqiu-records in a rather pragmatic way. According to the *Zuo zhuan* explanation in these cases the scribe either forgot to write a word or he didn't get a certain information a. s. f. We thus neither get any information about how Confucius compiled the historical material of the *Chunqiu* nor, what is more important, any information about his attitude towards it. Since the *Zuo zhuan* doesn't answer clearly to our question we may conclude that it doesn't reflect on the attitude towards the unknown we found in the *Lunyu*. The transmission of this attitude is obviously no matter of concern for the *Zuo zhuan*.

In this respect, the *Gongyang zhuan* clearly differs from the *Zuo zhuan* (whether the *Guliang zhuan* in this point is similar to the *Gongyang zhuan* remains to be investigated).

1. Among the approximately 140 entries concerning calamities or anomalies (zaī yì 灾异) only two entries reflect the cause of these natural

calamities and anomalies. ①In both Heaven is said to answer to certain human actions or to send a warning. These two statements show that a relation between natural deviations and human conduct is conceptualized. However, there is no attempt to formulate any more specific theory nor is this point elaborated any further. Instead most of the entries about natural calamities or anomalies are not commented at all. The *Gongyang zhuan* at the most only explains that this is an entry concerning a natural calamity or anomaly but never comments its cause. In my view one can take this silence as a practice of not talking about supernatural phenomena.

2. The *Gongyang zhuan* purports a very clear vision about the process of the Chunqiucompilation. The readers are not only told the principles and rules of composition they are also told how Confucius rewrote the original material, that is, they are told what he preserved and what he changed and according to which principles he changed or preserved which parts of the entries. Because the information about the special details of the compilation process is essential for a credible reading and exegesis of the *Gongyang zhuan* and hence enforces the reliability of the Gongyang-exegesis this information has to be given to the reader in detail. Through reconstruction we may know how the author of the *Gongyang zhuan* imagined Confucius to have compiled the *Chunqiu*, we thus also may know how the author of the *Gongyang zhuan* imagined Confucius' attitude toward the old historical material. I can't go into a detailed reconstruction of this imagination here, therefore I want to sum up its results. ②

According to the *Gongyang zhuan* Confucius compiled the *Chunqiu* of older material written itself according to certain historiographical principles and rules. Confucius took over most of these traditional historiographical rules. The *Gongyang zhuan* tells us that Confucius especially took over the listing-order of the participants of covenants or meetings as contained in the

---

① Wen 15. 11, Xuan 15. 9 (probably also Ai 14. 1).

② For further details see my *Das* Gongyang zhuan: *Auslegung und Kanonisierung der* Frühlings- und Herbstannalen, Wiesbaden: Harrassowitz, 2001.

original historiographical material. He further took over in at least one instance a historiographical rule according to which the intent and not the real action is written down in an entry. Confucius thus sometimes even took over the moral judgement of the scribe of the original material if he could share it. According to the information the *Gongyang zhuan* gives us we may assume that Confucius used most of the historical material and composed the *Chunqiu* out of it, the *Chunqiu* thus to a great extend seems not to differ fundamentally from the original Chunqiu of Lu. Confucius changed entries only in their wording, and sometimes he omitted parts of entries which seemed fantastic and not reliable to him. According to the *Gongyang zhuan* Confucius had two major matters of concern in his compilation.

. He wanted to express his own judgements on certain entries.

. He wanted to keep the reliability of the *Chunqiu* as a historical source.

The requirement was thus a contradictory one: He wanted to change the text without changing it, or, to be more precise, he wanted to add his own judgements to the text without changing its historical content. The Gongyang zhuans' imagination of how Confucius entered his judgements into the text of the Annals grows out of this specific tension between these two requirements. According to the *Gongyang zhuan* Confucius leaves the content of the historical text nearly untouched. His judgements are reduced to slight changes which occur only in very small text-units such as single words, mostly words which don't touch upon the historical content of an entry like, for example, the dating (at the beginning of an entry), the mentioning of a certain place or the naming of the historical actors. In that way he succeeds on the one hand in preserving the annalistic text as a reliable historical source and at the same time on the other hand manages to implement his own judgements on the historical cases in this same text.

From the above reconstruction of the Chunqiu compilation process as imagined by the author of the *Gongyang zhuan* we can infer how the author imagined the attitude of Confucius towards the old material and its transmission to be. We have seen that one of the two main aims of Confucius in his compilation of the *Chunqiu* was to transmit it as a reliable historical source. The second aim was to implement his own judgements. According to the exegesis of the *Gongyang zhuan* Confucius realizes both aims with the help of a genious compromise. He thus doesn't violate one of the two aims in order to realize the other. We may thus conclude that his respect for the text and its transmission is that high that he has to find a very sophisticated and complicated method to implement his own judgements into it. From the exegesis of the *Gongyang zhuan* it becomes clear that Confucius doesn't want to violate the historical text for the sake of his own historical judgements. The preservation of the old text is thus the first premise in his compilation.

We often find expressions of exegetical uncertainness in the *Gongyang zhuan*. The *Gongyang zhuan* admits in many cases that it doesn't know any explanation for a certain matter. Moreover, sometimes two alternative explanations are given by the *Gongyang zhuan*, informing the reader that it doesn't know whether explanation a or explanation b is true. We thus find the same attitude of explicit admissions of missing knowledge, of confrontation with contingency as noted in the *Lunyu* above also in the exegetical practice of the *Gongyang zhuan*.

Let me summarize the above argument. Within the *Gongyang zhuan* we find an attitude which we may describe as caution in respect to speak about or even to explain supernatural phenomena. We find furthermore an extremely careful respect for the original annalistic text which in major parts is taken over into the new compilation with minor changes only. These changes do scarcely interfere with the historical content of the text in order to transmit it as a reliable historical source. Finally, we do find the confrontation with contingency, the open admission of not knowing certain things rather than the hermetic answering of all questions within the exegesis of the *Gongyang zhuan*, too.

In the exegesis of the *Gongyang zhuan* we thus find exactly the same attitudes which we found as unique attributions to Confucius in the *Lunyu*. Unlike the *Lunyu*, however, the *Gongyang zhuan* doesn't talk about these attitudes and doesn't attribute them explicitly to Confucius. We only find them implicit in the exegetical practice of the commentary, so to speak, in the silence of the lacking explicit theoretical statements.

III

I move on to the third and last point of my paper.

There are no references to the *Lunyu* in the Gongyang zhuan which would suggest that these exegetical attitudes were taken over from it. Therefore it seems plausible to assume that these attitudes result from different sources. In my view the attitude towards old texts and their transmission reflects a common practice among scribes in the historiographical tradition.

If we follow Confucius statement in*Lunyu* 15. 25 that he can still remember the days when a scribe left blank spaces the same might also be true for the attitude of clearly pointing out the limits of the own knowledge.

This practice might be a professional attitude of methodological caring about a reliable transmission within an early Chinese historiographical tradition. The attitude of not talking about supernatural things might just be an analogous attitude with regard to another invisible sphere which we cannot have any knowledge about.

It might also reflect the attitude of ritual experts who, if we follow Falkenhausen's analysis, had a strict division of labour with the so called shamans whose job was the interaction with spirits and demons whereas the ritual experts entirely kept out of this realm[1]. From the *Lunyu*-image of Confucius it is obvious that he was well versed in the ritual traditions and a ritual expert himself. The exegesis of the Gongyang zhuan mainly operates with ritual rules and follows a formulaic-ritualistic reading of the Chunqiu that focuses on record patterns and their deviations. It can thus be taken as a

---

[1]   Lothar von Falkenhausen, "Reflections on the Political Role of Spirit Mediums in Early China: The *Wu* Officials in the *Zhou li*," in *Early China* 20 (1995): 279 – 300.

ritual commentary. We might therefore assume that the above mentioned attitudes explicitly ascribed to Confucius in the *Lunyu* and being a part of the implicit exegetical practice of the Gongyang zhuan are not necessarily connected with each other but might rather derive independently from two traditions which used to cultivate them as part of their professional profile. If this is the case and the Gongyang-exegesis is not influenced by the *Lunyu*-tradition in this respect, it is evident that the specific character of the *Lunyu*-construction of Confucius lies in its ascribing to him professional attitudes possibly found in the realm of historiography and ritual expertise. These attitudes basically have in common the confrontation of contingency rather than the coping with or managing of contingency which we find in all the other Confucius constructions transmitted to us.

This sceptical attitude seems in the first place to be an attitude of professional methodology, not of personal belief. Many passages of theAnalects give a very clear expression of Confucius' personal belief in an active power of Heaven, in destiny and the supernatural sphere. However, this is not part of his teaching as reflected in the *Lunyu* and the Gongyang zhuan. The fact that the cultic veneration of Confucius as a sage ancestor becomes part of the Confucian tradition as Thomas Wilson has shown so clearly in his recent publications does not contradict the basic careful and sceptical attitude of the Confucian teaching that seems to confront contingency only in the *Lunyu* and the Gongyang zhuan.

Teaching *Lunyu* from the National University of the Liang to the Periphery of the Tang Empire

Bernhard Fuehrer (SOAS, London)

Though not always classified as a "classic" (jing 经) in the technical sense historically, the utterances of Master Kong as transmitted in the *Lunyu* (Analects 论语) have undoubtedly been one of the most prominent teaching materials used in Chinese education since the Early Han (206 BC – 23 AD) period. For later periods of imperial China the transmitted source material on the transmission of learning of crucial educational works such as the *Lunyu* provides us with some amazing insights. We have, for example, direct access to the textbook on the Si Shu(Four Books 四书), compiled for a young boy who later became Emperor Kangxi (1661-1722), an annotated version of the Four Books that represents an edited version of readings explained and expounded upon in the context of his future leadership role. [1] In addition, the relevant historical source material also documents his teaching schedule including not only the names of the tutors but also the topics of their lectures. [2] Similarily, we have easy and direct access to the readings of the Four Books established by Zhang Juzheng 张居正 (1525-1582

---

[1] See La ś ari [Lashali] (? – 1679) *et al.* : *Rijiang Lunyu jieyi* (日讲论语解义)(1677).

[2] This can be reconstructed from the relevant *shilu* (实录) and *qijuzhu*(起居住)records; cf the articles by Liu Jiaju in *Dongwu Daxue xuebao* 9 (1991), 83 – 102 and *Dongwu daxue xuebao* 10 (1992), 109 – 143.

in his lectures to Zhu Zaihou (1537-1572), the later Longqing (1567 – 1572) emperor, and his son Zhu Yijun (1563-1620), the later Wanli (1573-1620) emperor. ① Given Zhang Juzheng's prominent political role, then historical material provides insights into interesting political aspects of teaching, even tensions between tutor and pupil in a complex hierarchical environment. ②Teaching material used in the education of princes and rules are not only important in the sense that they provide insights into how political leadership was perceived and the ways in which scholars tried to shape future (or present but young) political leaders. They are also important because, in one way or another, this teaching material was later also applied in educating the scions of the gentry, thereby providing guidance and leaving a mark not only on the top leader but also on the wider political and bureaucratic elite.

Reconstructions of the environment in which commentarial literature was put together show that a good deal of the reading traditions on the Four Books, and thus on the *Lunyu*, originates from teaching material. Whether or not this is still reflected in and clearly visible from the transmitted material, or, in what respect, the available material still exhibits characteristics associated with its origin as teaching material, depends largely on the later career of these texts.

Some of the earlier teaching material is not handed down directly but only in fragments, mainly integrated in compilations of explanatory material. An early example here would, of course, be the readings suggested by Bao Xian 包咸 (7 BC-65 AD), an imperial tutor, whose explanations have, at

---

① His *Lunyu zhijie* 论语直解 (1573) is to be found in the *Zhang gelao Si shu zhijie* 张阁老四书直解, a work first brought to Europe by Jesuits missionaries. An abridged version prepared by Yao Yongpu 姚永朴 (1861 – 1939), which in part differs substantially from the version found in the *Zhang gelao Si shu zhijie*, is included in the *Wuqiubeizhai Lunyu jicheng* 无求备斋论语集成, edited by Yan Lingfeng 严灵峰 (Taipei: Yiwen yinshuguan, 1966). We observe an increased interest in Zhang Juzheng's readings in the PRC but the two most recently published monographs are based on Yao Yongpu's version and offer little insights into more specific aspects of Zhang's commentary.

② For some insights see the article by Li Zeqi in *Lishi yuekan* 43 (1991), 79 – 81 and Ray Huang's *1587. A Year of No Significance* (New Haven, 1981).

least partly, been integrated in the *Lunyu* jije, a summary of primarily Han explanations of the *Lunyu* compiled under the general editorship of He Yan 何 晏（190 – 249）. Clearly, a comprehensive list of similar cases would go beyond the scope of what I attempt to do here, and it may suffice to refer the reader to various introductions to individual commentaries on the *Lunyu* in which this aspect is made topical and features prominently.

But important insights on how the *Lunyu* was taught can not only be gauged from the documentation of interpretations addressed to the very top of society. Unfortunately, the earliest textual witness of the *Lunyu*, the bamboo strip manuscript which dates from 55 BC and was found in in Dingzhou 定州 n 1973, offers no clues for our investigation. [1] Similarly, the famous manuscript by a Tang period student known as Bu Tianshou 卜天寿 only shows the main text and Zheng's commentary-which is interesting and important for a number of other reasons-with corrections in red ink by another hand, presumably his teacher, but, again, all this provides little clues for an investigation into the mechanics and down-to-earth issues involved in the teaching of the *Lunyu*.

With regards to the transmitted material, the various fragments of Zheng Xuan's 郑玄（127 – 200）*Lunyu* commentary and the *Lunyu* jijie 论语集解 （preface 242）as well as the various Han glosses and readings scattered all over the relevant material but not included in the *Lunyu* jijie, attest to the co-existence of a number of textual strata, an enormous synchronic and diachronic diversity of interpretations and reading traditions, as well as critical reflections upon textual and philosophical issues and so forth, but they provide little insights into teaching aspects on a more practical level.

It is only with Huang Kan's 皇侃（488 – 545）*Lunyu* yishu 论语义疏 （also known under the title *Lunyu* jijie yishu 论语集解义疏）that we gain glimpses into a classroom in which the *Lunyu* was taught. The transmitted text

---

[1]　See *Dingzhou Hanmu zhujian Lunyu* 定州汉墓竹简论语（Beijing: Wenwu chubanshe, 1997）.

of the *Lunyu* yishu, a sub-commentary on the *Lunyu* jijie, clearly derives from lecture notes on the *Lunyu* in which glosses transmitted in the *Lunyu* jijie are examined, discussed critically, and alternate readings are established. Clearly, the *Lunyu* yishu shows features of classroom dynamics and exhibits a number of pedagogical features, such as the tutor's dealing with the age-old problem of his audience's attention-span, and it should not be read as a straight-forward transcript of Huang Kan's lectures but as an edited form of lecture notes. In addition, the *Lunyu* yishu also shows how students were instructed to make the text accessible to themselves through cross-referencing within the *Lunyu* and other core readings. It is in this sense that the *Lunyu* yishu provides us with a certain degree of insights into orality, i. e. the way in which the *Lunyu* was made accessible to students and explored as teaching material trough oral instructions delivered by Huang Kan's in his classroom during the Liang period. [1]

But our insights into late medieval teaching practices of the *Lunyu* do not stop there. If the *Lunyu* yishu offers us one level of orality, i. e. Huang Han's teaching, the Tang fragment (P 3573) of the *Lunyu* yishu provides us with a second layer of orality, i. e. the teaching of an unknown tutor in Dunhuang based on Huang Kan's explorations. The manuscript fragment thereby offers a textual snapshot of an oral teaching tradition which is only scarcely documented otherwise.

At this point, a few words on this highly significant witness for our understanding of the transmission and learning of the classics, may be in order. The manuscript fragment was brought to Europe from Dunhuang by Paul Pelliot (1878-1945) and is now held at the Bibliothèque Nationale in Paris as manuscript P 3573. It represents the by far oldest textual witness of the *Lunyu* yishu, a text once lost in China and reintroduced to China during

---

[1]   On these issues see also my "Exegetical Strategies and Commentarial Features of Huang Kan's *Lunyu* yishu: A Preliminary Overview", in: Huang Junjie (ed.): *Dongya* Lunyu *xue: Zhongguo pian* (Taipei: Guoli Taiwan Daxue chuban zhongxin, 2009), 273 – 296.

the reign of emperor Qianlong. ① The manuscript fragment indicates the title as *Lunyu shu*(语义疏) at the beginning of the second scroll, Chinese sources tend to refer to it as *Tang xieben Lunyu yishu*(唐写本论语义疏). ② Together with photographs of other Dunhuang fragments in the collection of the Bibliothèque Nationale it was first made available in *Kanda Kiichirō's*(神田熹一郎,1897 – 1984) *Dunhuang miji liuzhen xinbian*(敦煌祕籍留真新编) (preface by Lu Zhihong 陆志鸿 dated 1947), an album-like reproduction of photographs taken at the *Bibliothèque Nationale.* ③ Fragment P 3573 is also reproduced in the *Yan Lingfeng's Wuqiubeizhai Lunyu jicheng*(1966), and the photographs first published in the Dunhuang miji liuzhen xinbian have seen a number of more recent reprints. ④ As part of the International Dunhuang Project led by the British Library, a scanned version is now made available online by the Bibliothèque Nationale in electronic format which is the by far best reproduction of this manuscript fragment. ⑤

The manuscript shows two dates, year 9 of the reign-period Zhenming(贞明,923) and the reign-period Longde (龙德,921 – 923) of the Hou Liang period (后梁,907 – 923), neither is believed to relate to the actual text of the *Lunyu* yishu or to the manuscript copy itself. ⑥ As it exhibits the typical

---

① On the return of the LYYS to China during the *Siku quanshu* preparation period see my "' The Text of the Classic and the Commentaries Deviates Greatly from Current Editions'. A Case Study of the *Siku quanshu* Version of Huang Kan's *Lunyu yishu*", in: Führer, Bernhard (ed.): *Zensur. Text und Autorität in China in Geschichte und Gegenwart.* Wiesbaden: Harrassowitz, 2003, 19 – 38.

② The beginning of the manuscript and of LY 1. 1 is damaged; the fragment ends with LY 4. 18. Before the beginning of LY 3. 1 the manuscript states: *Lunyu shu di er* (论语疏第二).

③ For the *Lunyu yishu* fragment see Kanda Kiichirō: *Dunhuang miji liuzhen xinbian*, vol. 1, p. 59-96. The original *Dunhuang miji liuzhen xinbian* is notoriously difficult to locate but National Taiwan University Library holds a copy which can easily be accessed.

④ See the reproductions of the *Dunhuang miji liuzhen xinbian* in modern collectanea such as *Dunhuang congkan chuji* (1985) or *Zhongguo Xibei wenxian congshu* (1990).

⑤ See idp. bl. uk.

⑥ Note that according to the official calendar the reign-period Zhenming only lasted for six years from 915 to 921 when it was changed by the last emperor of the Later Liang to Longde, a period which lasted up to the take-over by the Later Tang (Hou Tang 后唐) in 923 when the reign-period Tongguang (同光) was proclaimed.

Tang (618-907) taboo graphs the manuscript is believed to originate from that period, though an alternate possible explanation for the conflict in dates could be due to the author continuing to use taboo graphs after the fall of the dynasty, either out of habit or perhaps even as a political statement. ①

However, the fragmentcarries a total of thirty-eight sections (*zhang* 章) from the first four chapters (*pian* 篇) of the *Lunyu* yishu with the main text (*jingwen* 经文), excerpts from Huang Kan's sub-commentary and from the *Lunyu* jijie commentary in which the names of the commentators cited by He Yan and his collaborators are omitted. A comparison with the wording of the *Lunyu* jijie as transmitted, as the first commentarial level (zhu), in Xing Bing's (邢昺,931 – 1010) *Lunyu zhushu*(论语注疏,999) or in the Japanese text traditions of the *Lunyu* yishu reveals that the jijie-commentary in this manuscript fragment is substantially abridged. As far as the textual arrangement is concerned, the commentary part is written in small half-size graphs; it is often introduced by *zhu yun*(注云, the commentary states) and finishes with *yun yun*(云云, and so on), a formula indicating the omission of the rest of the commentary and widely attested on other Tang manuscripts. As these excerpts from the jijie-commentary often consist of its first few graphs only, they seem to have served as an aide-mémoire so as to prompt the wording of the commentary which the student/reader would have been expected to have memorised. Textual sequences and even whole sections (zhang) of the main text (jingwen) are missing, on a number of occasions the sub-commentary is shortened significantly and the introductory remarks in the sub-commentaries at the beginning of each chapter (*pian*) are omitted entirely. ② The text shows corrections in black and red ink, the latter is believed to represent corrections made by a teacher. Based on a comparison of P 3573 with the Zhibuzuzhai congshu(知不足斋丛书) versions of the *Lunyu*

---

① As for the taboo graphs see e. g. *ren* 人 for *min* 民 in LY 1. 5, 1. 9, 2. 1, 2. 3, 3. 21, 3. 24 and 3. 25 in *Tang xieben Lunyu yishu*.

② Out of a total of 84 sections from LY 1. 1. to LY 4. 18, the manuscript omits 46 and only carries 38 sections, 12 of which carry incomplete versions of the main text.

yishu Wang Zhongmin 王重民 (1903-1975) believed textual discrepancies in these two text traditions to be caused by alterations made by Japanese scholars before the text was reintroduced to China, and suggested the Tang manuscript was a fairly truthful representation of the original condition of the *Lunyu* yishu. ① He also maintained that those parts which appear in the Japanese text tradition (and the redactions which derive from it) but not in the Tang manuscript should be identified as interpolations made in Japan. However, apart from the obvious consequences of the Tang manuscript presenting substantially shortened versions of the yishu part, some of these discrepancies relate to passages attributed to earlier scholars and quoted by Huang Kan in the Japanese text tradition of the *Lunyu* yishu. ② Such omissions are found in the sub-commentaries on about twenty of the thirty-eight sections that survived in manuscript form and include citations from Li Chong 李充 (mid-fourth cent.) in the sub-commentaries on LY 3. 7 and LY 3. 20, from Sun Chuo 孙绰 (c. 314-c. 371) on LY 2. 4, LY 3. 22 and LY 3. 24, from Wang Bi 王弼 (226-249) on LY 2. 4 and LY 3. 4, from Fan Ning 范宁 (339 – 401) on LY 1. 15 and LY 3. 7 and so forth. As Li Fang has argued, it is rather unlikely that these passages are interpolations in the Japanese text tradition (from which the two Zhibuzuzhai congshu versions derive) . ③ Jiang Xi's 江熙 (fourth cent.) Jijie *Lunyu* 集解论语 (Collected Explanations of the Analects; 10 scrolls) and Li Chong's *Lunyu* zhu 论语注 (Analects, with a Commentary; 10 scrolls) were both lost at the time of the Northern Song period (960-1127), and since there is no record of them being transmitted to Japan, quotes from these commentaries are highly unlikely to be insertions by

---

① See Wang Zhongmin: "Bali Lundun suo cang Dunhuang canjuan xulu", p. 4 and Wang Zhongmin: *Dunhuang guji xulu*, p 73. Wang Zhongmin used a copy of the original (1776-1823) version of the *Zhibuzuzhai congshu*.

② Two examples may suffice: Compared with the versions transmitted in Japan the subcommentaries on LY 3. 7 are reduced from over 830 to around 370 (approx. 45%) and on LY 3. 4 from about 220 to about 90 (approx. 41%) characters in the *Tang xieben Lunyu yishu*.

③ See Li Fang: "Tang xieben *Lunyu* Huang shu de xingzhi ji qi xiangguan wenti", p. 51 and Tang Minggui: "Dunhuang ji Tulufan chutu Tang xieben *Lunyu* zhuben yanjiu gaishu", p. 33.

Japanese scholars. ① Like so many other portions of the Lunyu yishu which do not appear in the Tang fragment, we shall regard these citations simply as (probably deliberate) omissions in the P 3573 manuscript. There is little doubt that compared with the text versions preserved in Japan, the manuscript version shows considerable differences not only in the textual arrangement but also in the segmentation and wording of the main text and the subcommentary. ② Rather than regarding the manuscript P 3573 as a fair representation of the original version of the *Lunyu* yishu, the idiosyncrasies of the Tang manuscript suggest it derived from "an outline of [or for] lectures on Huang Kan's *Lunyu* yishu". ③ It should thus be perceived as a text genetically related to but not slavishly adhering to the *Lunyu* yishu.

A closer look at the manuscript fragments reveals a number of features in support of the view that the manuscript text and its amendments are primarily related to teaching practices and purposes. To start with, the manuscript often shows a more colloquial wording than the Japanese text tradition, a feature shared among a wide range of manuscript copies that can also be interpreted as supporting the view that it served a rather practical purpose and is closely related to the oral delivery of lectures. Of the twenty-eight sections there are twelve in which the main text (jingwen) is incomplete, some are missing the beginning (such as LY 1.7), some omit the end (such as LY 1.8), and others show both beginning and end but do not contain central segments (such as LY 2.3), but most importantly, there seems to be little pattern in these

---

① The titles of both works vary slightly in the bibliographic chapters of the dynastic histories from Sui to Tang. For the *Jijie Lunyu* and the *Lunyu zhu* see *SS*, 32: 936, the commentary on which records also a *Lunyu shi* 论语释 (1 scroll) by Li Chong which was however already lost at the time of the compilation of the bibliographical chapter; see *SS*, 32: 936. Neither Jiang Xi's nor Li Chong's work on the *Lunyu* appears in Fujiwara Sukeyo: *Nihonkoku genzaisho mokuroku* which records the *Lunyu yishu* (35: 8a). For more details on these commentators see chapter three in my forthcoming *Medieval Lecture Notes on the Analects: The Story of Huang Kan's Lunyu yishu* (Harrassowitz; Wiesbaden).

② The subcommentary in the Tang manuscript fragment separates quotes, indicates a change of topic or speaker by leaving one space empty (on some occasions with an additional circle ○), a practice not seen in the *yishu*-part of the other text traditions.

③ See Li Fang: *"Tang xieben Lunyu* Huang shu de xingzhi ji qi xiangguan wenti", p. 55.

omissions. Given the overall textual arrangement, it seems likely that these omissions derive from intentional general amendments rather than errors during the transcription process. ①

As regards the textualarrangement of the manuscript fragment, the yishu section comes after a short reference to the jijie-commentary (which is dropped entirely on a number of occasions), and is introduced by the formula ci ming 此明 (this explains / makes plain) with ci 此 written in the same size as the main text and ming 明 in half-size. ② It has however been noted that the manuscript is far from providing a complete copy of Huang Kan's sub-commentary but has about 60% less of it that the versions transmitted via Japan. ③

But perhaps more importantly, the Tang manuscript fragment carries another kind of revealing insertions which are absent from all other text traditions of the *Lunyu* yishu. Some of these additions to the sub-commentaries are marked by yang jie … zhe 仰解 … 者, yang shi … zhe 仰释 … 者, yang or ming … zhe 仰明 … 者 ([kindly] note the explanation …) etc. and present summaries offered to the students by the tutor who used the term yang 仰, a form of imperative in transmitting orders or advice to inferiors. ④ Other similar expressions

---

① See for example LY 1.7 where the explanations and commentaries in the manuscript only refer to the short excerpt (7 graphs) of this section in which the rest of this otherwise 38 graph-long section (in the transmitted text version) is omitted.

② Note that *ci ming* and *ci zhang ming* 此章明 (this section explains / makes plain) which introduce the *yishu*-commentary's synopses of sections appear quite frequently in the *Lunyu* yishu versions transmitted in Japan: for *ci ming* see e. g. LY 1.5, 1.9, 2.1, 4.2, 6.6, 7.7, 7.11, 7.16, 7.22, 7.32, 8.5, 8.9, 9.11, 9.26., 11.22, 14.11, 15.35, 16.1, 16.5, 20.1; for *ci zhang ming* see e. g. LY 1.5, 2.4, 2.10, 2.11, 2.12, 2.14, 2.22, 3.7, 3.9, 3.10, 7.6, 8.2, 8.8, 9.30, 16.1. There are however minor divergencies: For example the subcommentary on LY 1.5 reads *ci ming* in the *LYYS* (Taitokudō), 1: 5b whereas *LYYS* (Genji), 1: 6b has *ci zhang ming*, and the sub-commentary on LY 1.9 has *ming* in the *LYYS* (Taitokudō), 1: 10a where *LYYS* (Genji), 1: 11a reads *ci ming*. As Wang Zhongmin: "Bali Lundun suo cang Dunhuang canjuan xulu", p. 5 noted, there are however 17 cases in which the Tang manuscript shows the formula *ci ming* and where it is does not appear in other textual witnesses.

③ See Li Fang.

④ See for example the tutor's supplementary explanations to the sub-commentary on LY 1.1 and 1.5 (*yang jie … zhe*), LY 1.9 and 2.5 (*yang shi … zhe*), LY 3.2 and 3.16 (*yang ming … zhe*) in *Tang xieben Lunyu yishu*.

are yen 言 … zhe 者 or suoyi 所以 … zhe 者 which are equally used to mark the tutor's summaries and pointers which are written in single column graphs but smaller than the main text. See for example the addition to the sub-commentary on LY 1.5 which is clearly marked by the formula yang jie … zhe:

> Kindly note the explanation for being frugal in expenditure and loving of people: Although a country's wealth may be affluent, it is not permissible to be wasteful and extravagant; thus the expression "being frugal in expenditure". Although the residents may be noble and lofty, it is not permissible to be arrogant and slow; thus the expression "love".

And in his explorations of the term peng 朋 in LY 1.1, the tutor's yang jie peng you zhe 仰解朋友者 (kindly note the explanations of [the terms] peng [and] you) draws the pupil's attention to the semantic differences between the terms peng and you as explained at length by Huang Kan in his sub-commentary, a direct quotation that follows the emphatic formula yang jie … zhe. Other examples include the passage yang shi Zhongsun mingzi zhe: Zhongsun shi qi shi 仰释仲孙名字者：仲孙是其氏 (Kindly note the explanation of the name Zhongsun: Zhongsun is his clan name) in the explanations on LY 2.5 or the more in depth use of this formula in LY 1.9 where the tutor elaborates on the issues of "forgetting ancient matters" and "recalling the past" via a direct reference to the Book of Songs (Shijing 诗经).

Further to this, the sub-commentary in the manuscript fragment shows interpolated explanations offered by the tutor. One such example is found in the sub-commentary on LY 3.6 where the famous Mount Tai (Taishan 泰山) is simply introduced as "Mount Tai of Lu" in the Japanese text tradition. [1] The Tang manuscript records the following excursion:

---

① See *LYYS* (Genji), 2: 5a: 泰山鲁之泰山也；*LYYS* (Taitokudō), 2: 4b reads: 泰山, 鲁之大山也.

How do we know Mount Tai is in Lu? Regarding Mount Tai, the [Book of] Songs state: "Mount Tai is so very lofty, [it is] looked up to by the state of Lu." How do we know Lin Fang is from Lu? As Mount Tai is a mountain in Lu, so Lin Fang is a person from Lu."[1]

An interesting point here is that the Japanese text tradition shows that Lin Fang 林放 is first introduced in Zheng Xuan's commentary on LY 3.4 in the *Lunyu* jijie, a text portion dropped in the Tang manuscript.[2] As Huang Kan's sub-commentary on LY 3.4 does not provide further details on Lin Fang or establish any relation between mount Tai and Lin Fang, but focuses on the "roots of ritual practices" (li zhi ben 礼之本), the tutor behind the manuscript fragment seemingly provided the student with instructions on how to deduce information from the otherwise scarce material provided in the commentarial traditions. The common theme of ritual practices in LY 3.4 and LY 3.6 was probably perceived as a perfect opportunity to create a parallelism between the "Lu mountain" (Lu shan 鲁山) and the "Lu person" (Lu ren 鲁人) which supposedly aims at improving the learner's capability to extract background knowledge from the given source material. What the tutor in Dunhuang offered is, in fact, showing his students a way towards deductive reasoning and intertextual comparison that can be used in order to gain deeper understanding of the main text and its message.

Another example of the tutor seizing the opportunity to use elaboration and clarification to guide students through a course of deductive reasoning so as to gain a clearer understanding of the text and enhance their analytical skills id found in LY 3.9 where the rather complex matter of the succession of

---

① See *Tang xieben Lunyu yishu* [LY 3.6.]: 何知泰山在鲁家? 泰山者,诗云:泰山巖巖,鲁邦所詹。何知林放鲁人者? 泰山既鲁山,则林放是鲁人. For the point of reference in the "Odes of Lu" see *Mao Shi zhengyi*, 20B: 13a [p. 782]. Compare *LYYS*, 1: 4b-5a which does not contain this passsage.

② See *LYYS*, 1: 3b: 林放鲁人也.

power is clarified in complementary commentaries by the tutor in Dunhuang. On other occasions, such as in the sub-commentary on LY 3. 10 and LY 3. 11, the tutor summarises previous or ongoing debates on matters of context and interpretation to provide focused guidance to his students. The Tang manuscript, which reads 3. 10 and 3. 11 as one section, has the following additional remark which serves as an agent to clarify the lecture and to impart a more fixed structure to the oral lecture. The insertion is then followed by a direct quotation from the *Lunyu* yishu which details the numerous different theories on the pouring of libations:

> Earlier scholars proposed different explanations [of the meaning] of the pouring out of the libation. From the sub-commentary [these differences] become very clear. ①

Remnants of oral tradition are perhaps most prominently represented in the rhetorical question and answer format Huang Kan employs in his sub-commentaries on LY 1. 11, 1. 13, LY 7. 14 and so forth in the text version transmitted via Japan. To show this on just one example, we may refer to LY 7. 17, a passage discussing the influence of music upon people and vice versa, on which Huang Kan notes:

> Someone asked: "If music changes in compliance with the lord, and it the lord's heart is good, then the music becomes good, [and] if the heart is lewd, then the music becomes lewd. Now, the lord of Qi was not with the Way, but the music did not change and still flourished, how can this be so? Moreover, if the music kept flourishing, then the people of Qi ought to change with the music, but the people of Qi remained fierce and did not change in compliance with the music, how can that be

---

① See *Tang xieben Lunyu yishu* [LY 3. 10 11]: 先儒说灌法不同,依疏明显者也 and compare the sub-commentary in *LYYS*, 2: 8b-10b.

so?" I [Huang Kan] answer: "The music that follows the lord and thus changes is only the music in the time of a [real] king, that's it. "

The question answer format is a recurring teaching practice in the *Lunyu* yishu which serves a dual purpose. It gives the lecture structure and divides the material up more cleanly, and it serves as a method of retaining students' attention. The example in the sub-commentary on LY 7. 14 is fairly lengthy but shows a clearly constructed dialogue which elaborates on the core point. There are, however, many less developed rhetorical interjections, often consisting of no more than as simple hezhe 何者 (why is this?), a short interjection that seems to offer nothing more than to ensure the students' attention stays focussed, and thereby providing us with a fascinating insight into aspects of oral transmission as experienced in a classroom situations throughout the ages.

In the given context the rhetorical question answer format is certainly far from exclusive to the *Lunyu* yishu or to Huang Kan's teaching practice, and there are also numerous examples of rhetorical questions in the Tang manuscript fragment. These include LY 1. 10 where Zigong (520 – 446) discusses the master's methods of inquiring information. While the sub-commentary in the *Lunyu* yishu transmitted via Japan builds up a rather standard topic-comment, with a wording almost identical to that found in the manuscript, the manuscript shows the passage he zhi yu ren zhi qiu yi ye 何知与人之求異也 (How [do we] know [Confucius] is different to others in his seeking [of information]?), an insertion that originates from a real-life classroom situation.

In the two versions of the *Lunyu* yishu, we also find examples ofboth texts using rhetorical questions in the same place, but for different purposes. In LY 2. 22 for example, Confucius equates a man's trustworthiness (xin 信) to the crossbar of a chariot. Both versions of Huang Kan's sub-commentary make reference to Jiang Xi who quoted Chen Yansheng saying "A carriage relying upon its clamps and crossbar to move is similar to men relying on trustworthiness to stand [firm]". But whereas the manuscript introduces this quotation in a manner in which the topic is laid out by giving a clear direction of the discourse, the version transmitted via Japan uses parallel rhetorical questions as a means for textual emphasis:

> If a chariot does not have clamps or a crossbar, what can it then use to move?! If someone does not have trustworthiness, what can he then use to make a stand?!

The manuscript reads:

> How do we know that a man's being in accordance with trustworthiness is similar to a carriage's dependance on clamps and crossbar?

In other words, whereas the rhetorical question here serves as an emphatic element in the versions received via Japan, the manuscript appears to use the very same technique to add structure and direction to the discourse, presumably to assist the students in their learning to access the material.

To sum it up: The omissions, interpolations and amendments in the sub-commentary version from Dunhuang do not result from alterations made in Japan but are primarily related to amendments made by the tutor delivering his lecture on the *Lunyu* based on Huang Kan's readings. ① It thus follows that although the Tang manuscript is the earliest textual witness of and an invaluable source material for the *Lunyu* yishu, it represents what might be described as a "working manuscript" either taken from or used for lectures based on the *Lunyu* yishu at the periphery of the Tang empire. It offers valuable insights into teaching practices and manuscript culture but it does, unfortunately, not qualify as a faithful and trustworthy representation of the "original" textual condition of the *Lunyu* yishu.

---

① Due to the lack of further textual witnesses it remains however unclear to what extent these amendments are to be associated with one specific tutor or whether they can be taken as indications for a wider trend in teaching material related to the *Lunyu* and the *Lunyu yishu* at the time.

The versions of the *Lunyu* yishu handed down in Japan and re-introduced to China during the reign of Qianlong allow for glimpses into Huang Kan's classroom at the National University of the Liang where his lectures were attended by fairly large numbers of students. This version represents what we may call "edited lecture notes" which take the *Lunyu* jijie as its exegetical starting point and develop an intellectual environment in which the openness of the main text is emphasised over and over again by Huang Kan who discusses and allows for diverging, sometimes even contradicting, readings and interpretations of the Master's utterances. The transmitted text shows plenty of remnants of the oral teaching tradition, and offers telling insights into teaching practices. The Tang manuscript fragment builds on Huang Kan's elaborations and shows a second layer of oral transmission of teaching the *Lunyu*. The additional elucidations of the tutor in Dunhuang also offer windows into what was expected of students of the *Lunyu* in a specific environment during the late Tang. The tutor not only provides pointers and focused summaries but also additional references where he sees the need for doing so due to the students' perceived lack of familiarity with more advanced readings. On the other hand, the manuscript clearly indicates that the students' familiarity with the *Lunyu* jijie was a prerequisite, and that the main text was read and explained with reference to both, the *Lunyu* jijie and the *Lunyu* yishu. Although the appearance of main-text-cum-commentary editions is most widely associated with the printing business during the Song, it is clear that the main text of the *Lunyu*, the explanations recorded in the *Lunyu* jijie, the further elaborations, discussions of and addenda to it in Huang Kan's *Lunyu* yishu, as well as the tutor's take on all these materials were all substantial components of the teaching that took place in Dunhuang. The written outline of these teaching session, presumably recorded by a pupil, most certainly never aimed at later generations but, by coincidence, later emerged as the earliest textual witness of the *Lunyu* yishu that fills some of the gaps in our knowledge on how readings of the classics were passed down from generation to generation.

Delinquent Fathers and Philology:
Lunyu 13. 18 and Related Texts

Oliver Weingarten[1]

Introduction

Confucius is commonly regarded as one of the most influential thinkers of China, if not humanity. For two millenia, his words were carefully memorised and studied by Chinese literati, and they are still widely known and cherished. One of the most valued sources on the personality and teachings of the historical Confucius is the *Lunyu*, which is also widely considered to be one of the first, if not the first philosophical work in Chinese intellectual history. This view needs to be reconsidered. Philological studies of the *Lunyu* have thrown up a host of problems relating to the text's stratification, to the dates of its individual layers, and the date of its compilation. Such problems frequently are not given the attention they deserve, especially in discussions of *Lunyu* passages that focus on their philosophical significance and interpretation.

A full discussion of the textual stratification and dating of the *Lunyu* is beyond the scope of this paper.[2] However, I would like to explore on the

---

[1] ow208@ cam. ac. uk.

[2] For a more extensive assessment of textual studies of the *Lunyu* see Weingarten 2009a. 2.

basis of a single *Lunyu* passage and some related materials the possibilities that a revisionist approach to the *Lunyu* offers with regard to its appraisal as an historical source. I am convinced that a more systematic study of one of the foundational texts of Confucianism will ultimately lead to a reassessment of its origins and, possibly, of its significance in the earliest stage of its reception in Han China.

I have chosen *Lunyu* 13.18, the well-known passage about the man who testifies against his father, to illustrate the possibilities of a revisionist reading of the *Lunyu*. There are two reasons for this choice. First, there exist two important parallels to this text in pre-Qin sources which indicate, if carefully compared to the *Lunyu* version, that the latter is of a later date than the other two versions. Second, the *Lunyu* passage has attracted a certain amount of attention among students of comparative philosophy, who point out similarities with Plato's "Euthyphro". [1] One may wonder, among other things, whether such comparisons would still be viable should it turn out that the words attributed to Confucius in this passage are unlikely to have ever been spoken by him. At least, the comparisons would need to be framed in a different way.

In the following, I will briefly introduce recent views of The *Lunyu* and how they are likely to encourage a change in scholarly perspectives on the value of the *Lunyu* as a source on the historical Confucius. I will then present and discuss parallels to *Lunyu* 13.18 in Han Fei zi and Lü shi chunqiu as well as quotations of and allusions to it in Han texts. Finally, I will address the question of how evidence such as that presented in this paper can change the way we read the *Lunyu*.

Recent Scholarly Views of the *Lunyu*

It is commonly assumed that the *Lunyu* provides its reader with the most

---

[1] See Murphy and Weber 2010.

reliable picture of the historical Confucius, of his personality and his
teachings. ①After all, in what is probably a quotation from Liu Xiang's 刘向
(79 – 8 BCE) catalogue of the Imperial Library of the Han, Ban Gu 班固
(32 – 92) states that the *Lunyu* consists of the records and memories of
Confucius's disciples. ② The *Lunyu* itself tells us that Zizhang once "noted
down [the Master's words] on [his] sash", which suggests that disciples did,
indeed, keep records of Confucius's utterances. ③ Consequently, the *Lunyu*
has received more attention as a source of information on the historical
Confucius than other, non-canonical or even canonical writings. ④

However, the problem of the early history and authenticity of The *Lunyu*
has recently come to the fore in Western Sinology. About a decade ago, the
Bruce and Taeko Brooks summed up several centuries' worth of critical
scholarship from China, Japan and the West. As a result, they controversially
concluded that philological methods allowed them to identify distinct textual
layers of separate origins in the *Lunyu* and to rearrange them in their original
chronological sequence. ⑤For very good reasons, only few scholars have
agreed with the Brookses. Their reconstructions are based on arbitrary criteria
and an unsubstantiated account of the early history of Confucianism and the
Confucian "school". ⑥ These reservations notwithstanding, their work does
raise intriguing questions. Philological considerations not entirely different

---

① His biography is a different matter entirely. Sima Qian"s vita of the Master (*Shiji* 47) is the
earliest account that approaches the format of a conventional biography. It is widely acknowledged to be
unreliable, but for a lack of alternatives, it is still habitually used as a source.

② *Han shu* 30. 1717.

③ *Lunyu* 15. 6

④ The historian Zhu Weizheng estimates that only a few out of four to five hundred research
articles on Confucius published between 1949 and the middle of the 1980s in Mainland China are based
on source materials other than the *Lunyu* (Zhu Weizheng 2002, p. 98).

⑤ Brooks and Brooks 1998.

⑥ The discussion in English publications is summarised for a Chinese scholarly audience in Jin
Xueqin 2009, which ends on a skeptical note. A detailed discussion of the entire problem is presented
in Weingarten 2009a, ch. 1. Misgivings about the concept of "schools" in ancient Chinese thought have
been voiced over the last one or two decades in Western Sinology.

from theirs as well as the increasing methodological sophistication in the study of excavated manuscripts will undoubtedly change the way scholars read the *Lunyu* in the future and assess its source value. Recent scholarship tends to emphasise the fluidity and malleability of early writings that was due to scribal practices and the nature of the most commonly used writing supports, strips of bamboo or wood, that allowed readers and copyists to easily modify, enlarge or shorten the manuscripts that they used. [1]

According to research by Zhu Weizheng and John Makeham, it is likely that the date of compilation of The *Lunyu* was as late as the middle of the second century BCE, which means that individual textual units may have entered the *Lunyu* at any time up to that point. [2] Not all parts of the *Lunyu* can be assumed to speak about the historical Confucius with the same degree of authority, and the identification and dating of textual layers will remain an important problem that requires much further study. One may certainly wonder whether the *Lunyu* really had any direct relationship with Confucius and his disciples at all. There is no need to take Liu Xiang's word for it, given that he lived four centuries after Confucius's death.

It is an open question whether scholars will ever reach a consensus on the nature of textual layers in The *Lunyu*, on the individual dates of these layers, and on the problem of the date and nature of the entire compilation. Nevertheless, scholars who are interested in a critical investigation of the early Confucian tradition cannot ignore these problems indefinitely. They will have to engage in a critical study of their sources and will eventually have to address problems of a kind that have been explored by students of the New Testament for over a century. [3]

---

[1]   On the influence of manuscript studies on changing concepts of early writings and especially of the *Lunyu* see Scarpari 2007 and *id.* 2010, pp. 31 – 37 and 40 – 45. For a few remarks on the relationship between the *Lunyu* and the stock of fairly fluid maxims and other small textual units in pre-imperial times see also Li Ling 2007, pp. 35 – 36, and id. 2008, pp. 477 – 478.

[2]   Zhu Weizheng 1987, p. 168; Makeham 1996.

[3]   See e. g. Webb 2009 for a recent summary of and introduction to historical research on Jesus.

So far, scholars tend to concede that The *Lunyu* consists of heterogeneous textual strata, but they still customarily utilise different parts of the text more or less indiscriminately as evidence for whatever point they wish to make. ① Doubts exists as to whether the *Lunyu* deserves the elevated status it has enjoyed for such a long time. So far, however, such scepticism has not given rise to a significant body of scholarship that explicitly addresses these problems.

One way to approach the *Lunyu* from a new angle and to take its heterogeneous nature into account is to investigate textual parallels, instances of shared language or motifs that are too similar to be due to coincidence. A fair amount of such shared textual material exists and can be conveniently accessed. ② New evidence containing such a parallel suggests strongly that some of the texts assembled in the *Lunyu* may represent fragments or excerpts of longer writings rather than complete textual units. ③ So far, however, scholars have not made much use of these precious materials. Generally speaking, whenever parallels between the *Lunyu* and other texts are identified, it is assumed that these texts quote or allude to the *Lunyu*. But the problem is not so straightforward, and the heterogeneous nature of the materials in the *Lunyu* should alert scholars to the possibility that different paragraphs entered the text at different times and from sources with very different characteristics. Moreover, there is neither internal not external evidence to demonstrate that the *Lunyu* existed in anything approaching its

---

① Scarpari 2010, pp. 58 – 60, outlines the tension between critical philological approaches and a basic trust in the unity of the *Lunyu*'s philosophical outlook. For a recent attempt to reconcile philological considerations with a belief in the fundamental usefulness of the *Lunyu* as a source see Slingerland 2009, pp. 107 – 109. In spite of the numerous unsolved historical and philological problems, to Slingerland "it seems best to stick to whatever facts we might glean from the Analects itself" (p. 107).

② For illustrations of this approach see Richter 2002 and 2005; for an example specifically relating to the *Lunyu* see Weingarten 2009b. For editions that record textual parallels to the *Lunyu* see Yang Shuda ed. 1955, Hayashi Taisuke ed. 1971, Chan and Ho ed. 2007 .

③ See the parallel to *Lunyu* 13. 2 in the manuscript text "Zhonggong" 中弓 [= 仲弓] held by the Museum of Shanghai (see Chen Tongsheng 2006 for the textual evidence).

present form prior to the second century BC, let alone that it was regarded as an authoritative text—if it existed at all. We may therefore assume that a fairly free exchange of textual units took place between different traditions that were later incorporated into compilations considered to belong to different "schools". I believe that we will learn a lot about the *Lunyu* if we consider these phenomena carefully. To make a first, tentative step into this direction, I will examine textual parallels to our *Lunyu* passage about the thieving father and his upright son.

Thieving Fathers in and outside the *Lunyu*

A well-known *Lunyu* passage tells us about an encounter between Confucius and a noble from the southern state of Chu.

叶公语孔子曰:吾党有直躬者,其父攘羊,而子证之。孔子曰:吾党之直者异于是。父为子隐,子为父隐,直在其中矣。

The Master of She told Master Kong: "In my village there is a straight-bodied person. His father stole a sheep, and he, the son, testified against him. " Master Kong said: "Straight men in my village are different. Fathers cover for their sons, and sons for their fathers. Therein lies straightness. "[①]

The above passage is not the only one that refers to this, or a very similar-event. Two more early texts exist about a father who steals a sheep and is given up to the authorities by his "straight-bodied" son: the Han Fei zi and the Lü shi chunqiu. The following is the version found in Han Fei zi. It forms part of a longer discussion in the chapter "Five Pests" (Wu du 五蠹).

儒以文乱法,侠以武犯禁,而人主兼礼之,此所以乱也。夫离法者罪,而诸先生以文学取;犯禁者诛,而群侠以私剑养。故法之所非,君之所取;吏之所诛,上之所养也。法趣上下四相反也,而无所定,虽有十黄帝不能

---

① *Lunyu* 13. 18. The "Master of She" is Shen Zhuliang 沈诸梁, adult name Zigao 子高 from Chu who may have encountered Confucius in 489 BCE. Scholars disagree over whether *zhi gong zhe* 直躬者 is a description or a nickname, "a certain, straight Gong". I assume that it is the former and have chosen a literal translation to differentiate it from the following *zhi zhe* 直者.

治也。故行仁义者非所誉,誉之则害功;文学者非所用,用之则乱法。楚之有直躬,其父窃羊而谒之吏,令尹曰:杀之,以为直于君而曲于父,报而罪之。以是观之,夫君之直臣,父之暴子也。鲁人从君战,三战三北,仲尼问其故,对曰:吾有老父,身死莫之养也。仲尼以为孝,举而上之。以是观之,夫父之孝子,君之背臣也。故令尹诛而楚奸不上闻,仲尼赏而鲁民易降北[=败]。上下之利若是其异也,而人主兼举匹夫之行,而求致社稷之福,必不几矣。

With their embellishments, the Ru plunge the law into disorder; with their martiality, the knight-errants oppose restrictions, and yet the ruler embraces them and treats them according to ritual propriety. For this reason there is disorder. He who diverges from the law is guilty, but all those gentlemen [i. e. the Ru] are selected because of their embellished learning. He who opposes restrictions is executed, but the group of knight-errants is fed because of the swords that they privately own. And so it is those condemned by the law that the prince selects; it is those who the officials execute that the highest one feeds.

While shuttling back and forth between the highest and [his] inferiors, the laws are repeatedly reversed (?) and lack firm ground. Even if there were ten Yellow Emperors, they would be unable to impose order on this. Therefore: The one who implements benevolence and righteousness is not to be praised; praise him, and his will prove harmful to achievements. Those of embellished learning are not to be employed; employ them, and this will plunge the law into disorder.

When there was a straight-bodied man in Chu, and his father stole a sheep and he reported him to the officials, the chancellor said: "Kill him. He believed himself to be straight toward his ruler, but [in fact] behaved deviously toward hisfather, so he reported him and implicated him in a crime. " From this point of view, a ruler's straight subject is a violent son to his father.

A man from Lu followed his ruler into battle, and in three battles he was defeated thrice. When Zhongni enquired about the reason, the man replied:

"I have an elderly father, and should I die, nobody would nurture him. "
Zhongni considered him filial and promoted and honoured him. From this
point of view, a father's filial son is a subject that spells defeat for his ruler.

Therefore: The chancellor ordered an execution and crimes in Chu were
not reported to the superiors[anymore]. Zhongni ordered a reward and the
people of Lu easily submitted to defeat. To such extent do the respective
benefits of the highest and his inferiors diverge, and if the ruler embraces and
promotes the conduct of ordinary men in order to secure blessings for the
altars of soil and grain, this will inevitably lead to failure. [1]

To summarise the discussion in this passage: Both the Ru—or
"Classicists"—and the "knight-errants" undermine the rule of law, the Ru
through their teachings and the knight-errants through their willingness to
employ illegal violence for their own, private ends. Nevertheless, both groups
enjoy the support of the ruler. Such inconsistency in the application of the law
causes unrest, so the ruler needs to change his treatment of these groups and
throw the book at them if they misbehave. This is the central concern of the
passage.

Han Fei (ca. 280 – ca. 233 BC)—provided that he wrote this—then
uses two illustrations to drive home his point that moral considerations should
not be allowed to interfere with the application of legal regulations. The first is
the anecdote about the "straight-bodied man" from Chu and his father. It
looks rather different from the *Lunyu* version in that the straight-bodied man is
punished by the chancellor for the betrayal of his father. As a result of this
emphasis on a family-centred ethics, Han Fei points out in his conclusion,
crimes were not reported anymore in the state of Chu. The second illustration
involves Confucius. He reccommends a soldier from his homestate of Lu for
shying away from fighting because he fears that his father might wind up
without support if he falls on the battlefield. Again, such emphasis on filial
piety is harmful to the state, Han Fei concludes, because it will reduce its

---

[1] *Han Fei zi* 49. 1057.

military strength.

The second parallel to The *Lunyu* passage about the "straight-bodied man" is found in the Lü shi chunqiu chapter "Dang wu" 当务:

楚有直躬者，其父窃羊而谒之上，上执而将诛之。直躬者请代之。将诛矣，告吏曰：父窃羊而谒之，不亦信乎？父诛而代之，不亦孝乎？信且孝而诛之，国将有不诛者乎？荆王闻之，乃不诛也。孔子闻之曰：异哉直躬之为信也，一父而载[＝再]取名焉。故直躬之信，不若无信。

In Chu there was a straight-bodied man. When his father stole a sheep, he reported him to the superiors, and the superiors had him arrested and were going to execute him. The straight man begged permission to replace his father. Just when he was about to be executed, he addressed the officials: "Did I not indeed prove my trustworthiness when I reported my father after he stole a sheep? Does it not indeed show filial piety that I am taking the place of my father who was going to be executed? If you are actually going to execute someone who is not only trustworthy but also filial, would anyone in this state be spared execution?" The king of Jing heard this and, as a result, spared him.

When Master Kong heard this, he said: "Peculiar indeed is this straight-bodied man is trustworthiness. He twice gets a reputation out of a single father!" Therefore: Rather than having that straight-bodied [man's] trustworthiness, it is better not to have any at all. ①

The situation described here diverges from the anecdote narrated in the Han Fei zi. First of all, the outcome is very different. The "straight-bodied man" ends up dead in the Han Fei zi because he has acted against the principle of filial piety. In the Lü shi chunqiu, nobody gets punished; both father and son emerge unharmed from the events. The son proves his trustworthiness by reporting his father, but he also demonstrates his filial piety by offering to have himself executed in his father's stead. The text concludes

---

① *Lü shi chunqiu* 11/4. 603.

with a critical comment by Confucius: using one and the same person in order to get a good reputation out of him twice-that is "peculiar indeed"! What this gruff statement implies is, of course, that you cannot have your cake and eat it too. Either you report your father and accept that he will suffer punishment, or you cover up for him to save him-as the Confucius figure of the *Lunyu* suggests. But you can't have it both ways.

A brief inspection of some annotated *Lunyu* editions suggests that commentators have not usually paid much attention to the textual parallels. Some space is devoted to glosses of individual words (e. g. rang 攘, ye 谒, or zheng 证), and the moral of the passage is duly considered. On the whole, though, the commentators seem barely concerned with the ethical conundrum implied in the situation that is set out in the *Lunyu* paragraph. They all agree that it is right not to testify against one's father and do not consider collusion with the authorities a serious alternative. ① Only the Qing scholars Zhai Hao and Song Xiangfeng point out the parallels, and of these two only the latter discusses them in more detail:

两书所记，一诛一不诛，異者。盖其始，楚王不诛，而躬以直闻于楚。叶公闻孔子语，故当其为令尹而诛之。

What the two books [i. e. Han Fei zi and Lü shi chunqiu] record-that in one case [the son] was executed, but in the other he was not-is different. Presumably, the king of Chu did not execute him initially, and Gong became known in Chu for his straightness. The Master of She heard Master Kong's words, therefore he punished [Gong] when he served as chancellor (lingyin). ②

---

①　This is based on the commentaries reproduced in Liu Baonan ed. 1990, p. 536f. ; Cheng Shude ed. 1990, pp. 924 – 926; Huang Huaixin ed. 2008, pp. 1194 – 1198. Among the writings quoted are commentaries and philological notes by He Yan 何晏 (ca. 190 – 249), Huang Kan 黄侃 (488 – 545), Xing Bing 邢昺 (932 – 1011), Zhu Xi 朱熹 (1130 – 1200), Wang Fuzhi 王夫之 (1619 – 1692), Zhai Hao 翟灝 (d. 1788), Song Xiangfeng 宋翔凤 (1779 – 1860), and Yu Yue 俞樾 (1821 – 1907).

②　Quoted in Liu Baonan ed. 1990, p. 536. So far I have been unable to locate the passage in Song's *Guo ting lu* 过庭录 (ed. Liang Yunhua 梁运华, Beijing: Zhonghua shuju, 1986), from which the quote is taken.

Song assumes that the texts reflect events that took place in a certain chronological order. According to this view, the "straight-bodied man's" behaviour went unpunished at first (Lü shi chunqiu). Then the Master of She learned from Confucius what really constitutes straight behaviour (Lunyu), and when he became chancellor-as he did according to the Zuozhuan-he acted according to the Master's judgment and had the man executed (Han Fei zi).

This reading reflects an attempt to harmonise the sources by creating a temporal sequence between the pieces of information they contain. This approach allows all three of them to be regarded as historically true-true with regard to the state of affairs at different points in time, that is. This approach does not appear very convincing and seems to suffer from a certain inclination toward "face-valuism" in the reading of historical texts.

Interestingly, however, the sequence of events as arranged by Song does not correspond to the usual assumptions about the dates of the sources. The Lunyu is commonly regarded as the oldest of the three texts, but according to Song Xiangfeng, the events it relates happened after those recorded in the Lü shi chunqiu, while the Han Fei zi, which is, at least according to the age of its purported author-likely to be slightly older than the Lü shi chunqiu, narrates what happened last.

How, then, do the three versions of the anecdote relate to each other? The compilation date of the Lüshi chunqiu-ca. 239 BC—is a fairly straightforward matter. [1] But let us for the moment remain agnostic with regard to the dates of the compilations Lunyu and Han Fei zi and also, more specifically, with regard to the dates of the textual units under discussion. [2]If one assumes a lineal transmission from one of the texts to one of the other

---

[1] See Loewe ed. 1993, p. 324.

[2] Confucius lived earlier than Han Fei, who was roughly contemporaneous with Lü Buwei. However, Confucius did not write the Lunyu, which might have been compiled as late as the second century BCE, and the Han Fei zi in its present form was compiled under the Han. Individual textual units might have entered any of these texts at any point prior to the editorial work that fixed their extant form, and these textual units might have been quoted from sources written at any point before they were included in these works.

two, and then from the second to the remaining third, there are, in principle, six different routes that the anecdote could have taken. ① However, the assumption of a lineal transmission process is far from self-evident. Theoretically, two or all three of the texts may have drawn on a common source that has since disappeared, or they might have been derived from dissimilar versions of the same source. Even the influence of oral transmission with its inherent instability cannot be excluded. These considerations show that intertextual relationships in pre-imperial writings pose complex problems, and that there are limits to what philological studies of these texts can achieve. One thing is certain, however, and is worth emphasising: it is not sufficient to simply surmise that the presumably older and more authoritative text does in any case represent the oldest version of a given textual unit that is then quoted by other writings.

Leaving aside all the theoretically possible complications in the transmission process of the "straight man" episode, is it possible to arrive at a plausible scenario for the relationship between the three extant versions? Let us compare the texts in more detail.

In Han Feizi, Confucius is not directly associated with the case of the "straight man" from Chu. Rather, he comments on a contrasting anecdote, the one about the man from his homestate, Lu, who shies away from fighting because he wants to stay alive to be able to look after his father. The chancellor of Chu executes the "straight man" and, as a result, "acts of treachery" go unreported in Chu. Confucius encourages filial piety and Lu's military power is depleted. Both actions are condemned as harmful to the state by Han Fei.

TheLü shi chunqiu, a book that originated, like Han Fei zi, in Qin and was compiled during Han Fei's lifetime, presents a Confucius figure who

---

① These are: (1) *Lunyu* [LY], Han Fei zi [HFZ], Lü shi chunqiu [LSCQ]. (2) HFZ, LY, LSCQ. (3) LSCQ, HFZ, LY. (4) LY, LSCQ, HF. (5) HFZ, LSCQ, LY. (6) LSCQ, LY, HFZ.

13

criticises the "straight man" because he proves his allegiance to the powers that be by testifying against his father while he also tries to cling on to his credentials as a filial son by offering to undergo the punishment for his father's crime. Confucius condemns his actions, but he does not object so much to the man's betrayal of his father, but rather to his duplicitousness. The issue is not his lack of filial piety, but of "trustworthiness" (xin 信). Only in the *Lunyu* version does Confucius oppose the man's testimony against his father per se, because father and son are supposed to "cover up" each other's misdeeds.

I think there is good reason to believe that The *Lunyu* version developed as a result of the influence of an anecdote identical with or similar to the Lü shi chunqiu version, possibly also under the influence of the Han Fei zi. In spite of their dissimilarities, all three versions contain correspondences that indicate a close textual relationship. They all call the son who reports on his father a "straight" or "straight-bodied man". *Han Feizi* and *Lü shi chunqiu* share the use of ye(谒) to report, while the *Lunyu* speaks of zheng(证), and they both use qie(窃)forstealing, while the *Lunyu* has rang(攘). Han Fei zi and Lü shi chunqiu expressly identify the son as a denizen of Chu; the *Lunyu* does so implicitly by making him a villager in the domain of the "Master of She", a place located in Chu. Finally, all three versions use the word yi (異), although, tellingly, with different connotations—a symptom of the malleability of the tradition. Han Feizi concludes that the interests of superiors and inferiors "diverge" (yi) from another. The Confucius figure of the Lü shi chunqiu considers the "straight man's" brand of trustworthiness "peculiar" (yi), and that of the *Lunyu* claims that "straight persons" in his village are "different" (yi) from the "straight man" of Chu. Note that this last utterance implicitly contrasts the mores of Chu and Lu. The comparison is reminiscent of the Han Fei zi paragraph but unrelated to the Lü shi chunqiu version.

In its condemnation of the chancellor of Chu's decision to have the unfilial son executed, the Han Feizi shows approval of the "straight man's" action, an attitude that chimes in with the legalist interest in a strong state. However, Confucius is not associated with this case. The Confucius figure enters the text as part of a separate narrative. In the Lü shi chunqiu, Confucius is made to comment on the "straight man", and this might well result from the close juxtaposition of the two anecdotes in Han Fei zi. However, the Lü shi chunqiu does not show any particular interest in the man's unfilial behaviour. The issue is rather his dishonesty.

The *Lunyu*, in contrast, merges two aspects that are kept distinct in the other two versions: (1) the condemnation of the straight man for implicating his father-this corresponds to the attitude of the chancellor of Chu in the Han Fei zi; (2) the use of the Confucius figure as a critic, a feature of the Lü shi chunqiu, but not the Han Fei zi. The ideological thrust of the Master's judgment in the *Lunyu* is diametrically opposed to the moral of the Han Fei zi version. The Ru do not wish to strengthen the state, they rather want to protect clan solidarity against the invasive meddling of the state. The *Lunyu* version combines a formal feature of one version (Confucius as a commentator in Lü shi chunqiu) with an ideological position that is reported, though not endorsed, in another (the condemnation of the "straight man" in the *Han Fei zi*).

We may now ask what is more likely: that the Han Fei zi and Lü shi chunqiu versions developed in reaction to the *Lunyu* version, or vice versa. It appears unconvincing that Han Fei should have responded to the *Lunyu* version with the text that we find in today's "Wu du" chapter. Surely, a reaction to the *Lunyu* would have adressed Confucius's judgment on the "straight man". Instead we find two anecdotes, one that involves the "straight man" of Chu, and another, unrelated one about Confucius's attitude toward a man in Lu. And although Confucius is criticised in the Han Fei zi, he is not censured for his judgment on the "straight man's" behaviour, because he is mentioned in connection with a different figure. Why should Han Fei have deconstructed the *Lunyu* passage by disassociating some of its elements from each other and relating them separately in his own text?

It is far more likely that the author of The *Lunyu* paragraph was influenced by a version closer to that in the Lü shi chunqiu. Here we find

Confucius directly associated with the "straight man" case, and he acts as a commentator who passes a negative moral judgment. We may therefore assume that the Han Fei zi with its juxtaposition of the "straight man" anecdote and the anecdote about Confucius's positive judgment on the man in Lu gave rise to a version that conflates the two elements-the anecdote and Confucius as a source of a judgment-as the Lü shi chunqiu does. The Lü shi chunqiu or a version very similar to it then influenced or inspired the author of the text that is now part of the *Lunyu*. In the *Lunyu*, the anecdote assumes an ideological colouring that is not identical with the Lü shi chunqiu, but nevertheless much closer to it than the Han Feizi.

Admittedly, this sketch of the anecdote's route of transmission remains fuzzy. I would not necessarily insist that Han Fei zi led directly to Lü shi chunqiu, and that the author of the *Lunyu* version read the Lü shi chunqiu exactly as we now have it. It is impossible to know, and rather unlikely, that all the relevant evidence is still extant. As indicated above, it is likely that various other versions of this anecdote existed that were transmitted either orally or in writing. But I would contend that the Han Fei zi version was conceived prior to Lü shi chunqiu, and in this instance, the influence might have been fairly direct given that both texts originated in Qin at around the same time. The case for the connection between Lü shi chunqiu and *Lunyu* is less clear, but I doubt that the *Lunyu* version could have come into being without the influence of a version that displayed some of the same elements as the Lü shi chunqiu version.

Allusions and References in Han Sources

In addition to the sources discussed so far, a number of Eastern and Western Han texts quote Confucius's judgment about the "straight-bodied man" or allude to it. These references provide an impression of how Han scholars used and understood the text of the *Lunyu*.

A passage in theHuainan zi combines two allusions, one to the "straight-bodied man", and one to Wei Sheng, who proved his trustworthiness when he drowned because he had arranged to meet with his wife in a place that became inundated, but he was unwilling to leave because of the commitment he had made:

直躬,其父攘羊而子证之。尾生与妇人期而死之。直而证父,信而溺死,虽有直信,孰能贵之。

The straight-bodied [man]—his father stole a sheep, but [he], the son, testified against him. Wei Sheng had a date with a woman and died for it. To be straight and yet to testify against one's father, to be trustworthy and drown-even though [these two men] were straight and trustworthy, who could appreciate it?①

The judgment on the "straight-bodied man" is negative, although, contrary to Confucius, the author of this passage does not fundamentally question the man's "straightness". Rather, his particular brand of straightness does not inspire much admiration. Confucius is not mentioned in this passage, and one may assume that the source of the allusion was not considered very important. A passage in the Zhonglun(中论) of the Eastern Han scholar Xu Gan(徐干,170 – 217) uses the same two examples, among others, to illustrate that there are more and less desirable varieties of certain virtues. 2②

A short paragraph in theHan shi waizhuan, a text that was compiled around the middle of the second century BCE, contains some similarities with the *Lunyu* paragraph:

子为亲隐,义不得正;君诛不义,仁不得爱。虽违仁害义,法在其中矣。诗曰:优哉游哉。亦是戾矣。

If a son covers up for his father, justice is not being upheld ['kept correct']. If a prince executes an unjust person, benevolence is not being held dear. But even though [the one] acts against benevolence and [the

---

① *Huainan zi* 13, p. 1402.

② For the original text and an English translation see Makeham 2002, pp. 80 – 83.

other] harms justice, the law lies therein. The Ode says:

"How mild, how happy, / Is their coming here! "①

The passage alludes to the words attributed to Confucius in The *Lunyu*. The term ' to cover up' (yin 隐) occurs in none of the other versions, and the concluding statement that precedes the quotation from the Odes imitates the phrasing of Confucius's comment on straightness (zhi zai qi zhong yi 直在其 中矣). Interestingly, however, the passage points out that it is not "just" (yi 义) to conceal one's fathers misdeeds and that an "unjust [person] " (bu yi 不义) deserves to be punished even though this runs counter to the ideal of "benevolence" (ren 仁). Moreover, the text emphasises the rule of law (fa 法) in a way that is diametrically opposed to the lesson one is supposed to draw from the *Lunyu*. Whoever wrote this clearly had very different ideas about the relationship between state law and family values than the author of the *Lunyu* paragraph. If the author of the Han shi waizhuan passage reacted to a statement that he associated with Confucius-which is not evident from this passage—he certainly did not conceive of him as an unassailable authority.

Another passage in theHan shi waizhuan with a parallel in Lü shi chunqiu narrates the story of a "man of service" (shi 士) called Shi She(石 奢) in Chu. ② The concept of straightness that is central to *Lunyu* 13. 18 recurs in both of these texts. Shi She is known for being "public-spirited and fond of straightness" (gong er hao zhi 公而好直) according to the Han shi waizhuan or, in the Lü shi chunqiu version, for being " public-spirited, straight and free from selfishness" (gong zhi wu si 公直无私). One day, he observes a murder on the street and pursues the killer, only to come face to face with his own father. He lets him escape, but presents himself at court and commits suicide, although the king of Chu pardons him. The demands made on him by his different roles as son and subject are irreconcilable, as he

---

① *Han shi waizhuan* 4, pp. 397 – 398; the quote is from *Shi* no. 222 [trans. : Legge via Hightower]. Cf. the translation in Hightower 1952, pp. 143 – 144. Hightower suggests the emendation of *ai* 爱 to *shòu* 受 [du?] but seems to translate it like *shŏu* 守 [hju?] ("*jên* is not being adhered to").

② *Han shi waizhuan* 2, pp. 160 – 161; *Lü shi chunqiu* 19. 2, p. 1256.

states in his final speech (here in the Han shi waizhuan version) :

不私其父，非孝也；不行君法，非忠也；以死罪生，不廉也。君欲赦之，上之惠也；臣不能失法，下之义也。

Not to be partial toward one's father is impious. Not to carry out the prince's law is illoyal. To live with a guilt worthy of death is not being upright. That Your Majesty wishes to pardon me is the expression of a superior's generosity. That I, Your subject, cannot evade the law, conforms to what is right for a subordinate.

As a son, Shi She is not supposed to capture and incarcerate his father, but as his ruler's subject, he ought not to shirk the responsibility for ignoring the law either. The only solution to this conundrum is his death.

The same story is also found in Xin xu, in a version that is mostly identical with and probably derived from Han shi waizhuan, and in a strongly condensed form in Shiji. ①There are no parallels to the *Lunyu* in either the Lü shi chunqiu or the Shiji versions, and Sima Qian does not quote or allude to the conclusion of the Lü shi chunqiu, that conveys the moral of the anecdote in a few verses. ② Only the Han shi waizhuan and the version derived from it in Xin xu quote Confucius's words as they are recorded in the *Lunyu*. Yet, they do not mention the work expressly but rather introduce the quotation with the phrase "Master Kong said" (Kongzi yue 孔子曰). The Lienü zhuan, like the Xin xu a work that was compiled by Liu Xiang, quotes the sentences explicitly from the *Lunyu*. ③

In the Chunqiu fanlu attributed to the scholar Dong Zhongshu(董仲舒， 179[?] – 104[?] BC), a parallel is constructed between the obligations

---

①   *Xin xu* 7, pp. 949 – 953; see *Shiji* 119, p. 3102, for the anecdote, and *ibid.* , p. 3103, for Sima Qian's brief appraisal of Shi She. It is not clear which version of the anecdote Sima Qian used.

②   The end of the *Lü shi chunqiu* version reads: 正法枉必死。父犯法而不忍 [n？ n？]，王赦之而不肯 [khêN]，石渚之为人臣也 ｜gin}，可谓忠且孝矣。"When the proper laws are bent, death inevitably follows. [Shi She's] father violated the law, but he did not bear [to punish him]; the king pardoned him but [he] did not accept-as a subject, one may call Shi Zhu [= She] both loyal and filial. "

③   *Lienü zhuan* 5. 5. 13/49/26.

towards one's father and those towards the state:

礼，子为父隐恶。今使伐人者，而信不义，当为国讳之。

According to ritual propriety, sons cover up the misdeeds of their fathers. Now, if one lets an attack on others happen even though it is, indeed, unjustified, one should keep it hidden for the sake of the state. ①

The sentence in question is associated with "ritual propriety" in general rather than with the authoritative figure of Confucius, and the writer of this passage might have been influenced by ritual prescriptions such as this one recorded in the Liji:

事亲有隐而无犯。

In serving one's parents, one should cover up [for them], and there should be no disobedience. ②

This statement closely echoes Confucius's utterance in the *Lunyu*, but it is not specifically ascribed to him.

The Yantie lun, which purports to record a series of economic and political debates held at the Han court in 81 BCE, quotes the sentences attributed to Confucius as part of the contribution by the "scholars" (wenxue 文学) to a dispute about punishments. However, the sentences are merely introduced by "[I] heard" (wen 闻) without any explicit attribution. ③ Intriguingly, the contribution is framed as a response to an edict issued by Emperor Xuan 宣 (91 – 49 BC; r. 74 – 49 BC) in 66 BCE, fifteen years after the salt and iron debates were held. The edict stipulates that some relatives can hide the crimes of their kin with impunity, while others will be subjected to the jurisdiction of the emperor. The guiding concept behind this law appears to be that those regarded as the weaker part in a kinship relationship such as sons, wives, or grandsons, were automatically spared punishment if

---

① *Chunqiu fanlu* 25, p. 500.

② *Liji*, "Tan Gong shang", p. 165. The extant version of the *Liji* might have been compiled as late as the first century CE, but very likely contains older materials (see Loewe ed. 1993, pp. 293 – 295).

③ *Yantie lun* 57, p. 584.

they covered up for the superior and more authoritative part such as their parents, husbands, or grandparents, but not vice versa. [1] It is to this edict that the "scholars" object by stating that "since the law about ' taking the lead in hiding' [misdeeds] and mutually incriminating one another has been established, the kindness between close kin [' bone and flesh'] has been cast aside, and crimes and punishments have multiplied". (自首匿相坐之法立, 骨肉之恩废, 而刑罪多矣。) [2] They then bolster their argument by quoting the statement on fathers and sons covering up for each other.

TheBaihu tong, based on court discussions held in 79 CE, contains an explicit quotation of *Lunyu* 13. 18, and in another part of the book, the question of why "a father [should] cover up for his son" (fu wei zi yin 父为子隐) and "a son [should] cover up for his father" (zi wei fu yin 子为父隐) is explored within the framework of the "Five Phases" (wu xing 五行) theory. [3] The Han shu likewise quotes Confucius's words, but under the incipit "a tradition says" (zhuan yue 传曰). [4] He Xiu's 何休 (129 – 182 CE) commentary on the Gongyang zhuan quotes the sentences as well. [5]

Finally, Gao You (高诱,ca. 168 – 212) states in his commentary on the conclusion in the Lü shi chunqiu's parallel to *Lunyu* 13. 18 that "rather than having that straight-bodied man's trustworthiness, it is better not to have any at all" (zhi gong zhi xin, bu ruo wu xin 直躬之信,不若无信):

父为子隐,子为父隐,直在其中矣。信而证父,故曰:不若无信也。

Fathers cover up for their sons and sons for their fathers, therein lies straightness. [He] was trustworthy and yet testified against [his] father, therefore [the text] says: "It is better not to have any trustworthiness at all. " [6]

---

①   *Han shu* 8. 251; see Dubs trans. 1944, p. 224.

②   *Yantie lun* 57, p. 584.

③   *Baihu tong*, *juan* 4, p. 196, and *juan* 5, p. 241.

④   *Han shu* 80. 3322.

⑤   See Chan and Ho ed. 2007 under *Lunyu* 13. 18.

⑥   *Lü shi chunqiu*, p. 609 n20.

The syntax of one of the phrases echoes the remark in Huainan zi that the straight-bodied man "was straight and yet testified against his father" (zhi er zheng fu 直而证父). Possibly, Gao was influenced by the other great book to which he wrote a commentary. More importantly, it is obvious that he makes the connection with Confucius's words without, however, explicitly referring to him. As this quotation and the one in Han shu demonstrate, even during the Eastern Han, the authority of the *Lunyu* might not have been so widely recognised that a writer would automatically refer to it by title to lend his arguments more weight.

Conclusion

From the entire body of evidence presented so far, one can draw the following—necessarily tentative—conclusions. The pattern of *Lunyu* parallels and quotations in pre-Qin and Han sources fits the hypothesis of a late appearance of the *Lunyu*. The Han Fei zi presents a version of the anecdote that is entirely different from and very likely older than the version that the *Lunyu* transmits. The *Lü shi chunqiu* shares two intertextual links with the *Lunyu* passage, one of them direct, the other one indirect. In one paragraph, a version of the anecdote about the "straight-bodied man" is narrated, but it differs substantially from the *Lunyu* version. In another one—the anecdote about Shi She—the topic suggests an association with Confucius's pronouncement on "straightness" and, indeed, the early Han text *Han shi waizhuan* does make this connection by quoting the words of "Master Kong" as a comment on the *Shi She anecdote*. But the *Lü shi chunqiu* itself does not, and neither does Sima Qian, even though he lived only a few decades after the compilator of Han shi waizhuan and his chapters on Confucius (Shiji 47) and the disciples (Shiji 67) demonstrate clearly that he must have been familiar with some version of the *Lunyu*.

In subsequent Han texts, we can observe a heightened attention to Confucius's words, which are quoted or alluded to in several works, and which are even used in an Eastern Han commentary to elucidate the Lü shi chunqiu parallel to *Lunyu* 13. 18. The *Lunyu* text now seems to have become more widely known among scholars, although its title is rarely referred to, and the authors of the texts surveyed above do not appear to be particularly keen to avail themselves of the Master's authority. One of the two Han shi waizhuan passages does not mention the source of its quotation, and neither do the authors of the Huainan zi paragraph, the Chunqiu fanlu and the Yantie lun, or Ban Gu and Gao You.

Inthe case under consideration, the extant testimony does not bear out the notion that the *Lunyu* was very influential-or even widely known at all-during the late Warring States period. Furthermore, both in the Western and Eastern Han scholars do not appear to have paid much attention to the *Lunyu* as an authoritative source. They rather used it as a repertory of Confucius sayings whose authoritative character was due to the fact that they were attributed to the Master. But so were many other materials, and the *Lunyu* itself was merely a "tradition" (zhuan) among others. All this suggests to me that the relative status of the *Lunyu* in comparison to other sources that were available in the Han was not necessarily very high. But the question certainly awaits further study.

Finally, I would argue that it will prove fruitful to put more emphasis on the contextualisation of The *Lunyu*. We may read the *Lunyu* as a text that gives us direct access to the mind of the historical Confucius and treat other pre-Qin and Han works as supplementary materials that help us to achieve this aim. As far as I can see, this is so far the most common approach to the *Lunyu*. But it rests on a debatable pair of assumptions: that the *Lunyu*, or the material contained in it, is older and that it has a stronger claim to authenticity than other texts. Once we reconsider these assumptions, which are not supported by much hard evidence, we are free to approach the *Lunyu* in a different manner. We can explore the textual relationship between its components and other pre-Qin and Han writings, as I have done in this paper. In fact, I am convinced that this should be done for each single *Lunyu* paragraph. More importantly, we can then proceed to contemplate how issues touched upon in individual *Lunyu* passages relate to the historical, cultural and intellectual background of early China more generally. The tension between clan solidarity on the one hand and loyalty toward ruler and state on the other that is impressionistically sketched out in the *Lunyu* paragraph about the "straight-bodied man" is, after all, not a trivial matter. However, regardless of whether Confucius actually commented on the case or not, the *Lunyu* paragraph in itself does not offer much to go on beyond the initial impulse to consider the problem. To arrive at a more nuanced understanding of how people in ancient China conceived of such conflicting obligations, we need to look at sources outside the *Lunyu* like, for instance, the Shi She anecdote. The *Lunyu* would then lose its status as a privileged source on the historical Confucius and rather become a source among others that can be used to explore wider topics in early Chinese culture.

Works Cited

Baihu tong: Chen Li 陈立 ed. 1994. Baihu tong shuzheng 白虎通疏证, Beijing: Zhonghua *shuju*.

Brooks, E. Bruce, and A. Taeko Brooks. 1998. The Original Analects: Sayings of Confucius and His Successors. New York: Cornell University Press.

Chan, Hung Kan [= Chen Xionggen 陈雄根], and Ho Che Wah [= He Zhihua 何志华] ed. 2007. Citations from the Zhouyi, *Lunyu* and Mengzi to Be Found in Pre-Han and Han Texts. Hong Kong: Chinese University Press.

Chen Tongsheng 陈桐生. 2006. "Kongzi yulu de jieben he fanben: cong Zhonggong kan *Lunyu* yu qishi zi houxue sanwen de xingshi chayi" 孔子语录的节本和繁本：从《仲弓》看《论语》与七十子后学散文的形式差异. Kongzi yanjiu 2006. 2, pp. 116 – 122.

Cheng Shude 程树德 [1877 – 1944] ed. 1990. *Lunyu* jishi 论语集释.

Beijing: Zhonghua shuju.

Chunqiu fanlu: Zhong Zhaopeng 锺肇鹏 ed. 2005. Chunqiu fanlu jiaoshi 春秋繁露校释. Rev. ed. Shijiazhuang: Hebei renmin chubanshe.

Dubs, Homer H. trans. 1944. The History of the Former Han Dynasty: Translation, Volume Two. First Division: The Imperial Annals, Chapters VI – X. London: Kegan Paul, Trench, Trubner & Co.

Han Fei zi: Chen Qiyou 陈奇猷. 1958. Han Fei zi jishi 韩非子集释. Beijing: Zhonghua shuju.

Han shi waizhuan: Qu Shouyuan 屈守元, ed. 1996. Han shi waizhuan jianshu 韩诗外传笺疏. Chengdu: Bashu shushe.

Han shu: Ban Gu 班固 [32 – 92 CE]. Han shu 汉书. Beijing: Zhonghua shuju, 1962.

Hayashi Taisuke 林泰辅 [1854 – 1922] ed. 1971. Rongo genry? 论语源流. Tôkyô: Kyûko shoin.

Hightower, James Robert. 1952. Han Shih Wai Chuan: Han Ying's Illustrations of the Didactic Application of the Classic of Songs. Cambridge, Mass. : Harvard University Press.

Huainan zi: Zhang Shuangdi 张双棣 ed. 1997. Huainan zi jiaoshi 淮南子校释. Beijing: Beijing daxue.

HuangHuaixin 黃怀信 ed. 2008. *Lunyu* huijiao jishi 论语彙校集释. Shanghai: Guji chubanshe.

Jin Xueqin 金学勤. 2009. "*Lunyu* chengshu 'cenglei lun' ji xifang hanxuejie xiangguan pinglun"《论语》成书"层累论"及西方汉学界相关评论. Kongzi yanjiu 113 (2009. 3), pp. 21 – 29.

Liji: Sun Xidan 孙希但 ed. 1989. Liji jijie 礼记集解. Beijing: Zhonghua.

Li Ling 李零. 2007. Sangjia gou: wo du '*Lunyu*' 丧家狗—我读《论语》. Rev. ed. Taiyuan: Shanxi renmin chubanshe.

——. 2008. Jianbo gushu yu xueshu yuanliu 简帛古书与学术源流. Second, rev. ed. Beijing: Sanlian.

Liu Baonan 刘宝楠 [1791 – 1855] ed. 1990. *Lunyu* zhengyi 论语正

义 . Beijing: Zhonghua shuju.

Loewe, Michael ed. 1993. Early Chinese Texts: A Bibliographical Guide. Berkeley: The Society for the Study of Early China and The Institute of East Asian Studies, Univ. of California.

Lü shi chunqiu: Chen Qiyou 陈奇猷 . 2002. Lü shi chunqiu xin jiaoshi 吕氏春秋新校释 . Shanghai: Shanghai guji.

Makeham, John. 1996. "The Formation of *Lunyu* as a Book". Monumenta Serica 44, pp. 1 – 24.

—— trans. 2002. Balanced Discourses: A Bilingual Edition. New Haven and London: Yale Univ. Press, Beijing: Foreign Languages Press.

Lienü zhuan: D. C. Lau ed. 1993. Gu lienü zhuan zhuzi suoyin 古列女传逐字索引 . Hong Kong: Commercial Press.

Lunyu: D. C. Lau, ed. 1995. *Lunyu* zhuzi suoyin 论语逐字索引 . Hong Kong: Commercial Press.

Murphy, Tim, and Ralph Weber. 2010. "Confucianizing Socrates and Socratizing Confucius: On Comparing Analects 13:18 and the Euthyphro". Philosophy East and West 60. 2, pp. 187 – 206. 26 Richter, Matthias. 2002. "Self – Cultivation or Evaluation of Others?: A Form Critical Approach to Zengzi Li Shi". Asiatische Studien 56. 4, pp. 879 – 917.

—— . 2005. Guan ren: Texte der altchinesischen Literatur zur Charakterkunde und Beamtenrekrutierung. Bern [etc.]: Peter Lang.

Scarpari, Maurizio. 2007. "Zi yue, 'The Master Said . . . ', or Didn't He?". In Guru: The Spiritual Master in Eastern and Western Traditions, Authority and Charisma, ed. Antonio Rigopoulos, 437 – 469. Venice: Venetian Academy of Indian Studies, and New Delhi: Printworld.

—— . 2010. Il confucianesimo: i fondamenti e i testi. Torino: Einaudi.

Slingerland, Edward. 2009. "Classical Confucianism (I): Confucius and theLun-yü". In: History of Chinese Philosophy, ed. Bo Mou, pp. 107 – 136. London and New York: Routledge.

Yantie lun: Wang Liqi 王利器 ed. 1992. Yan tie lun jiaozhu 盐铁论校注 . Beijing: Zhonghua shuju.

Webb, Robert L. 2009. "The Historical Enterprise and Historical Jesus Research". In: Key Events in the Life of the Historical Jesus: A Collaborative Exploration of Context and Coherence, ed. Darrell Bock and Robert L. Webb, pp. 9 – 93. Wissenschaftliche Untersuchungen zum Neuen Testament 247. Tübingen: Mohr Siebeck.

Weingarten, Oliver. 2009a. "Textual Representations of a Sage: Studies of Pre-Qin and Western Han Sources on Confucius (551 – 479 BCE)". Ph. D. dissertation, University of Cambridge.

—— . 2009b. "Confucius and Pregnant Women: An Investigation into the Intertextuality of the *Lunyu*". Journal of the American Oriental Society 129. 4, 597 – 618.

Xin xu: Shi Guangying 石光瓓 ed. , Xin xu jiaoshi 新序校释, Beijing: Zhonghua shuju, 2001.

Yang Shuda 杨树达 [1885 – 1956] ed. 1955. *Lunyu* shuzheng 论语疏证. Beijing: Kexue chubanshe.

Zhu Weizheng 朱维铮. 1987. "Lishi de Kongzi he Kongzi de lishi" 历史的孔子和孔子的历史. In Kongzi yanjiu lunwenji 孔子研究论文集, ed. Zhonghua Kongzi yanjiusuo 中华孔子研究所, pp. 156 – 172. Beijing: Jiaoyu kexue chubanshe.

—— . 2002. Zhongguo jingxue shi shi jiang 中国经学史十讲. Shanghai: Fudan daxue chubanshe.

On "Dao" and "Virtue"[①]

LIN An-wu[②]
Translated by LEE Yen-Yi[③]

Prolegomenon

"Confucianism and Daoism both grow from the Dao as it was in its wholeness. Both of them are complementary to each other in the process of civilisation. Both of them should exist in integrative harmonisation as the positive and negative forces to serve the civilisation. "

---

① We are indebted to Mr. Michael Stein Lenihan, PhD Candidate of Politics and International Studies at the University of Warwick, for having proofread the English translation of this article. the subtitte of this essay is A Philosophical Interpretation of the Thesis That Confucianism and Daoism Develope from the Same Root And Are Complementary to Each Other: An Investigation on the Implications of "I Set My Heart on the Dao and Based Myself on Virtue" of Confucian *Analects* and of "Dao Bears Myriad Things While Virtue Nourishes Them" of *Laozi Daodejing*

② LIN An-Wu is the director of the Institute of Religious and Cultural Studies of Tzu Chi University, Taiwan and the Professor at the Department of Chinese at National Taiwan Normal University. He is also a member of the council of Chinese Association for General Education and that of International Confucian Association. He earned his PhD. degree from the Department of Philosophy at the National Taiwan University and was Fulbright scholar from 1993-1994. He served as the director and professor of the centre of general education at National Tsing-Hua University, the director of the institute of philosophy of Nan-hua University, chief editor and director of *Legein Monthly* (*Er-hu yeh-kan*) , chief editor of *Thought and Words: Journal of the Humanities and Social Science.*

③ LEE Yen-yi is a PhD Candidate of the School of Philosophy, Theology and Religion at the University of Birmingham.

Abstract

Dao refers to "the root of the totality" and "the totality of the root" while Virtue denotes to "the innate nature" in which "the nature is intrinsic. " "Dao bears myriad things and Virtue nourishes them" implies that it is the manifestation of the totality of the root of beings and its nourishment and shaping of those beings that conceives the innate nature. "I set my heart on the Dao and base myself on the virtue" refers to the self-awareness of the subject and directs oneself towards the totality of the root of beings, participates and councils it to open up, for the purpose to inherit the goodness of the root to nourish one's own nature to be the good virtue and eventually embody it in his or her practical life.

Daoism pays more attention to and is more aware of the tendency of things (events shape them and power completes them) caused by "the intervention and operation of language. " It stresses the ideas of "clarifying the inner vision, " "the practice of Dao constitutes daily diminishing, " "attaining complete emptiness and clinging to the inner peace" and "returning to the root of its original state" to overcome "the alienation of language" to "negotiate the problems of being. " Confucianism highlights the real feeling that results from the interaction and interweaving of "the self-awareness of the subjects (lean upon Ren for support). " Besides, it emphases the vision of "Ren as being in wholeness and totality" that is formed by leading a life of cultivating oneself by arts (behaving in accordance with Ren and taking recreation in the arts), by the ideas of "rectifying the name to accord with the reality" and that of "Ren and Rites are identical. "

There are four great entities in the universe. Heaven, earth and man are being regarded as the three geniuses. Man resides between heaven and earth. His participation in "the realm of the real existence" and interaction with others leads to the manifestation of "the root of the totality, " which "covers and pervades the universe, reveals its patterns, " "helps the completion of everything and shapes them by name. " Nonetheless, there is something essentially identical between Heaven and man. Man can only harmonise and complete his or her own virtue by means of "taking him or herself and Heaven as the dwelling place to and being in cooperation with each other" and of "knowing myriad things and warding over their root and honouring the Dao and respecting the virtue. "

Keywords: Real existence, the realm, root, totality, intrinsic nature, innate, inter-subjectivity, three geniuses, being, language, alienation, therapy, harmony and compatibility, phenomenon, appliance, name and reality, being and non-being

Text

1. Dao refers to "the root of the totality" and "the totality of the root. "

1. 1. "Dao" is "the effably ineffable. " "Ineffable" refers to its "initial silent state" and "effable" to its "manifestations through language. " With the aid of "language" it produces "everything. "

1. 1. 1. "Dao" is "ineffable" in the sense that it is "the emptiness of therealm" and " the transparency of human consciousness. " It is the circumstance that can be expressed as "the state of namelessness is the inception of heaven and earth. "

1. 1. 2. "The emptiness of the realm" and "the transparency of human consciousness" are the status of indeterminable silence of "both the vision and consciousness are being eliminated (jing-shi-ju-min) , " which can be understood in the sense of "stillness" of the Commentary on the Book of Changes.

1. 1. 3. The silence of the "stillness" indicates that human beings are "living beings" partaking in life in a condition of unhappiness, which is not a "perishing situation" but a "lively and active void. "

1. 1. 4. In other words, there is a possibility of "being stimulated and

responsive" in the status of "stillness. " "Stillness is being stimulated. "
Stillness and being stimulated are not dual positions.

1. 2. "Dao" is "the source of language" and transcends it. It is
"speechless. " It is different from "Logos" as "the source of language, "which
is itself "the speech. "

1. 2. 1. "Dao" can refer to "discourse, " "way, " "thinking, " "being, "
etc. . All these meanings can be integrated into and be traced back to a
"source of language, "which is a speechless source of language.

1. 2. 2. The understanding and interpretation of Dao was transformed by
shaman in light of "the dynamic process of Qi" into a philosophy: it is a
transition from God (di) through Heaven (tian) to Dao.

1. 2. 3. "God (di) " refers to "an entity regarded as of holiness and of
power; " "Heaven (tian) " denotes "something universal and pervasive; "
"Dao" indicates something that works as "the root of the totality" and as "the
totality of the root" in the sense that "Heaven, Earth and Man communicate
and cooperate with one another. "

1. 2. 4. "Heaven, Earth and Man communicate and cooperate with one
another" presents that the Dao maintains a discreet distance from this world
and to myriad things. It is understood in the context of the idea of "the
continuity of being. "

1. 3. Since the Dao is grasped in the context of the idea of "the
continuity of being, " it could not necessarily be discussed by the pair of
concepts "the transcendent" and "the immanent" and might be understood
more accurately in terms of "the root of the totality" and "the totality of the
root. "

1. 3. 1. "The continuity of being" implies "the essential union of
Heaven, Earth, Man and myriad things. " Its worldview is of one-world, not
of a bi-tier world. Only within the bi-tier worldview emerges the question of
the tension between the transcendentand the immanent.

1. 3. 2. Therefore, to interpret the Dao through the pair of concepts "the
transcendent and the immanent" can be avoided. Dao is the root and the

totality. It is of wholeness. It is the Dao of this-world: the disjunction between this-world and that-world can not be found in its vision.

1. 3. 3. Dao as "the root of the totality" emphasises the dimension of the root. It is in the sense that the Dao is playing a role of an "Ideal. " It further reveals the implication of "being, " "meaning" and "value" of Dao.

1. 3. 4. Dao as "the totality of the root" highlights the dimension of the totality. It is understood in that Dao is "pervasive and universal. " It also reveals the implication of "being, " "meaning" and "value" of Dao.

1. 4. Dao denotes "the identity of Being and Value, " which is different from Logos that refers to "the identity of Being and Thinking".

1. 4. 1. In terms of its fundamental significance, there is a harmonious relationship between "being, " "meaning" and "value. " The identity of them should be understood in this way. The identity in the context of "integrative harmonisation" is distinct from that under the background of "equivalence".

1. 4. 2. The identity in the context of "integrative harmonisation" is the identity of"the two opposites being agreeable and interactive with each other. " It is an identity interwoven in a dialectical way. It is not the identity in the sense that "the subject" prehends "the object, " neither the identity of the "equivalence" of two things.

1. 4. 3. The phrase of "the reciprocal process of yin and yang is called the Dao" in the Commentary of the Book of Changes can be said to be an ultimate idea. It shows the "*rhythm of the Dao of being.* " It also presents the way the two opposites are in sync and interact with each other, the way they function as the dwelling place for each other and the energy of development for each other.

1. 4. 4. The Dao in this sense is not the Dao of an"Abstract Ideal" and "Pure Form. " It is the Dao as the realm for the living being to dwell in. It is the Dao formed by the mutual reception of both sides. The Dao is "real, " "living, " "concrete, " "fundamental" and "ideal".

1. 5. "The theory of the Dao" can also exhibit a cosmological and ontological implication. However, it is dissimilar to the cosmology and

ontology of the main stream of Western philosophy.

1.5.1. "The Ontology" of "the theory of the Dao" isthe Ontology concerned with "the vivid experience of the subject. " The human beings in this context are the living beings that disclose the perplexity of the Dao by their own personal experience. It is the Ontology in the context of "It is the Man who is capable of promoting and unfolding the implication of the Dao (ren-neng-hong-dao). "

1.5.2. This ontological substance is not something congealed, firm and transcendental. Rather, it is the ontological substance as the root and totality that consists of the interaction and communication of the myriad things. Put differently, this type of ontology is relevant to the philosophy of life, theory of practice and axiology.

1.5.3. "The cosmology" of the theory of the Dao is the cosmology of"My mind is not separated from the cosmos and vice versa. " "The cosmos is composed of two respects: Space and Time. Space (yu) connotes in all directions while time (zhou) refers to the past, the present and the future. " This cosmos is not the cosmos in the sense of objective and physical universe. It is the cosmos of the inter-subjectivity.

1.5.4. The cosmos is not the cosmos of pure principle or as an objective object. It is a world that is full of affection and feeling and a world of the pleasure of fulfilling nature. It is also a cosmos of getting back to the root and returning to the suchness. This type of cosmology is relevant to the philosophy of life, theory of practice and axiology.

1.6. The theory of Dao is neither an "ontological substance- centred theory," a "cosmology-centred theory," a "subject-centred theory" nor an "object- centred theory. " The theory of Dao is not a theory centred on a particular dimension. It is a theory based on the "inter-subjectivity (hu-ji) ".

1.6.1. It is reasonable to understand the Dao in a " decentred perspective. " What is implied here is the idea of " diversity " and "difference. " The despotism and monism of China was not the outcome of the theory of the Dao. On the contrary, it is the theory of the Dao that moderates the "despotism" and "monism" of China.

1. 6. 2. What's more interesting is that the "diversity" and "difference" do not indicate the status of being scattered but the situation of interaction and communication. It reveals the pattern of "diversity in unity (a plurality within an organic whole). " It is properly stated in the phrase of "As all in the world come to the same end, though the roads to it are different, so there is an ultimate congruence in thought, though there may be hundreds of ways to deliberate it" of the Commentary on the Book of Changes.

1. 6. 3. "The theory of inter-subjectivity (hu-ji-lun) " can be understood as "being the dwelling place for each otherand the energy of development for each other. " Furthermore, "being the dwelling place for but still retain autonomy from each other at the same time; be the energy of development for each other while self- nourished at the same time. " The relationship between Heaven and Earth, that between the object and subject and that between others and self can be understood in this context of "the synthesis of two opposites (liang-duan-er-yi-zhi) " of the theory of inter-subjectivity.

1. 6. 4. This type of inter-subjectivity differs from the theory of inter-subjectivity in recent Western philosophy, which marks a linguistic turn in the West and intends to make a breakthrough of "the division of the subject and object. " The theory of inter-subjectivity in the context of the Dao-theory signals a return towards a theory of being.

1. 7. "Dao bears myriad things" refers to the inception from "the totality of the root" and "the root of the totality. " It is a transition from "both the vision and consciousness that are being eliminated" to "both the vision and consciousness that are being manifested. " They manifest in their own way. It can be called "non-created bearing (*bu-sheng-zhi-sheng*). "

1. 7. 1. The "non-created bearing" is not like theBrahma in Hinduism that gives rise to everything and not like God's act of Creation. It is also unlike the emanation by "the One" of Plotinus' philosophy. It is a bearing that results from the " inter-subjectivity" of "the human beings as living beings".

1. 7. 2. In other words, the "bearing (sheng)" is not the bearing that could be traced back to and be done by an "other. " It is a bearing unfolding in the context of "inter-subjectivity" in the sense of "I and Thou. " It is the general idea shared by Confucianism and Daoism.

1. 7. 3. Authors (e. g. Prof. MOU Tsung-san) may explain Confucian "bearing" as "establishing a moral value of things (dao-de-de-chuang-sheng) . " This does not contradict an understanding in the context of inter-subjectivity in the sense of "I and Thou. " Besides, only in this way can it evade the tendency and the problem of moral subjectivism. Prof. Mou's understanding was coloured by moral subjectivism while it is possible for XIONG Shi-li's approach of interpretation under the background of "primordial creativity and the unfathomable nature (qian-yuan-xing-hai) " to avoid such moral subjectivism.

1. 7. 4. "Dao bears myriad things" can be regarded as "the function and pervasion of Heaven is perpetually creative. " Its manifestation is universal, unlimited, creative and dynamic. It manifests under the background of the " inter-subjectivity " between Heaven and Man. Thus, it could be inappropriate to explain this idea as "establishing a moral value of things on the grounds of a moral Reality (dao-de-shi-ti-de-chuang-sheng) . "

1. 8. "I set my heart on the Dao" suggests that human beings as living beings will orientate themselves towards "the root of the totality" and "the totality of the root" and consequently establish a moral value of things.

1. 8. 1. "Will" means "determination, " "to dominate one's own mind. " It is the sublimation and upgrading of one's mind's intention toward the Dao. In this manner, it can be called "devotion (yi-zhi) ".

1. 8. 2. When it relates to the idea of "it is the Man who is capable of promoting and unfolding the implication of the Dao, " this stresses the self-awareness, self-determination, and self-mastering of human beings. Nonetheless, human beings as living beings are always participants and stimulators. Human beings should not become the centre of the cosmos.

1. 8. 3. The main idea of the phrase "It is the Man who is capable of

promoting and developing the Dao. It is not the Dao that is capable of promoting and developing the Man" is the "subjective dynamics of human beings. " Specifically, it refers to the "inter-subjectivity" between Heaven and Man in the sense of "the synthesis of the two opposites, " that of "I and Thou. " Dao is consequently being revealed.

1. 8. 4. In other words, the "metaphysics" in the sense of "what is priori to physical form pertains to the Dao (xing-er-shang-zhi-wei-dao)" is not the "moral metaphysics" that is erected by human beings as moral subjects. Instead, it is a "theory of the Dao" constructed by the root of the totality as the interaction and communication between Heaven, Earth and Man.

1. 9. The theory of the Dao as the root of the totality formed by "the interaction and communication between Heaven, Earth and Man" is the result of Human beings' dwelling in the realm of Heaven and Earth and their mutual reception and reciprocal enrichment.

1. 9. 1. Simply indicates the idea of "sincerity is the way of heaven; to think of how to be sincere is the way of man" in the Doctrine of the Mean. The first part of it relates to "the root of the totality, " the source of the creation of the cosmos, "the identity between the being and the value. " The second part concerns the "self-awareness of the subject, " the subjective dynamics of the human beings, and the free will of man. In this manner, Heaven and man are not dual entities.

1. 9. 2. "Heaven and Man are not dual entities" can be understood in the context of WANG Yang-ming's idea of "Ren as forming one body with all things (yi-ti-zhi-ren) . " However, the "one body (yi-ti)" shall not be understood as the "subject" but the "substance" that comes from the "inter-subjectivity. " Ren originally implies the inter-subjectivity.

1. 9. 3. In other words, the Ren is not only the self-awareness of the subject but the self-awareness of the "inter-subjectivity. " The self-awareness is not viewed in the sense of solipsism but in the sense of interaction, communication and the nourishment of myriad things.

1. 9. 4. By "Dao bears the myriad things" it refers to "the totality of the

root. " By "I set my heart on the Dao" it indicates human beings as living beings that participate and assist in the operation of the Dao. Dao in both contexts is the Dao as " the totality formed by the interaction and communication between Heaven, Earth and Man: " it implies the root, the totality, the realm, disclosure, manifestation, creative creativity, spontaneity and integrative harmonisation.

2. By "Virtue" it means "the innate nature" and "the nature is intrinsic. "

2. 1. "The Dao is pervasive between Heaven and Earth while Virtue is the pivot of this human world. " The main idea of the Dao includes the Dao as the totality, as the root, as the realm while the key point of the Virtue is that Virtue is innate, the original nature and the subject. Virtue inherits from the Dao while the Dao is embodied in the Virtue.

2. 1. 1. The Dao as "the realm of the root of the totality" is revealed by means of the participation of human beings as living beings in its operation. It manifests and then is embodied in Virtue, which becomes the subject with an innate nature in terms of human beings.

2. 1. 2. "I set my heart on the Dao" therefore "the Dao bears my innate nature. " When the Dao is embodied in Virtue, "the virtue is being nourished by the Dao" and then "I base myself on the Virtue. " The Dao is realized in the Virtue of human beings. Human beings can nourish themselves on the ground of their virtue. It is because virtue can be nourished that it can be the foundation of human nature.

2. 1. 3. The Virtue can be nourished in the sense that the "nourishment" implies the ideas of raising, the innate and the grow-up. One can base oneself on the Virtue in the sense that the " basement " implies the ideas of foundation, following, and accumulation. It further has two ends: one is "cultivating oneself by keeping the attitude of respect (han-yang-yong-jing) " and the other is "investigating things and extending the knowledge (zhi-zhi-ge-wu) ; " both of them can be integrated as one.

2. 1. 4. "The realm of the root of the totality" can not be isolated from

"the innate nature as the subject of human beings. " Meanwhile, "the innate natureas the subject of human beings" can not be separated from "the realm of the root of the totality. " This can be understood in the context of the idea that "In the realm there are four great entities and humans is one of them. Humans learn and conform to the principle of Earth; Earth conforms to the principle of Heaven; Heaven conforms to the Dao; the Dao conforms to its natural self. " It can also be understood in terms of "The celestial force symbolises being strong and dynamic. In the same manner, the Junzi never ceases to strengthen his own character. The terrestrial forces can be considered being compliant and receptive. In this manner, the Junzi with his generous virtue carries everything. "

2. 2. "To behave in accordance with your virtuous mind (zhi-xin-xing-zhi)" incarnates the idea of virtue, which is understood in terms of connecting back the root of human nature. "Being watched by ten eyes (shi-mu)" symbolise "being unconcealed (zhi) ; " which implies a public socio- political body.

2. 2. 1. "To behave in accordance with your straight mind, " tracing back to the root of human nature and then embody it in the practical life, practicing it as it is in its sensitive and compassionate state to the surroundings. This is the original and fundamental meaning of human nature. In this context, the aspect of its orientation (ding-xiang) , not that of its essence (ban-zhi) should be highlighted. It is expressed in the phrase of "Below the mountain emerges the spring: this constitutes the image of juvenile ignorance. In the same way, the Junzi makes his actions resolute and nourishes his virtue" of hexagram Meng of the Commentary of the Book of Changes. It is also stated in the phrase "The spring is surging. Nothing could withstand it" of Mencius.

2. 2. 2. In this manner, the ideas of the orientation, the origin and the foundation of human nature in Pre-Qin Confucianism led by Confucius and Mencius should result in "a theory of good orientation of human nature (ren-xing-shan-xiang-lun) , " not in "a theory of the orientation of human nature is toward good (ren-xing-xiang-shan-lun) . " The main idea of the theory of good

orientation of human nature is that the intrinsic human nature has its own root, not that there is an extrinsic and transcendent ideal for humans to pursue.

2. 2. 3. "To behave in accordance with your straight mind" incarnates the idea of virtue. It is realised in the real moral feeling among humans. This can be called Ren, which integrates the moral practice and moral Ontology into one.

2. 2. 4. When it comes to the public socio-political body, that is to say, under circumstance of "being watched by ten eyes, " moral practice is closely related to the ideal and the general will of social totality. It is also about the norms of the realm of human life, which can be regarded as the Rites (Li). In this manner, the Ren and the Rites are not dual entities.

2. 3. Virtue is the virtue in terms of the idea of being stimulated and responsive and nourishing myriad things of *Ren* and of property as being regulated by the Rites; The *Ren* and the Rites are not dual entities but originally as one. Both are from the Dao of the cosmos and become human virtue.

2. 3. 1. The main idea of Ren lies inthe meaning of subject, that of self-awareness and that of the act of creation while the concern of Rites is about the meaning of the object, that of the rule and that of completion by implementing. Both have been shown in Confucian Analects.

2. 3. 2. One of the intensions of Mencius is to transform the idea of Ren into that of "the Ren and Righteousness (Yi) are innate and immanent (ren-yi-nei-zai)" and to discuss the idea of that human nature is good on these grounds. This is the approach of "human nature is rooted in the moral mind (ji-xin-yan-xing). " In contrast, one of the purposes of Xunzi is to transfer the Rites into the idea of "comprehending the rules of categorisation of things (zhi-tong-tong-lei)" and to discuss the idea that "human nature is bad (xing-er). " This is the approach of "human nature should be regulated by the moral mind (yi-xin-zhi-xing). "

2. 3. 3. "What can a man do with the rites who is not of Ren? What can a

man do with music who is not of Ren?" "Ren" is about "correlation (gan-
tong) , " "Rites is about "appropriateness (fen-cun) " and "Music (yue) "
symbolises the idea of "integrative harmonisation (he-he) . " Rites and Music
are not dual entities. Ren, Rites and Music represent organic oneness.

2. 3. 4. "Apprehending the idea of Ren must be the first task for the
student. One who is of Ren is integrated organically oneself with Heaven,
Earth and the myriad things as a whole. " " The greatest rites are
corresponding to the rhythm of the Cosmos while the greatest music reflects
the process of the harmonisation of the Cosmos. " All these should be grasped
in terms of "the realm of real existence" and of "the root of the totality. "
"The realm of real existence" and "the root of the totality" are essentially
represented in a discreet relationship. Humans are participating in both of
them; in this manner, both of them can not be isolated from the self-
awareness of the subject of human beings.

2. 4. "The root of the totality, " "the realm of the real existence" and
"the self-awareness of subject" can be integrated into a wholeness. It is
because Dao is within that "Heaven and Earth, " "Heaven andEarth" nourish
myriad things and Humans are born and are dwelling in between Heaven and
Earth with their own awareness.

2. 4. 1. "The Dao is in Heaven and Earth" and is originally ineffable: it
is a statusof "both the vision and consciousness that are being eliminated, " a
status that can be described as "the state of Namelessness is the inception of
the Heaven and the Earth. " When it transits from the ineffable to the effable
state, it reaches the stage of "both the vision and the consciousness manifest
(jing-shi-ju-xian) . " Simply because of the effable comes the action of
speech, which is a status of "the consciousness grasps the vision (yi-shi-zhi-
jing) " and can be stated as "the state of Naming is the source of the myriad
things. "

2. 4. 2. The transition from the state of the ineffable to that of the effable
is the omen of the manifestation of the Dao. The omen results from human
beings' participation in the Dao. Originally, human beings are in the Dao.

This is because the Dao is the root of "the totality as the interaction and communication of Heaven, Earth and Man. "

2. 4. 3. The self-awareness of the subjectis key to the revealing of being, the key to the root of the totality. It manifests because of human inquiry. What it has manifested is "the realm of the real existence. "

2. 4. 4. It is because of the asking of the subject, the manifestation of the root of the totality and the realisation of the realm, that the intrinsic human nature appears. The root of the totality can be called the endowment of the Heaven (tian- ming). Thus the intrinsic human nature can be understood in terms of "What Heaven endows with man is called human nature (tian-ming-zhi-wei-xing). " When it is being realised, it can be described as "To follow such nature is conforming to the Dao (shuai-xing-zhi-wei-dao). "

2. 5. If the idea of "Dao and Virtue" is understood in light of the process of the practice of human nature, then it means that "the reciprocal process of yin and yang is called the Dao. That which inherits from the Dao is human goodness, and that which it embodies is human nature, " that "Heaven continuously endowed with humans and its nature which is being cultivated gradually" and that "when human nature has not reached its completion it is still possible for it to be formed. On the other hand, even when it has reached its completion, it is possible for it to be changed. "

2. 5. 1. In the phrase of "the reciprocal process of yin and yang is called the Dao. That which inherits from the Dao is human goodness, and that which embodies it is human nature" of the Commentary on the Book of Changes, the reciprocal process of yin and yang" denotes "the becoming formed in the process of the revealing and concealing of the Dao" and the opening of the root of the being: it refers to the dimensions of the manifestation and the openness of the Dao. "That which inherits from the Dao is human goodness" indicates human beings' inherence from and participation in the operation of the Dao. "That which embodies it is human nature" refers to the innateness and the completion of human nature. Then, the virtue in this sense should not be understood as something essential but as something to be grown up and

something changeable in the process of learning and practice.

2. 5. 2. All the ideas of "The becoming formed in the process of the revealing and concealing of the Dao, " "the openness and the manifestation of the Dao, " "human participation in, assistance of and inherence from the Dao" and " the implementing and completion of intrinsic nature " are essentially identical. The reason is that human beings are the pivot of these ideas. Without human beings, there would be no "becoming formed in the process of the revealing and concealing of the Dao, " no "openness and the manifestation of the Dao, " no "human participation in, assistance of and inherence from the Dao" and "the implementing and completion of intrinsic nature" and that the virtue is being formed in the process of creative creativity.

2. 5. 3. In the phrase of "human nature is completed in the process of learning, " "human nature" indicates the original and fundamental nature while "learning" means "being completed with practice" and "the exhibition of what is intrinsic in the nature. " In a word, "human nature is completed in the process of learning" denotes the existence, exhibition and completion of original human nature with learning and practice. In this manner, the implication of Virtue should be understood in terms of becoming and continuation, not of essence, for the Dao, as creative creativity, is unfolded in the flux of time.

2. 5. 4. Therefore, the human nature in the idea of "human nature is good" should be understood in the context of "that which inherits from the Dao is human goodness, and that which embodies it is human nature, " of the realisation and completion of an orientation of the goodness. It does not mean something essentially good. It is because " the human nature is being contained in the goodness and the goodness is being included in the Dao (dao-da-er-shan-xiao, shan-da-er-xing-xiao) . " When human nature has not reached its completion it is still possible for it to be formed. On the other hand, even when it has reached its completion, it is possible for it to be changed. Preserving human nature and realising it in practical life is the

subtle key point of cultivating it.

2. 6. In terms of "the root of the totality" and "the totality of the root, " the Dao takes no action. In terms of the manifestation of the Dao, there is a "subtlety (*ji*)" that contains the possibility of being good or being bad. It is due to its non-action (*wu-wei*) there is no deceitfulness (*wu-wei*), which means genuineness without absurdity. In other words, it is "sincerity denotes no deceitfulness. Subtlety implies the possibilities of being good or being bad (*cheng-wu-wei, ji-shan-er*). " 2. 61. According to the idea of "integrative harmonisation of the Being and the Value" that has been discussed above, the Dao as the root of the totality isontologically non-action as being neither good nor bad. Its ontological dimension contains its value dimension. It can be called "the ultimate sincerity is being without deceitfulness. "

2. 6. 2. It is because the root of the being and the root of the value are one, that the natural dimension of the realm of Heaven and Earth can be transformed into the self-awareness of human beings. Further, the dimension of the spontaneity of Heaven and Earth is reflected in the self-awareness of human beings and is actualised in human freedom.

2. 6. 3. The interaction and communication of Heaven, Earth and Man form an indivisible totality, which implies being natural and spontaneous and being of self-awareness and of freedom. The establishment of a moral value of things by heaven and earth is thus being formed and that the human self-awareness and self-determination is fulfilled. This is the meaning of the phrase of "sincerity is the way of heaven; to think of how to be sincere is the way of man" in the Doctrine of the Mean.

2. 6. 4. The process from the establishment of a moral value of things by heaven and earth and the manifestation of the root of being to their realisation in human beings as living beings can be expressed in the phrase of "It is due to our nature that enlightenment results from the sincerity (zi-cheng-ming-wei-zhi-xing). " The process from the enlightenment of human self-awareness to the return to the root of creation and then to the opening of the omen of cultivation can be described in the phrase of "it is due to education that

sincerity results from enlightenment (zi-ming-cheng-wei-zhi-xing) . " All these notions exhibit the interaction and communication of Heaven, Earth and Man integrating as one body as Substance (ti) and developing one another in each one's function (yong) .

2. 7. The transition from the idea of "Heaven and Man are one(*tian-ren-he-yi*) " to the idea of "the virtue of Heaven and that of Man are essentially identical (*tian-ren-he-de*) " is a transition from "moral mysticism" to "moral rationalism. " It was accepted and approved by Pre-Qin Confucianism and Daoism.

2. 7. 1. Notably, the reason of Confucianism and that of Daoism were formed under the background of the worldview of "the continuity of being. " It is "the reason of continuity (lian-xu-xing de li-xing) " and is different from "the reason of discontinuity (duan-lie-xing de li-xing) " which is made in the worldview of the discontinuity of being.

2. 7. 2. It is due to the reason of continuity that there is no clear boundarybetween its mysticism and rationalism. They are in a continuous relationship. Generally speaking, however, though there is a dimension of mysticism of Confucianism and Daoism, it will be proper to take them as forms of rationalism.

2. 7. 3. Both Confucianism and Daoism can be understood in terms of Dao and Virtue. The difference between them lies in Daoism's emphasis on "the realm of real existence" while Confucianism stresses "the self-awareness of the subject"; both of them are in a reciprocal relationship and can be traced back to the Dao, "the root of the totality and the totality of the root. "

2. 7. 4. The manifestation and revealing of "the root of the totality and the totality of the root, " "what is being manifested is the phenomenon (xian-nai-wei-zhi-xiang) , " which is not a "vertical creation (zong-guan-de-chuang-sheng) " but, in actuality, "the manifestation of Being (cun-you-de-zhang-xian) . " The Being is the root of totality formed by the interaction and communication of Heaven, Earth and man.

2. 8. It is continuity in the sense of the indivisible totality as the interaction

and communication of Heaven, Earth and man. This is the idea of integrative harmonisation, not the idea of "the opposites of subject and object. "

2. 8. 1. In this manner, the moral theory of Confucianism and Daoism should neither be understood in the sense of establishing a moral value of things of self-awareness nor in the sense of the practice of self-cultivation towards a vision. It should be understood in terms of WANG chuan-shan's idea of "the synthesis of two ends. "

2. 8. 2. Or, the Confucian idea that details the establishment of a moral value of things by subjective self-awareness, which is highlighted in Contemporary Neo-Confucianism, could be moderated in the idea of Heaven and Earth or the realm to realise the idea of the interaction and communication as "being the dwelling place for each other and the energy of the development for each other. "

2. 8. 3. Or, the idea of the practice of subjective vision of Daoism stated by Contemporary Neo-Confucianism could be considered in the context of that heaven and earth or the realm to comprehend the implication of "the state of Namelessness is the inception of Heaven and Earth. The state of Naming is the source of the myriad things" and the "mystic identity (xuan-tong) " in the context of "Both come from the same root, " which is the status that "the hidden and the manifested give rise to one another. "

2. 8. 4. Further, both Confucianism and Daoism develop their philosophy in a philosophical model of being reciprocal to each other. Thus there is no opposition between the pattern of reality and that of the vision. There is no need to open any discourse or argument on this opposition. Reality is in the void and void is reflected by the reality. Reality and void can not be separated from each other. The void can be fulfilled in reality while reality can be encompassed by void. Reality and void are not dual entities.

2. 9. "Dao bears it and virtuenourishes it": the concern of Daoism is the realisation from "the manifestation of the root of being" to "intrinsic original nature. " "I set my heart on the Dao and base myself on the Virtue": the purpose of Confucianism is to participate and assist in the root of creation by

means of subjective self-awareness. In addition, it aims to fulfil the interaction and communication of Heaven, Earth and man with the self-awareness to complete the cultivation of human relationships.

2. 9. 1. Daoism pays more attention to and is much aware of the tendency of things (events shape them and the power completes them) caused by "theintervention and operation of language (hua-yu-de-jie-ru). " It stresses the ideas of "clarifying the inner vision (di-chu-xuan-lan), " "the practice of Dao constitutes daily diminishing (wei-dao-ri-sun), " "attaining complete emptiness and clinging to the inner peace" and "returning to the root of its original state" to overcome "the alienation of language" to "negotiate the problems of beings. "

2. 9. 2. Confucianism highlights the real feeling of existence that results from the interaction and interweaving of "the self-awareness of the subjects (lean upon Renfor support). " Besides, it emphases the vision of "Ren as being in wholeness and totality" that is formed by leading a life of cultivating oneself by arts (behaving in accordance with Ren and taking recreation in the arts), by the ideas of "rectifying the name to accord with the reality" and that of "Ren and Rites are identical. "

2. 9. 3. One of the main ideas of Confucianism is "construction (jian-gou). "However, it is not the construction in the sense that "the subject cognise the object (yi-zhu-she-ke)" and that "the perceiver grasps the perceived (yi-neng-she-suo). " It is the construction in the sense that the subject and the object are not a dual entities and that the perceiver and the perceived are in integrative harmonisation. One of the main ideas of Daoism is "deconstruction (jie-gou). " However, it is not the deconstruction in the sense that "the object is eliminated by the subject (min-ke-yu-zhu)" and that "the perceived is eliminated by the perceiver (min-suo-yu-neng). " It is the deconstruction in the sense that "both the subject and the object are eliminated (zhu-ke-ju-min)" and that "both the perceiver and the perceived are eliminated (neng-suo-ju-min). "

2. 9. 4. Confucian construction and Daoist deconstruction are in

integrative harmonisation. Theyare reciprocal to each other as a whole. Both are the manifestations ofthe root of the totality formed by the interaction and communication of Heaven, Earth and man. It is because of the elimination of the division of the subject and the object and that of the perceiver and the perceived that human beings understand tacitly the root of being. It is then lead the root of being to cover and pervade Heaven and Earth, to manifest itself and then to help the completion of everything and shapes them by name. At this final stage, it transits from "the manifestation of Being" with "the intervention of language" to "the determination of being by discourse."

3. As it has been shown above, when tracing back to the root, Confucianism and Daoism have the same root and are complementary to each other. Both are in an integrative harmonious relationship. Some have argued that Confucianism has been the main stream while Daoism is a tributary of Chinese philosophy. This is an untenable opinion. By contrast, some may claim that Daoism is the main current while Confucianism is the branch. This is an agitated idea to revolt against the previous one. All these can be understood and comprehended within and can be treated easily. All these can be reconsidered in the foregoing discussion.

Postscript

There was a croaking sound from a knot of frogs in the night of early summer. I was in an unexpected silence when the draft was finished.

(The draft of this paper was finished in the summer of 2002. It was then revised on 4th of August, 2010 at Yuan-heng Study at the East Coast of Taiwan)

The Forum on New Interpretation of Classics:
the English version If *Lunyu*

Virtue and New Explanation of the Concept

On Internal Ontogenesis of Virtues in the Analects: A Conceptual Analysis

Chung-ying Cheng
(University of Hawaii at Manoa)

Introductory Remarks

In any theory of the development of the concept of human self we must recognize that the human self has to have an inner content which enables itself to know and respond to the world in such a way that we may find eventually an autonomy of will which can make moral choice and adopt a norm to follow in action. This does not mean that human person may not act without an inner consciousness or a will which makes normative decisions. He could for example simply pursue an end but not worry about the way of pursuing. But as a human being qua human being its understanding of inner self as a source or its interaction with the world is rather important for the assertion of the meaning and purpose of moral life. In the Western tradition we can see that the belief in human soul has been assumed when the Greek came to speak of the human self. But as to how this inner self is composed we have to wait for Plato to give it an ontological articulation and logical distinction. What we have is an ontology of the human self whose genesis may appear metaphysical and a mystery.

In the case of the Chinese philosophy, it is important to note that a human being is normally capable of recognizing the outer world and then responding and reflecting on his knowledge of the world so that he may also recognize his own identity as a human self. This human self is to be seen as having a mind capable of questioning what one wants and seeking what one pursues and thus making a distinction between what is good and bad relative to his needs and conception of what he wishes to achieve in the end. The process of formation of this concept of self is not transcendent nor transcendental but empirically ascertained on experiential grounds of observation and reflection or feeling and perception. What we have is an experience-induced onto-genesis of various feelings and dispositions under a fundamental conception of self which presents itself in practice and performance of virtues. I shall call this Chinese metaphysics "onto-generative metaphysics" (本体形上学) or generative ontology (发生本体论) in distinction from the ontological metaphysics (存有形上学) or simply ontology (存有论) of the Greek kind.

In this article I shall describe how Confucianism has formed an important notion of the onto-generative self in terms of reflective internalization of virtues in an germinating nature of the human person. It will be suggested that it is through the interplay of the function of mind as cognitive ability with the function of heart as affective ability in response to the outside world. It is on the basis of this interplay that the classical Confucian philosophy gradually comes to a full exploration of mind in a deep experiential understanding of the mind in the human person or human self. (We shall see zhi 知 or understanding or knowing as capable of deeply experiencing the self) . We could see such a process in the received texts of the writings of Confucius and his school up to Mencius and even to Xunzi. But it is not obvious and evident how this process takes place and finds its way until we come to possession of the excavated texts of the Boshu(帛书) and Zhujian(竹简).

I shall further show how Confucius must have inspired his disciples to identify the process and structure of human self called *xin* (heart-mind 心) and how the human self will cultivate itself in embodying and developing virtues within itself and eventually practicingvirtues as potential ways for full self-realization of the self in the Wu Xing Chapter 五行篇 (abbrev. WX) of the Boshu and Zhujian and Xingzhimingchu 性自命出 (abbrev. XZMC) and Xingqinglun 性情论(abbrev. XQL) in the Zhujian.

In the following I shall first make a conceptual and onto-hermeneutic analysis of the underlying self (ji 己) structure in the Analects and its born nature and mind as content. In the process of the appraisal of the internality and activity of mind we shall see emergence of the internal activity of heart-mind as feedback of the human nature and as a background condition for the emergence of autonomous will as basis of moral value affirmation. We shall also see how moral disposition and moral conduct will be formed in such an understanding, and how the external good is discovered as equally rooted in the intrinsic nature of the human person. On the basis of this approach we come to see how a moral psychology of virtues is founded and how such a moral psychology has implications for moral onto-generative metaphysics 本体形上学 and onto-generative ethics 本体伦理学 .

Self (自 – 己) and Virtue of Humanity (人 – 仁) in the Analects

If there is one word which can characterizes the essence of Confucius's teaching, it must be the word "ren" (仁) . If there is one word which can characterize the spirit of his philosophy and provides the unity for his teaching, it is still the word "ren". In the Analects we find one brief passage which seems to adequately describe's Confucius as a philosopher: 9. 1 子罕言利 , 与命 , 与仁 . (Confucius rarely speaks of profits, giving himself to destiny and "ren") ① . How does Confucius give himself to destiny? He simply let *ming* 命 determine his life and death and let heaven determine whether he

---

① Notice that the Chinese word "与" is used as a verb and means "give in" or "is given to" or "join with".

becomes g poor or wealthy (12. 5). He says that at fifty he came to know the mandate of heaven (2. 4). Apparently, it is *tian* 天 that determines one's destiny as if it is by a mandate. But we should not forget that it is also *tian* which determines the nature of humanity *xing* 性 as we see in Zisi's Zhong Yong 中庸 : It says as its first sentence that "What *tian* determines is nature". Nature unlike *ming* is what enables us to freely choose the right over wrong, and in an important sense to follow nature is follow the *dao*. For Confucius, no doubt, *ren* must be a force both presenting and defining *dao* in the world as well as an ability and a vision arising from oneself, and consequently a virtue conceived as acquired or inherited from the dao.

In fact, it could be due to Confucius's own influence, that Zhong Yong, affirms a positive and creative ability which follows the *xing* (率性) and which because of this, develops the *dao*. *Ren* must be such a positive and creative ability and power from the nature and has a root in the ultimate source of life and nature. It is no wonder that later Yizhuan 易传 comes to hold that the great virtue of heaven and earth is life-producing and that "继之者善也,成之者性也" (What succeeds the heaven is good; what accomplishes the tian is nature). The nature of man is therefore a continuer and accomplisher of the creativity of heaven and earth, under a more naturalist description of the natural power than a more personalistic description of heaven in early Confucian thinking.

Confucius is known for his explanation of *ren* in terms of his own experience of *ren* in his own self: There are several occasions that Confucius comes to creatively define *ren* either directly or indirectly. We have the following selective statements (translation by James Legge):

A . 子贡曰:"如有博施于民而能济众,何如? 可谓仁乎?"子曰:"何事于仁, 必也圣乎! 尧舜其犹病诸! 夫仁者, 己欲立而立人, 己欲达而达人。能近取譬, 可谓仁之方也已。"(6. 30)

Zi Gong said, "Suppose the case of a man extensively conferring benefits on the people, and able to assist all, what would you say of him? Might he be called perfectly virtuous?" The Master said, "Why speak only of virtue in connection with him? Must he not have the qualities of a sage? Even Yao and Shun were still solicitous about this. Now the man of perfect virtue, wishing to be established himself, seeks also to establish others; wishing to be enlarged himself, he seeks also to enlarge others. To be able to judge of others by what is nigh in ourselves-this may be called the art of virtue. "

B. 樊迟问知。子曰："务民之义，敬鬼神而远之，可谓知矣。"问仁。曰："仁者先难而后获，可谓仁矣。"（6.22）

Fan Chi asked what constituted wisdom. The Master said, "To give one's self earnestly to the duties due to men, and, while respecting spiritual beings, to keep aloof from them, may be called wisdom. " He asked about perfect virtue. The Master said, "The man of virtue makes the difficulty to be overcome his first business, and success only a subsequent consideration-this may be called perfect virtue. "

C. 子曰："仁远乎哉？我欲仁，斯仁至矣。"（7.30）

The Master said, "Is virtue a thing remote? I wish to be virtuous, and lo! virtue is at hand. "

D. 颜渊问仁。子曰："克己复礼为仁。一日克己复礼，天下归仁焉。为仁由己，而由人乎哉？"颜渊曰："请问其目。"子曰："非礼勿视，非礼勿听，非礼勿言，非礼勿动。"颜渊曰："回虽不敏，请事斯语矣。"（12.1）

Yan Yuan asked about perfect virtue. The Master said, "To subdue one's self and return to propriety, is perfect virtue. If a man can for one day subdue himself and return to propriety, all under heaven will ascribe perfect virtue to him. Is the practice of perfect virtue from a man himself, or is it from others?" Yan Yuan said, "I beg to ask the steps of that process. " The Master replied, "Look not at what is contrary to propriety; listen not to what is contrary to propriety; speak not what is contrary to propriety; make no movement which is contrary to propriety. " Yan Yuan then said, "Though I am deficient in intelligence and vigor, I will make it my business to practice this lesson. "

E. 仲弓问仁。子曰："出门如见大宾，使民如承大祭。己所不欲，勿施于人。在邦无怨，在家无怨。"仲弓曰："雍虽不敏，请事斯语

矣。"（12.2）

Zhong Gong asked about perfect virtue. The Master said, "It is, when you go abroad, to behave to every one as if you were receiving a great guest; to employ the people as if you were assisting at a great sacrifice; not to do to others as you would not wish done to yourself; to have no murmuring against you in the country, and none in the family." Zhong Gong said, "Though I am deficient in intelligence and vigor, I will make it my business to practice this lesson."

E. 有子曰："其为人也孝弟，而好犯上者，鲜矣；不好犯上，而好作乱者，未之有也。君子务本，本立而道生。孝弟也者，其为仁之本与!"（1.2）

The philosopher You said, "They are few who, being filial and fraternal, are fond of offending against their superiors. There have been none, who, not liking to offend against their superiors, have been fond of stirring up confusion. The superior man bends his attention to what is radical. That being established, all practical courses naturally grow up. Filial piety and fraternal submission! -are they not the root of all benevolent actions?"

F. 子曰："弟子入则孝，出则弟，谨而信，汎爱众，而亲仁。行有馀力，则以学文。（1.6）

"The Master said, "A youth, when at home, should be filial, and, abroad, respectful to his elders. He should be earnest and truthful. He should overflow in love to all, and cultivate the friendship of the good. When he has time and opportunity, after the performance of these things, he should employ them in polite studies."

G. 子曰："富与贵是人之所欲也，不以其道得之，不处也；贫与贱是人之所恶也，不以其道得之，不去也。君子去仁，恶乎成名? 君子无终食之间违仁，造次必于是，颠沛必于是。"（4.5）

The Master said, "Riches and honors are what men desire. If it cannot be obtained in the proper way, they should not be held. Poverty and meanness are what men dislike. If it cannot be avoided in the proper way, they should not be avoided. If a superior man abandon virtue, how can he fulfill the requirements of that name? The superior man does not, even for the space of a single meal, act contrary to virtue. In moments of haste, he cleaves to it. In seasons of danger, he cleaves to it. "

H. 8. 7 曾子曰：“士不可以不弘毅，任重而道远。仁以为己任，不亦重乎？死而后已，不亦远乎？”（4. 5）

The philosopher Zeng said, "The officer may not be without breadth of mind and vigorous endurance. His burden is heavy and his course is long. Perfect virtue is the burden which he considers it is his to sustain is it not heavy? Only with death does his course stop is it not long?"

Among these sample statements on *ren*, we notice that there are three standing out which gives both a content of *ren* and a subject of the *ren*. We can see that almost in all the statements Confucius speaks of a person or a superior man as having *ren* in reference to his behavior or conduct with other people. But there are three statements among all his statements on *ren* which addresses the activities of *ren* by addressing to the subject "self" (*ji* 己) and the subject "myself" (*wo* 我) which is the self which anyone can identify with his own being from experience. This amounts to defining *ren* in terms of some powerful internal activities in oneself which are exhibited in feelings or attitudes in the self of a person.

Thus Confucius twice speaks of "己所不欲勿施与人"（7. 30）"for anything any self does not wish for his self (or herself) he or she will not wish for others". Next, he also speaks of a benevolent person as "己欲立而立人，己欲达而达人"（In wishing to establish oneself any self would wish others to establish themselves, in wishing to reach for an end oneself any self would wish others to reach for an end". The reference to a self is also manifest in speaking of "克己复礼为仁。一日克己复礼，天下归仁焉。为仁由己，而由人乎哉". "To subdue one's self and return to propriety, is perfect virtue. If a man can for one day subdue himself and return to propriety, all under heaven will ascribe perfect virtue to him. Is the practice of perfect virtue from a man himself, or is it from others?" It is obvious that in all these three statements Confucius refers to a human self who is a subject of desiring, wishing and willing and who is capable of controlling himself for doing something or not doing something and in this case not to impose on others what he does not wish or desire for himself. It is made clear that in being capable of restraining himself one would be made possible to practice and perform rituals (*li* 礼) in relating to others and this is necessary for a society to function harmoniously.

Finally, we come to the most significant statement. 子曰:"仁远乎哉? 我欲仁,斯仁至矣。"The Master said, "Is virtue a thing remote? I wish to be virtuous, and lo! virtue is at hand. "Here we see that *ren* is not only an object and goal of one's will and desire, it is this desire and will which we can call *ren*. The statement identifies the human self in such a way that anyone can call forth and experience *ren* at will. We can see that the language conveys the meaning of the I (*wo* 我) as an active force which can bring out what is felt inside itself because it is its own hidden or deep identity. With this said, we may say that for Confucius humanity is individualized in human persons but all individual persons have in themselves an identity which wishes to relate and identify with others and this is expressed in the negative will and wish of a person to not harm others as well as the positive wish to help others, as *ren* can be experienced and willed by any human self reflectively. It is in his insight and insistence on this will and wish to relate to others that he sees the rise of virtue *ren*. For what is a virtue if it is not what is already rooted in the human self or humanity of the self? In fact, as Confucius sees it, *ren* must be the root and source of all virtues or any virtue which have to arise in human's dealing with others. It is also seen that the practice of *ren* leads to many different virtues addressing to various circumstances and this process of implementing *ren* makes it possible to say and project *ren* as a perfect virtue.

As the term *ren*(仁) indicates, *ren* should take place when one person is confronted with another person. How to overcome the harmful feelings between myself and another person or between any self and other self is a first step toward ren. Human relationships can be many sorts, and yet they may have analogical structures. Thus one virtue for one relationship could lead to different yet analogous virtues for different analogous relationships. It is on this basis that Yuzi speaks of(1.2). 有子曰:"其为人也孝弟,而好犯上者,鲜矣;不好犯上,而好作乱者,未之有也。君子务本,本立而道生。孝弟也者,其为仁之本与!" The philosopher You said, "They are few who, being filial and fraternal, are fond of offending against their superiors. There have been none, who, not liking to offend against their superiors, have been fond of stirring up confusion. The superior man bends his attention to what is radical. That being established, all practical courses naturally grow up. Filial piety and fraternal submission! —are they not the root of all benevolent actions?"

In saying that filial and fraternal loves as the source of *ren*, it is actually to say that filial and fraternal loves are sourced in the human self of *ren* and hence come to be what they are. Then it becomes possible to say that "孝悌" is the source of *ren*, which consists of more the same and other manifest realizations of the benevolent one (仁者). It is clear that we should make the distinction between root as empirical basis or starting point for realization of ideal virtue and root as the onto—cosmological origin in one's self or nature which makes empirical virtues possible. In this way we can envision a system of virtues springing out from the deep source and these virtues are bases and even inspirations for performing other virtues. One may imagine some process and structure of the following at work, a process and structure in which a particular virtue rooted in the human self becomes the empirical origin of other virtues which are also rooted in the original source which provides the similarity, analogy and extendability in the first place. [1]

Ren as humanity < --→filial and fraternal pieties →other virtues of ren

It is on this line of thinking that we can see not only that there is an internal source of *ji* which gives rise to our feelings and will of *ren* but that this source produces a basis for developing other virtues because of analogies

---

[1]   In fact this is the underlying way of generating the world of things in both theory of "太一生水" and the Yizhuan onto-cosmology as I have brought out.

among human relationships. In this fashion, we may easily identify *ren* as a foundation and fountainhead or source for all virtues because *ren* is rooted in self as the root 本 *ben*. In so far as all other virtues can be shown to derive and depend on *ren*, they have an internal basis and can be said to be differentiation of *ren* relative to relationships and circumstances. One may also argue that in so far as our intelligence and wisdom are able to make distinctions among things, we are to experience presentation of different virtues through the work of *ren* and its related wisdom *zhi*.

Given the above illustration of Confucian thinking in relation to *ren* as a source virtue, I wish to stress that for Confucius he has implicitly present the internality of virtues such as *ren* because of his experience and reference to the self and myself. In this manner we can see that the human self's internal feelings and reflective thoughts are the sources of virtues. Similarly, we can see other virtues as dispositions and activities as rooted in the root activity of the root virtue 仁, which is manifested in the process of desiring *ren* and gaining *ren* 欲仁得仁. In this connection we must point out the relevance of *zhong* 忠 and *shu* 恕. As an intuitive understanding we can see that *zhong* is a matter of integrity and loyalty to oneself, and thus the capacity to think of others as myself. On the other hand we can see *shu* as a matter of sympathy and empathy with others so that one can think of myself as others or in other's place. These two capabilities constitute what we may call a relation of reciprocity between the self and others so that we can derive from them rules of no harm (the Silver Principle) and the rules of benefit (the Golden Principle) which constitutes the concretization of the *ren* as a feeling and will. ① Here we see again a process of generation of the *ren* in specific applications

Ren as feeling and will of humanity → reciprocity of integrity and care (zhongshu) → the Silver principle and the Golden principle

It is only when the virtue becomes concretized in rules of action that the

---

① In the Da Xue it is applied to generate the so-called the way of measuring (xiejuzhidao 絜矩之道) in defining human actins relative to a relationship.

internal source of *ren* become externalized in action.

One final question relates to how it is difficult for people to maintain*ren* even if they have come to grasp it by desire-will and disciplining of one's selfish or private desires. To explain this requires further insight into how the self functions. It is clear to Confucius that people have to meet demands of life and survival at all the times, and thus people tend to be reduced to the routinized everydayness (to use a Heidegger's term) or habitual survival at most of time and lost sight of what Mencius calls the original heart-mind or the original nature. Thus for maintaining one's true self or original nature it is important for a person to hold to a way he has learned and devoted to the practice of de (志于道, 据于德 devoted to the dao and grounded on virtue) so that he could depend on and follow his *ren* instinct or *ren* feel to be awakened by a tradition of moral actions. This takes great effort and great attention so that we have to cultivate oneself for the transformation and thus restoration of the original nature of a person. Those who can do this and wish to do this are called the *junzi* 君子, and those who refuse to do this or fails to do this are called xiaoren 小人.

It must be noticed that there are many references to human self (*ji* 己) which may not immediately relate to ren. One of these is Confucius's saying that"古之学者为己, 今之学者为人" (In ancient times people learn for themselves; in present time people learn for others) (14-24). One can see that "learning for oneself" and "learning for others" are in contrast with the implication that one should use learning to concentrate on establishing oneself (立己) and accomplishing oneself (成己) instead of trying to please others. This means also that the self has its moral identity and moral purpose which it is capable of achieving by learning. As a matter of fact and without citing details, I like to give the following characterization of *ji* based on all statements related to *ji* in the Analects: 1) *Ji* can be expressed in first person, second person and third person and thus can be considered an subject-existence which any person can identify by reflection and reflexive thinking. In this sense *ji* is perceived to be a presentation of human existence which manifests many functions and activities; 2) Apparently, this human self identified as ji (己) has an independence and activity capable of initiating thinking and desiring in relation to others or to the human self. Thus a human self can be said to desire many things which he also desire for others or not to desire anything which he does not desire for others; 3) He is able of restraining and controlling himself so that he could achieve a goal of relating to others in proper order; 4) The human self is capable of learning for himself so that he may become established and accepted by society and who can further teach others what he has learned ; 5) The human self can cultivate himself toward respect for oneself and care for people at large. We have to see that the process and activities of cultivation of oneself (xiuji 修己) have to be explicitly explored and formulated in some important way; 6) It is clear that this human self is not only flexible in cultivated transformation, but is capable of reaching for the highest point of self-realization in accordance with the *dao* so that one's life can be said worthwhile and significant.

In light of above, we can see that the human self has an indefinite potential for making self-transformation and the transformation required of a human being is moral transformation from being human to being virtuous and moral. But we must also note that although the human self could have a rich content, it is necessary that we shall ask what makes it becoming aware of its constitutional agency or its identity as human self. This as we shall see will lead to our discovery that the human self could be eventually identified with mind and nature of the human person.

Function of Mind as Content of Human Self

While it is said that Confucius seldom speaks of the human nature and the way of heaven, we also find that Confucius did not talk much on the function of human heart or mind. But throughout the Analects there are six places where *xin* 心 (heart-mind) as a whole is mentioned and where important aspects of *xin* are revealed. The most well-known statement is where Confucius speaks of " At seventy l let my heart pursue what it likes(*cong xin suoyu* 从心所欲) and it will not trespass any rules of right (*er bu yuju* 而不逾矩). "(2. 4)

Zhu Xi sees this statement as one letting go one's heart- and- mind and yet it will naturally attain a state of virtue. ① It is obvious that *xin* has the status of feeling which may respond to anything within or without the human self, and yet it has the function of desiring and liking on its own strength which may have to do what one decides to do or what one decides not to do. Here we can see that *xin* can be in a state of freedom or free action which may be at the same time the result of education and self-discipline. In light of what Confucius has said about the process of his own moral growth, this state of freedom of heart mind is better seen as a result of self-discipline, reflective experience and deep knowledge embodying emergent awareness of one's destiny 命 . That is, it is knowing of the *tianming* 天命 (mandate of heaven) at fifty in his life. ② Based on this observation, one can see how this freedom of *xin* is also an exhibition of the regulation and limitation (*ming*) of heaven and that is also the reason why it cannot trespass any rule of right. From grasping this single statement in the Analects, we have come to grasp a deep understanding of *xin*, namely *xin* as a feeling which is capable of grasping the law of heaven. But *xin* is still basically our ability to feel and respond to the world and a capacity to know the world in terms of both unity of multiplicity of things. As later Xunzi explicitly says: 心知道然后可道 (the *xin* knows the *dao* and consequently can speak of the *dao*) ③. This means that *xin* has

---

① See Zhu Xi's 四书集注 in corresponding chapter and section.

② On this we must mention the novelty of Confucius' understanding: one has to see that the tianming was used to speak of the legitimacy of a political rule in the Shujing, but here Confucius uses the term creatively to address to what he feels he is destined to do, a role which is only justified in terms of tian's authorization as tian is considered the ultimate source of life and purpose of existence. It is clear that the knowledge of one's tianming is achieved by one's heart-mind and no doubt for Confucius knowing this is an achievement of one's heart-mind. zhuan onto-cosmology as I have brought out.

③ See Book of Xunzi chapter on *Jiebi* 解蔽 (removing obscurities) . Here Xunzi presents the sage as one who is capable of exhibiting all things in the world without discrimination and then comes to recognize a balanced point of view from which nothing is obscured by other things and this balanced point of view is called the "weighing measure 衡 *heng*" which warrants the revelation of order among things. The *dao* hence has two aspects for Xunzi: the natural order of things and the way of understanding this order without obscuring. Hence *dao* is both onto-cosmological and epistemological.

revealed itself as the will, the feeling and the knowledge because it combines the three things altogether and form an organic interdependence of the three as a whole. ① As such *xin* is implicitly perceived as the ruling subject of a human self in Confucius's own account of his moral growth. In other words, it testifies to his moral growth of his heart-mind into a moral personhood or moral self-identity. Later when Neo-Confucians have come to speak of *xin* as unifying and commanding the nature and feelings (心统性情)② it must be seen as a reflection of Confucian insight.

With this understanding of *xin* as both the feeling and active power of self-restraint, we see that *xin* can be intentional and have a direction of purpose for it is the nature of *xin* to seek a purpose and achieve value.

Thus when one strikes a bell there could be a some message intended for a audience to obtain, and this message could be manifest in certain context and obscure in other contexts. This also means that one could use one's mind to indicate one's intention or to achieve knowledge or do some significant thing. Here one may ask what is that which is to use one's mind (用心 or to focus mind on) as the term is used in the Analects. ③The natural answer is that it is the *xin* itself. Once we see this we see how *xin* can be an elusive subject when it uses itself as an object. But to say this is simply to say that the *xin* functions for a purpose in relation to an object. The last chapter of the Analects has cited the passage of the sage-king Yao which contains a reference to *xin* in the same paragraph, namely, "简在帝心" (the words are in the heart of the ruler) and "天下之民归心" (All the people under heaven return to the same heart). This has brought the notion of xin to a depth which

---

① It is in this sense I have first translated *xin* as heart-mind. See my paper "Some Aspects of the Confucian Notion of Mind", Bulletin of Literature History and Philosophy, National Taiwan University, Taipei, Taiwan, 1971, 491-510.

② See relevant writings of this proposition in Zhang Zai and Zhu Xi. See especially my essay "朱熹四书次第与其整合问题:兼论朱熹中和新旧说的内容与其涵义" (Zhu Xi's Integration of Four Books: Significccance of Old and New Theories of Centrality and Harmony),《朱子学刊》,黄山书社 2006 年版,第 110—132 页。

③ Confucius says: "饱食终日,无所用心,难矣哉,不有博弈者乎,为之犹贤乎。"(17. 20)

enables us to say that *xin* can contain maxims and principles in guiding oneself and others. It also shows how human minds could come together in a consensual support of a ruler in terms of their feelings and ideas.

With *xin* being now described as source, place and power of activities involving various feelings and cognition, *xin* can be said to feel, to know, to think, to learn, to will and to desire, and within each kind of these activities, we can also list many other more specific activities and feelings such as believing or doubting, complaining and praising etc. . ① We must see how it can be seen as a source, a place and a function and a ruling force for our internal consciousness. It can be seen as active realization of human self in the context and process of interaction with other things and people who have an internal structure of heart mind. Note what needs to be brought out is that for any *xin* activity there is both the feeling side and the knowing side. In other words, the feeling activity of mind presupposes the knowing as a base for response whereas the knowing activity of mind presupposes natural feeling arising from the knowing. But there is no reason why feeling and knowing cannot take place at the same time because each may arise from our central ability to feel for knowing and to know for feeling. The importance of feeling and knowing is that we have reacted as a whole and our action is dependent on the unison of the feeling and knowing. What is also significant to see is that we can feel what we know and we can also come to know what we feel so that we may make decision of action more efficiently and more consistently and this is hidden function of heart-and-mind as *yu* 欲 as *zhi* 志 or will. Confucius thus speaks of "博学笃志"(to learn wide and to be sincere in one's will" (19. 6) and "不降其志"(not to surrender one's will) (18. 8).

There is, finally, the consideration of *zi* 自 for the identity meaning of a source. From my earlier papers I have observed that this source idea forms an

---

① It is obvious that Xunzi simply comes to make these activities and functions of mind explicit in his description of mind as the ruler of body and the master of spirit and a commander of commanding without being commanded. See ibid. in the middle of this famous essay.

inevitable origin of the feelings and knowledge of the mind. It has been also independently used as a stand-in for human self. ① Thus the Analects comes to speak of reflective examination of oneself (内自省). Confucius says: "见 贤而内自省" (See the sagely and reflect on oneself) (4. 17) It is obvious that this *zi* 自 refers to the self as both a source for examining activity and an object for examination, and thus implies the self which can conduct this self-reflexive activity of self-reference. Similarly , Confucius speaks of 内自讼 (To litigate against oneself within the self) (5. 27) . This indicates that the human self could turn itself to be an object of one's activity which may be originally is directed to an object outside. The importance of this use of *zi* is indication that mental activities come from the self as source and hence from the heart-mind itself as the source.

Eventually, we come to name the human self as *zi-ji* 自己 or "from-self" which is a vivid description of how the human self can be self-reflective and self-reflexive and how there is an inside (内) in oneself which is to be contrasted with an outside (外) beyond the self. This is no doubt a main feature of the heart- mind which functions as a whole and in unity and which yet distinguishes between the inner in mind and the outer outside mind, the former referring to all activities and things in mind whereas the latter refers to all things in the world in so far as one ' s experience goes. In light of what we have said about the heart-mind in the Analects, this self as an activity is no better described as activities of the heart-mind and consequently to be functionally identified with the heart-mind of a person.

On the Nature (性 *Xing*) of the Human Self

As mentioned, Confucius has not talked much about *xing* and

①   See my article "A Theory of Confucian Selfhood: Self-Cultivation and Free Will. "*Komparative Philosophie: Begegnungen zwischen ? stlichen und westlichen Denkwegen.* Ed. Rolf Elberfeld. München: Wilhelm Fink Verlag, 1998, 51 – 86.

tiandao. But we must come to deal with the question of nature in some way as we find that there are places where the concept of nature is called for. Once we have heart-mind as based on human self we may now simply identify the human self as nature with function of mind or just as nature which is what mind come from and hence has a unique union with the human body. With this understanding of *ben* 本 (root, base) we see that every time he is speaking of activity of mind, he has touched the nature (*xing* 性) of the human person. We may therefore say that Confucius has related to human nature from the very beginning and his concern with human virtue is a concern with human nature because to be virtuous requires great effort of learning based on our ability to learn which no doubt is a characteristic of nature. That one can achieve virtue or maintenance of virtue from learning has also something to do with nature.

There are two places Confucius speak of human nature : The first place is where Zigong says that "夫子之言性与天道不可得而闻也" (It is seldom to hear the master 's talk on nature and way of heaven) (5-13) This does not tell anything about the content of Confucius's ideas of *xing* 性。But the second place is where Confucius did say something important : "性相近也,习相远也。唯上智与下愚为不移" (The natures of people are similar to each other. It is by habit they become apart. It is in supreme wisdom and extreme ignorance only that a person may not change his nature) (17. 2). Confucius did not say that all people have the same nature, but when they are born, they must have something in common, namely they are human. That is what makes them resembling each other and this can be certainly told by wide observation. Similarly, by observation it is also clear that people can become very different by later learning and adaption or habituation and acculturation in different environments and traditions. This shows that Confucius takes human nature to be transformable and changeable due to adaption and learning and this should be the foundation for his notion of "cultivation of self 修己". If our nature can be changed externally there is no reason why it cannot be changed internally or changed by the internal dynamics of our mind due to activity and autonomy. This would immediately lead to the question of acquisition and formation of *de* (德 virtue), the ability and disposition to do good and act right from the dao which also comes from the nature according to Zhong Yong.

When Confucius says that "天生德于予", he sees de as capable of being inherent from one's birth or in one's nature. But he may not make assumption that all people have inherent de. He stresses the importance of learning *xue* 学 and his disciple have stressed that for a good man (*junzi*) it is by learning that he has reached the *dao* where *dao* is understood as the way to lead a person to reach an ideal state of good (for what this means we shall see later). Of course, there are also good examples of virtuous action or conduct which we may follow as models or to learn to embody so that we may act right and achieve goodness. When Confucius says that "道之以德，齐之以礼，民有耻且格" If we guide people with virtue and regulate them with rites, people will have a sense of shame and a moral personality) (2. 3) We can see that the virtue is model of conduct which one finds in sage kings or in oneself which one is capable of cultivating. What is essential to a *de* is its embodiment in action and practice. In other words, *de* is not just a model of conduct or a figure of speech but one which one has to embody and act out (*xing* 行) in oneself. It is also obvious that such action will lead to resonance of the same and has an effect of transforming people and society from bad to good or from chaos to order, and from indifference to caring. It is how the *dao* becomes prevailing via action of *de*.

Among all virtues which eventually forms a system of learning and practice, Confucius singles the virtue of *ren* (仁 benevolence) as the source and basis for all other virtues. For Confucius, as explained in the above, *ren* is captured in the action of not wishing to do things to others what one does not wish others do to you. What really distinguishes *ren* from other virtues is that it is something coming from one's will and feeling of heart-mind. Although Confucius does not use *ren* in terms of *xin* 心 and *zhi* 志, his statement that "Is *ren* far away? If I desire *ren* and lo, *ren* arrives here. "

(7. 30) indicates that Confucius never thinks of *ren* or *de* for that matter as outside oneself. *Ren* as feeling of care for humanity and therefore a feeling of care for others rooted in ones's awakening of humanity in oneself. This makes *ren* an inevitable internal happening in a person. But when *ren* is thought to conceptually ground other virtues, one may not immediately see how those other virtues as internally sourced in one's self. Yet in order for a virtue to be a motivating force and an end to be pursued one has to see it being capable of being derived from some internal feeling through reflection. Thus when we come later to the dispute between Mencius and Gaozi on whether yi or righteousness is internal or external, it takes an argument based on experience of feeling for Mencius to make his point. For after all, without deep internal feeling for a just action, how could one relate justice to oneself or to *ren*? How could one come to choose to abide by law if there is no internal basis? It is possible that one may not immediately be aware of one's feeling for a positive value in oneself, for it may take efforts of one's mind to envision a good end and a will to develop an ability to perform the virtuous action. This process would be called the process of cultivation of virtues (修德 *xiude*) which is in effect a process of cultivation of *ren (修仁 xiuren)* or cultivation of oneself (修己 *xiuji*) or one's self as embodied (修身 *xiushen*).

Confucius even speaks of cultivating a civilian culture (*wende* 文德) to attract distant people for taking residence in one's state (16. 1) . In fact Confucius has spoken of virtue in terms of a system of virtues which he respectively explained in connection with his understanding and his own deep experience of *ren*.

From Confucius's own statement on xing in the Analects 17. 2 we also see that Confucius has linked transformation of nature with the notion of superior wisdom. If a man does not change his nature it is because he has reached a state of being capable to acting right and doing good in any circumstances so that he may not have to shape his character for adapting to his circumstances. But this means that he is able to do the adaption on his own and will not be subject to external forces for causing his adaption. This means that this wisdom is one which Confucius would identify with his mind at 70, where one meets one's demands from the world and yet satisfies them with creativity and freedom. The opposite of supreme wisdom 上智 is low ignorance 下愚 or sheer stupor which could not know right nor has the will to learn.

From this understanding we see that Confucius takes human nature to be malleable to change and transformation and the question is how it can be changed and what end it will attain in one's transformation of one's nature. These questions no doubt lead to the inquiry on how one could cultivate oneself and how one's nature could be open to influences from outside and inside, and eventually how nature is formed originally, and where it can be said to originate under what proper conditions. I believe that these implicit questions have led to inquires in the disciples of Confucius as shown in Daxue and Zhongyong. The discovery of the silk and bamboo manuscripts such as Wu Xing 五行 in 1973 and Xin Zi Ming Chu 性自命出 in 1993 provide us a clue as to how the theory of self-cultivation develops after Confucius. But I wish to point out that without deep reflective understanding of Confucius in the Analects we would not be able to gather the proper attention and insight for interpreting these excavated texts.

It is only when we have a deep reflective understanding as a background we may come to see how these texts are to be properly interpreted. In other words, without a basic model for understanding the Analects, we would not have a standard of judging what is what and how is how, and in particular how these texts under the guidance of the Analects could have given rise to received Confucian texts such as the Da Xue and the Zhong Yong as one may like to see. ① This means that we must take Analects seriously for integrative

---

① One may let the texts speak for themselves, but no texts simply speak for themselves without a coherent pre-understanding and a coherent post-understanding. One of the critical issues for evaluating the excavated texts is to see how they are related to other relevant texts such as Daxue and Zhongyong. It is evident that they must arise after the Analects and they could not develop after Daxue and Zhongyong if we have reason to believe that Daxue and Zhongyong are more settled ideas than the excavated texts. They could of course develop at the same time of Daxue and Zhongyong or even after Daxue and Zhongyong. But there is no indication that that is the case.

understanding of what constitutes human nature and how human nature is the root for forming virtue and how it can eventually be regarded as intrinsically and onto-generatively good. This means that we shall show how Confucius's view of human nature will move from awareness of its potential to active cultivation to recognition of its being intrinsically rooted in goodness in a certain onto-cosmic sense. This indicates an issue of interaction of ontology and cosmology of nature with epistemology of knowing nature and morality of cultivating nature, which points to a unity of existence, knowing and goodness as the ideal base for human development and an ideal for human beings to cherish and achieve.

Let us focus on one singular significant statement in the Analects which is an implicit comment on the goodness of nature of human being and which has been completely neglected in the discussion on Confucius's attitude toward human nature. This statement says: "人之生也直,罔之生也幸而免" (Man is born straight; if born as crooked the survival of the person is a matter of luck) (6. 19) If a person is straight (zhi 直) by birth, it means that he is straight by nature. For we can say that the once a person was born, his nature is given at his birth. Hence one can know the nature of a person by knowing what he is endowed with at birth. It is may be the essential meaning of "生之谓性" (What is born is called nature) as held by Gaozi in the Book of Mencius. But we may still do not know what type of a nature a person may have even his nature was already given at his birth. Gaozi falls short of telling us what this born nature is. It has to take observation to tell what a person's nature is in light of what we know about good and bad. For we may want to know whether human nature is good or bad, or to be more precise, to be judged good or to be judged bad. In this case Confucius 's statement tells us more than Gaozi, for he says that a person is straight by birth. His claim must be based on his observation and reflection. He must come to know that for all people he knows were straight by birth and if not it would take much effort to survive not to say to develop. The implication is that most of people are straight by birth and those who may not be straight would normally perish.

What then is the meaning of "being straight"? Obviously, one meaning of *zhi* 直 *consists in one's natural disposition of honesty in telling what one feels when one feels without any intention to deceive others or oneself.* It is *zhi* which provides the basis for being honest and frank regardless whether one may cover up what one may not have. In this sense to be straight is a good thing to have and it leads to better results than being crooked and deceptive. ①
Thus the overall implication of Confucius statement is that he would have to say that human nature must be judged good in so far as being straight is good. ② In the Analects Confucius has consistently defends the practice of being straight and apparently considered it as a moral virtue. ③

With the above analysis in mind we must conclude by saying that Confucius has made a point about human nature and that point is that human nature is straight if it can be identified with the born nature. In this connection we must also notice that this born nature as straightness could be actually a matter of virtue. In the Analects *zhi* is contrasted with crookedness (枉 *wang)* which is characterized by deviousness and lack of candor when candor is called for. *Wang* needs not be regarded as dis-value or badness, but certainly not as desirable a quality in many human contexts. Given this contrast with *wang, zhi* is no doubt a preferable way of expression and conduct because it is germane to attaining good end of life or experienced as disposition toward

---

① Chen Baonan in his *Lunyu* Zhengyi quotes from Cheng Xuan: " The nature at birth is just (zhengzhi 正直)". Cheng Xuan's view apparently takes human nature to be virtuous in a fundamental sense. My interpretation of *zhi* as straightness may not go so far but sees *zhi* as a pre-virtue quality which is better than its absence and which provides for an initial condition for learning or developing virtue.

② As we shall see, *shan* as a concept refers to any action or character which gives us what we normally desire and which should please us or benefit us. In this sense any performance of *de* is good just as its acquisition. But to show how human nature contains dispositions to produce *shan* requires both experiential instances and interpretation of the meaning of those instances. This takes place later in Mencius. In so far as human nature has a virtuous disposition or an initial feeling which we can identify with ways to achieve good it is therefore good.

③ There is the famous passage on how a father hides a "theft of sheep" for his son and reciprocally. Confucius said that there is straightness (直) in there. See 13. 18. He also speaks of uplifting the zhi and putting aside the crooked in ruling a state. See 2. 19 and 12. 22.

such an end. In this sense it may not be too far-reaching to argue that the born nature of a human person is perceived by Confucius as basically good in an intrinsic and onto-generative sense of good because it contributes to a virtuous way of living than otherwise.

Here I may come as up against the most common prevailing view that Confucius does not take any view as to whether human nature is basically or good or bad. It is true that Confucius never takes any such view as he has not addressed to any such question. But this does not prevent us from identifying the presupposition and implication of the Confucian statement in the context of his observations of human condition. It is further necessary that we should look into what does the notion of good (善 *shan*) stand for in the Confucian Analects, and how it relates to virtuous action and human intention.

In the first place, we can see that Confucius has taken the notion of *shan* for granted in the Analects and use it and has not made any explanation of what shan is about. But in his use of term we see that he perceived the music of *shao*(韶) as perfectly beautiful and perfectly good while he perceived the music of *wu* (武) as perfectly beautiful and yet not perfectly good. According to Zhu Xi, what makes the music of *shao* perfectly good beside being perfectly beautiful is the fact the *shao* embodies or symbolizes the virtue of humility of the sage- king Xun , while the music of *wu* embodies and symbolizes the action of King Wu to make expedition and conquest of the cruel Zou of Shang. ①

Of course, what is called good can be good in a non-moral sense which need not to do with one's character or a desirable result as we may also distinguish between instrumental good and good as an end value. Here in the following text Confucius clearly speaks of a moral good and good as a moral end; "I worry about these: one's virtue is not cultivated, one's learning is not pursued, one does follow righteousness after knowing it, one does not improve

---

① See *Lunyu* Jizhu volume 2, in Sishu Zhangju jizhu, Beijing: Zhonghua Book Company, 2008.

one's lack of good. " (7. 3) Here we see clearly that Confucius takes *shan* to be a result of cultivating virtue and following righteousness and something to be learned from observing goodness in others. When he comes to say "善人为邦百年,亦可以胜残去杀矣。" (If a good person rules a country for a hundred years, he would be able to overcome cruelties and remove killings.) (13. 11) , it is clear that a good person must be a virtuous person or person of benevolence (*ren*) who is capable of overcoming cruelties and removing killings under his rule. From these instances we may suggest that the general meaning of *shan* as desirable qualities or states of being have been established long before any philosophers come to speculate wherefrom it originates. What a philosopher needs to do is to identify what are considered good in light of our common and intuitive understanding of good derived from general experience of life. This identification process for an outstanding instance of the good is also a process of defining and articulating the term and giving it a meaning so that we come to have better understanding of the term. This process actually takes place constantly in the Chinese Classical Writings of the time when we see how a term is identified in terms of the epithet "*weizhi*(谓之) " or "*zhiwei*(之谓) " "*yue*(曰) " . ① From these, it seems clear that we have good reason to consider goodness a part of human in the texts of the Analects.

In light of later development after the Analects, from the WX and XZMC bamboo texts to Liji inclusive of Daxue and Zhongyong, and further to Mencius and Xunzi, we should not forget the function and activities of heart-mind in the human self which are not explicitly articulated and focused on in discourse but which nevertheless remain looming behind the words of Confucius. It is perception and consciousness of these functions and activities of heart-mind which eventually give rise to the notion of human nature in Mencius in which goodness as a disposition and as a vision inevitably forms an

---

① We come across these epithets for defining or giving a meaning to commonly used term in all almost all classical texts of Confucianism, Daoism and Moism. This process of defining and redefining develops into a logical treatise of defining basic concepts of knowledge, value and existence in the Neo-Mohist Canons.

inevitable component.

Conclusion

In conclusion, the above analysis of Confucian concepts of self, mind, nature, virtue and good provides a framework of reference for raising questions and orienting responses and answers in the latter Confucian texts such as Daxue, Zhongyong and also those silk and bamboo texts we have excavated in contemporary times. It provides not only a basis, a scope and a limit for understanding the basic concepts involved, but offers a direction, a reason and a guidance for how to interpret those concepts and the related propositions. Given the Confucian reflection and expression in the Analects, it is clear that Confucius have left open unanswered many essential questions regarding nature and virtue of the human self, regarding source and origin of nature and mind, regarding how virtues must be rooted in one's nature, and whether human nature can be regarded as good or bad. All these questions have to be answered in an inquiry among Confucius's many disciples and their answers could be regarded as new discoveries or illuminations of the basic concepts of the mater therein the texts or in the mind of Confucius.

Rang or Yielding in Respect: Reflections on a Confucian Virtue and Its Relevance in the Cross-Strait *Realpolitik*

Yen-zen Tsai

(National Chengchi University)

Abstract

Rang 让 occurs seven times in the *Analects of Confucius (Lunyu)*. It is commonly translated as deference, yielding, giving up, or ceding to others. Although it has captured less attention than *ren* (仁) (benevolence, humaneness) or *li* (礼) (ritual, propriety) among modern scholars of Confucian studies, its importance, the paper argues, cannot be easily dismissed. Confucius regards it as basically a mental attitude and a sensitive way of dealing with other fellow beings. When it is manifested, it is often connected to or implemented in the ritual context. These classical denotations, however, undergo dramatic turns when this virtue meets with practical considerations. A good case in point is the recent signing of the Economic Cooperation Framework Agreement (ECFA) between China and Taiwan in which li (利)or profit is involved. The paper then analyzes how *rang* is used in the process of power negotiation and explicates its possible meanings in the present-day *Realpolitik*. By way of contrasting the internal with the external, the spiritual with the material, and the classical with the modern, the papers intends to unravel the subtle implications of this Confucian virtue.

I. Introduction

On June 29, 2010, Mainland China and Taiwan signed the landmark Economic Cooperation Framework Agreement (ECFA) which was intended to facilitate the development of mutual trading across the Taiwan Strait. [①] The event was widely held to be a positive step toward easing the tension between these two political adversaries. According to this liberalizing pact, The Mainland China will reduce tariffs on 539 items from Taiwan valued at US $ 14 billions and Taiwan will cut tariffs on 267 Chinese goods worth about US $ 3 billions. [②] The new China-Taiwan economic relation will bring significant benefits to both sides, preponderantly to Taiwan. Political economists estimated that by 2020, Taiwan would increase its GDP by 5. 3 percent thanks to the net effect of ECFA, which includes possible similar agreements that Taiwan might sign with the Association of Southeast Asian Nations (ASEAN). [③]

On the surface, ECFA was reached on the basis of "equal consultation and mutual benefits, "[④] China seemed to have exchanged economic favor for ulterior purposes. Wen Jiabao, Chinese premier, openly remarked that "we can give up our profits because Taiwanese compatriots are our brothers. "[⑤] In

---

[①]　For the news, see "China-Taiwan trade pact sparks street protest in Taipei, " BBC, June 26, 2010 (http: //news. bbc. co. uk/2/hi/world/asia_pacific/10423409. stm); "Taiwan weighs up historic China trade deal, " BBC, June 29, 2010 (http: //www. bbc. co. uk/2/hi/world/asia _ pacific/ 10434768. stm).

[②]　Pamela Boykoff, "Taiwan, China sign historic deal, " CNN, June 29, 2010 (http: // edition. cnn. com/2010/WORLD/asiapcf/06/29/china. taiwan. deal/index. html).

[③]　Daniel H. Rosen and Zhi Wang, "Deepening China-Taiwan Relations through the Economic Cooperation Framework Agreement, " in *Policy Brief*, no. PB 10-16 (Peterson Institute for International Economic, June 2010).

[④]　See "Taiwan and China sign landmark trade agreement, " BBC, June 29, 2010 (http: // www. cbbc. co. uk/2/hi/world/asia _ pacific/10442557. stm); The remark was quoted from Chen Yunlin, China's official representative.

[⑤]　See "Taiwan and China sign landmark trade agreement, " BBC, June 29, 2010 (http: // www. cbbc. co. uk/2/hi/world/asia _ pacific/10442557. stm); The remark was quoted from Chen Yunlin, China's official representative.

a situation where China and Taiwan has been political rivals for sixty years and mutual trust is yet to be established, his statement alarmed some in Taiwan. ECFA is thus not merely an economic deal, Taiwanese critics pointed out; it involves other political and nationalistic considerations. Significantly, Wen's coinage of *rang li* (让利), translated as "giving up profits" in the news report, deserves our special attention, as it touches upon an important virtue, *rang* 让 or yielding, in the *Analects of Confucius*. When *rang* is combined with *li* 利, however, the new compound reflects subtle implications with respect to human connections and international relations. This paper proposes first to analyze *rang* and *li* as presented in the *Analects* and intends to reveal the original meanings of these two terms in ancient China. It then proceeds to discuss *rang li* and shows how the term creates tension as well as possibilities in the context of the cross-Strait *Realpolitik*.

II. *Rang* (让) in the *Analects*

Rang occurs seven times in the *Analects*, but one repetition extracted, it is found in six different sayings. For the sake of our analysis and discussion, I list the full texts that contain this character in Chinese with English translations as follows.

1:10   子禽问于子贡曰:「夫子至于是邦也, 必闻其政, 求之与? 抑与之与?」子贡曰: 「夫子温、良、恭、俭、让以得之。 夫子之求之也, 其诸異乎人之求之与?」①

Ziqin asked Zigong, "When the Master arrives in a state, he invariably gets to know about its government. Does he seek this information? Or is it given him?" Zigong replied, "The Master gets it through being cordial, good, respectful, temperate, and

_____

① For the Chinese text and its modern punctuations, I basically follow Yang Bojun's 杨伯峻 version with my modifications unless noted otherwise; see Yang Bojun, translated and annotated, *Lunyu yizhu* 论语译注 (Beijing: ZhongHua Company, 1980).

deferential. The Way the Master seeks it is, perhaps, different from the way other men seek it. "①

3:7　子曰:「君子无所争。比也射乎! 揖让而升,下而饮。其争也君子。」

The Master said, "There is no contention between gentlemen. The nearest to it is, perhaps, archery. In archery they bow and make way for each other as they go up and on coming down they drink together. Even the way they contend is gentlemanly. "

4:13　子曰:「能以礼让为国乎? 何有? 不能以礼让为国,如礼何?」

The Master said, "If a man is able to govern a state by observing ritual propriety and showing deference, what difficulties will he have? If he is unable to govern a state by observing ritual propriety and showing deference, what good are the rites to him?"

8:1　子曰:「泰伯,其可谓至德也已矣。三以天下让,民无得而称焉。」

The Master said, "Taibo can be said to be of the highest virtue. Three times he renounced his right to rule over the empire, and yet the people could not find words to praise him. "

11:26　子路、曾皙、冉有、公西华侍坐。子曰：「以吾一日长乎尔,毋吾以也。居则曰『不吾知也!』如或知尔,则何以哉?」子路率尔而对曰:「千乘之国,摄乎大国之间,加之

---

① For the English version of the *Analects*, I follow D. C. Lau's translation with my own modifications unless noted otherwise; see D. C. Lau, *Confucius: The Analects* (Harmondsworth and New York: Penguin Books, 1979).

以师旅因之以饥馑；由也为之，比及三年，可使有勇，且
知方也。」夫子哂之。…（曾皙）曰：「夫子何哂由也？」
曰：「为国以礼，其言不让，是故哂之。」①

When Zilu, Zengxi, Ranyou, and Gongxi Hua were seated in
attendance, the Master said, "Do not feel constrained simply
because I am a little older than you are. Now you are in the
habit of saying, 'My abilities are not appreciated,' but if
someone did appreciate your abilities, do tell me how you would
go about things." Zilu promptly answered, "If I were to
administer a state of a thousand chariots, situated between
powerful neighbours, troubled by armed invasions and by
repeated famines, I could, within three years, give the people
courage and a sense of direction." The Master smiled at thim…
. [Zengxi] asked, "What did you smile at You (i. e. Zilu)?"
The Master said, "It is by observing ritual propriety that a state
is administered, but in the way he spoke You showed no
deference. That is why I smiled at him."

15∶36 子曰：「当仁，不让于师」

The Master said, "When faced with the opportunity to
practice benevolence, do not yield precedence even to
your teacher."

The *Shuowen jiezi* (《说文解字》) by Xu Shen (许慎) (fl. 100 CE),
the most authoritative and influential lexicon in the Chinese history, defines
the original meaning of *rang* as "to rebuke," but it further adds that its
denotation evolved into "to yield / to defer" as seen in the various ancient

---

①　11∶26 is the longest account in the *Analects*. To save space and for the particular purpose of
this paper, I only excerpt the passage most relevant to *rang*.

writings. ① *Rang* that appears in the *Analects* has more or less consistently the latter meaning. 1: 10 records a conversation between Confucius' two disciples about the Master's interest in government in relation to his personality. While Ziqin is perceptive that Confucius, upon entering a state, always seeks information about its governance, he is curious how Confucius gets it. Zigong the senior disciple affirms that the Master's way of getting information is different from that of others; he gets it by his personal qualities. These qualities, being cordial, good, respectful, temperate, and deferential, appear very akin to one another in their signification. ② They all point to a person spiritually well-cultivated and delicately cultured. They specifically refer to a type of temperament that is receptive, amiable, and even soft in nature. Once situated in human interactions, these qualities allure. That is the way Confucius obtains what he wants: people offer the information voluntarily because of the former's attraction. Thus so far as *rang* is used to describe human personality, it connotes amicability and refinement on the one hand, and, on the other, affective and catching power.

    3: 7 reflects Confucius' understanding of *junzi* 君子, gentlemen or, as Roger T. Ames and Henry Rosemont would put it, exemplary persons. ③ Confucius affirms that the real gentlemen never contend, and if they do, it

---

    ①   Duan Yucai (段玉裁), *Shuowen jiezi zhu* (《说文解字注》), (Taipei: Yiwen Publishing Company, 2005), pp. 100-101.

    ②   It is interesting to note that in translating these five Chinese characters, Sinologists hardly found their exact English equivalents. As a result, they chose words that are qualitatively abstract and comprehensive and often interchangeable among them. To correspond *wen* 溫, *liang* 良, *gong* 恭, *jian* 儉, *rang* 让, James Legge offered " benign, upright, courteous, temperate, complaisant," respectively; see his *The Chinese Classics*, vol. 1 (Taipei: Southern Materials Center, 1983), p. 142; Arthur Waley, "cordial, frank, courteous, temperate, deferential"; see his *The Analects of Confucius* (New York: Vintage Books, 1938), p. 86; Raymond Dawson, "warm, amiable, courteous, frugal, deferential"; see his *Confucius: The Analects* (Oxford: Oxford University Press, 1993), p. 4; Roger T. Ames/ Henry Rosemont, Jr., "cordial, proper, deferential, frugal, unassuming"; see their *The Analects of Confucius: A Philosophical Translation* (New York: Ballantine Books, 1998), 73; Edward Slingerland, "courteous, refined, respectful, restrained, deferential"; see his *Confucius: Analects* (Indianapolis/Cambridge: Hackett Publishing Company, 2003), p. 4.

    ③   Ames/ Rosemont, *The Analects of Confucius*, p. 83.

would only happen ritualistically. As archery is one of the Six Arts that the male aristocrats received for shaping their physical fitness and artistic dexterity in ancient China, [①] he graphically describes its process of competition. He emphasizes that from ascending to descending, i. e. , from the beginning to the completion, the two competitors bow and make way for each other, exhibiting mutual respectfulness. The entire competition in this way looks more like a graceful performance than a fierce contest. Etymologically *rang* 让 may be construed as another homophone, *rang* (攘) , meaning to push away or to decline, but in this account *yi rang*(揖让) as a compound indicates the gesture of raising hands for mutual greeting. [②] Thus *rang* (让) plays an important role in a ritualized context. What a ritual may prescribe for the gentlemen the right steps to follow, the spirit of deference seasons it from within. The function of *rang* therefore softens and harmonizes the ritual acts, leaning more heavily toward the participants' inward character than the framework that regulates them.

The dynamic relationshipbetween ritual and its spirit is emphatically expounded in 4: 13. In this saying, Confucius juxtaposes *li* (礼) and *rang* (让) , the only example in contrast to the common *ren li* (仁礼) (humanity and ritual propriety) dyad throughout the *Alanects*, treating them as an inseparable concept or principle highly relevant to governing a state. He believes that it is not too difficult to bring a state to order, as long as the ruler observes ritual propriety and shows deference. He quickly adds that if rituals and deference do not simultaneously function, the former alone cannot take real effect. In other words, ritual propriety may be important, the spirit behind it is even more vital. Zhu Xi (朱熹 1130 – 1200) , when commenting on this statement, exegetes *rang* as *li zhi shi* 礼之实 or "the substance of

---

① The Six Arts refer to *li* 礼 (rituals), *yue* 乐 (music), *she* 射 (archery), *yu* 御 (charioteering), *shu* 书 (writing), and *shu* 数 (mathematics); see *Zhouli zhushu* 周礼注疏, in *Shisanjing zhushu* 十三经注疏, 8 vols. , ed. Ruan Yuan 阮元 (Taipei: Yiwen chubanshe, 1985), *juan* 14 ("Paoshi"), p. 6b.

② See Qian Mu (钱穆), *Lunyu xinjie* (《论语新解》) (Taipei: Dongda tushu, 1988), p. 77.

ritual". ① Liu Baonan (刘宝楠 1791 – 1855) subscribes to Zhu's opinion and further says that ritual is 让之文 or "the embellishment of deference". ② Both of these two commentators see the precedence of *rang* over *li*, which should be the right understanding of Confucius' original meaning.

The background of 8: 1 tells of the incomparable virtue of Taibo, the oldest granduncle of King Wu (r. 1046 – 43 BC), the founder of the Zhou Dynasty. Legendary has it that, upon seeing that his youngest brother and nephew were more sagacious than he, Taibo renounced his right to inherit the throne and intentionally passed it to them. For three times he made excuses, even deserting to the barbarian south, to decline his mandate. These, to the exclusion of ordinary people's knowledge, all happened in the royal family and before the Zhou Dynasty was formally established. ③ Confucius was much impressed by this story and attributed Taibo's virtue of yielding to the highest kind. Zhu Xi interprets *san rang*(三让) to be *gu xun* (固逊), deferential with persistency. ④ Qian Mu(钱穆 1895 – 1990) comments that Confucius not only praised Taibo's extreme deference but also commended his purposeful concealment of what he had done, and the so-called "highest virtue" should include these two facts. ⑤ *Rang* in this context carries the meaning of sacrificing one's benefits to fulfill the higher common good and, moreover, hiding away one's meirt as if a secret.

The excerpt drawn from 11: 26 demonstrates the example of a lack of deference, *bu rang*(不让). While Confucius is conversing with four of his disciples, he encourages them to frankly speak up their life goals. Zilu takes the lead and immediately makes known his scheme to govern a state of "a thousand chariots" plagued by foreign invasions and famines. He is confident that after three years of his government, the state would be strengthened and

---

① Zhu Xi, *Sishu jizhu*(《四书集注》) (Taipei: Yiwen yinshuguan, 1980), *juan* 2, p. 11.

② Liu Baonan, *Lunyu zhengyi*(《论语正义》),(Taipei: Shijie shuju, 1968), p. 80.

③ Liu Baonan, *Lunyu zhengyi*, pp. 154 – 155; Slingerland, *Confucius: Analects*, p. 78.

④ Zhu Xi, *Sishu jizhu*, *juan* 4, p. 11.

⑤ Qian Mu, *Lunyu xinjie*, p. 272.

restored to its right track. In contrast to other disciples who humbly want to administer a much smaller state, to be a celebrant at a religious ceremony, or to simply bath in the river with fellow companions in the spring time, Zilu's political ideal seems pompous and ambitious. The Master does not deny Zilu's ability to run a big state, but he is conscious of the way this disciple expresses his intent. Here as in 4:13, Confucius confirms the importance of governing a state by observing ritual propriety, yet he at the same time reminds his interlocutor that the weight should be placed upon deference than upon ritual observance. Zilu's lack of deferential attitude or courtesy on this particular occasion reveals the weakness of his personality and casts a doubtful outcome on his grandiose plan. That is why the Master disapprovingly smiles at Zilu on hearing the latter's reply.

Bu rang(不让) in our last case, 15:36, is taken to illustrate a very positive virtue, *ren*(仁), the highest Confucian ideal variously translated as benevolence, humanity, humaneness, Good, or Goodness. ① In this general statement, Confucius envisages a situation in which one is offered the opportunity to practice *ren*. One is urged on to do it unreservedly, even to take precedence over one's teacher. The virtue of deference or yielding is somehow missing from the scene. What is valued, on the contrary, is the spirit of determinedness and bravery that is required to seize the moment and accomplish the task. Here *bu rang* is not related to the context of ritual propriety, and therefore it does not contradict the understanding that deferential attitude is more important than outer ritual expression. Rather, it is highlighted as an independent virtue that is also necessary for being a gentleman.

Rang in the six sayings or accounts analyzed above exhibits features worthy of our attention. First, it first and foremost centers about a person or persons, stressing his or their internal disposition. The reason why Confucius

---

① For an exposition of ren, see Tu Wei-ming, "The Creative Tension between Jen and Li, " in idem. *Humanity and Self-Cultivation* (Berkeley: Asian Humanities Press, 1979), pp. 5 – 16.

is attractive is because of his deferential attitude, a kind of irresistible power that enables whomever he meets to offer him information willingly (1 : 10). Likewise, Taibo merits the title of highest virtue due to his repeated renunciation of rulership and his intentional concealment of this feat (8 : 1). Deference or yielding with respect does not have anything to do with one's ability. Zilu may be a competent state administrator, but his rashness undermines the possible success of his great scheme to manage a big country (11 : 26). Gentlemen do not contend, and if they do in the situation of a ritual contest, they treat each other with the spirit of deference (3 : 7). These characteristics of *rang*, very often soft, restrained, and unassuming in orientation, however, do not deny the understanding that sometimes the gentlemen are supposed to be valiant and courageous when confronted with the demand to practice benevolence (15 : 36).

Second, *rang* is intimately connected to or inseparable from ritual propriety. As Confucius lived in an era distinguished by pervasive rites and ritual observances, ① this virtue in the *Analects* is adopted to reveal "the substance" behind them. Undeniably ritual propriety is required to govern a state, but without *rang* it alone is vain and empty (4 : 13; 11 : 26). When the two archers compete, they follow the ritual prescriptions of bowing to each other in the process and drinking a salute in the end (3 : 7). It is *rang* that enlivens human interactions as well as a society governed by *li*.

Third, *rang* in the *Analects* is almost invariably related to the political realm. Taibo manifests his highest virtue of repeated renunciation in the matter of royal heritage (8 : 1). Mild and meek Confucius is, his grave concern is how a state is governed. In this regard his deferential attitude facilitates his gathering of information effortlessly (1 : 10). When he elaborates on the relationship between *li* and *rang*, he has *guo* 国 , a state or states, in

---

① See Herbert Fingarette, *Confucius — The Secular as Sacred* (New York: Harper & Row, 1972); Benjamin I. Schwartz, *The World of Thought in Ancient China* (Cambridge: Belknap Press of the Harvard University Press, 1985), pp. 67 – 75.

mind, thus setting his philosophical ideas in the proper context (4:13). That Zilu shows no deference may be something personal, but he makes known his personality in relation to government. It is also in this political connection that the Master expresses his disapproval (12:26).

It is therefore clear that although *rang* may not appear too frequently in the *Analects*, it is laden with rich implications. Our analysis shows that it at least carries the personal, ritual, and political dimensions. These three, conceptually different, are actually interconnected. *Rang*, in sum, functions as a pivotal idea in Confucius' philosophical agenda.

III. *Li*(利) in the *Analects*

The character *li*(利) has dozens of meanings in Chinese, [①] but for our purposes in this paper, we focus upon its denotations with reference to "profit, benefit, advantage, gain" either as a noun or as a verb. As such, out of its ten occurrences in the *Analects*, we choose seven accounts for our analysis. I list their texts in Chinese with English translations as follows.

4:2 子曰：「不仁者不可以久处日，不可以长处乐。仁者安仁，智者利仁。」

The Master said, "One who is not benevolent cannot remain long in straitened circumstances, nor can he remain long in easy circumstances. The benevolent man is attracted to benevolence because he feels at home in it. The wise man is attracted to benevolence because he finds it to his advantage."

4:12 子曰：「放于利而行，多怨。」

The Master said, "If one acts with a view to profit, there

---

① See *Hanyu cidian* 汉语词典 (http://tw. 18dao. net) (accessed on Aug. 20, 2010).

will be much resentment. "①

4:16   子曰:「君子喻于义,小人喻于利。」

> The Master said, "The gentleman understands what is
> appropriate. The small man understands what is
> profitable."

9:1   子罕言利,与命与仁。

> The Master seldom talked about profit, but approved of Destiny
> and benevolence.

13:17   子夏为莒父宰,问政。子曰:「无欲速,无见小利。欲速,
> 则不达;见小利,则大事不成。」

> On becoming prefect of Jufu, Zixia asked about government.
> The Master said, "Do not be impatient. Do not see only petty
> gains. If you are impatient, you will not reach your goal. If you
> see only petty gains, the great tasks will not be accomplished."

14:12   子路问成人。子曰:「若臧武仲之知,公绰之不欲,卞庄
> 子之勇,冉求之艺,文之以礼乐,亦可以为成人矣。」曰:
> 「今之成人者何必然?见利思义,见危授命,久要不忘平
> 生之言,亦可以为成人矣。」

> Zilu asked about the complete man. The Master said, "A man
> is as wise as Zang Wuzhong, as free from desires as Gongchuo,
> as courageous as Zhuangzi of Bian, and as skillful as Ran Qiu,
> and is further refined by ritual propriety and music, then he
> may be considered a complete man." Then he added, "But to
> be a complete man nowadays one need not be all these things.
> If a man remembers what is appropriate at the sight of profit, is

---

① This is Dawson's translation; see his *Confucius: The Analects*, p. 73.

ready to lay down his life in face of danger, does not forget the words he lives by when in straitened circumstances for a long time, he may be said to be a complete man. "

20:2   子张曰:「何谓惠而不费?」子曰:「因民之所利而利之, 斯 不亦惠而不费乎?」

Zizhang asked, "What does it mean to be generous and yet not extravagant?" The Master said, "Give the common people those benefits that will really be beneficial to them—is this not being generous without being extravagant?"[1]

The main focus of 4:2 is about*ren* 仁, benevolence or humanity. According to Confucius, a man without benevolence is not able to stay long in adversity, because he does not have the inner quality needed to sustain him through the hardship. Nor is he able to enjoy pleasurable circumstances for any period of time, because he easily falls into corruption due to a lack of the supporting highest virtue. To state it positively, it is only the benevolent man who is able to succeed in these two contrasting situations. As a real benevolent man, he is unaffected by the external environments and dwells upon his own virtue unswervingly. Confucius at this point equates the wise man with the benevolent man, and confirms that the former analogically never departs from benevolence because his wisdom informs him how to profit from it. *Li* in this sense is used as a verb, meaning to take profit or advantage from somewhere. [2]

As a short axiom, 4:12 may be subject to various interpretations. Literally, Confucius says that if one acts expressly for one's personal profit, one will incur much resentment. Profit seems a dangerous thing. Zhu Xi

---

①   This is the translation by Ames and Rosemont; see their *The Analects of Confucius*, p. 228.

②   Some scholars interpret *li* as "to desire"; see Legge, *The Chinese Classics*, vol. 1, p. 165; Qian Mu, *Lunyu xinjie*, pp. 112 – 113. Although it has such a connotation in the text, but it seems an overstatement.

explains that if one concentrates on one's personal profit, one's selfishness surely disadvantages others; hence the origination of resentment. ① Liu Baonan sees Confucius' wisdom as a warning to those in power to stay in what is appropriate and avoid competing for profits with the commoners. ② Qian Mu cites " 〔 if one 〕 seeks benevolence and gets it; what resentment will there be?", an excerpt from 7: 15, as a proof text and asserts that 4: 12 is its counter expression. In Qian's opinion, once one pursues *ren* the highest virtue rather than personal profit, resentment is naturally out of the question. ③ These commentators all regard *li* in the negative sense, particularly when understood on the personal level.

4: 16 lays out two parallel but contrastive statements by Confucius. What sides with the gentleman is *yi*(义), popularly translated as righteousness, rightness, or appropriateness, ④ whereas the small man is associated with profit. There are no reasons given behind the distinction between them. It seems that the gentleman is conversant with what is right by his natural disposition, just as the mean person leans toward profit out of his instinct. That is why Cheng Yi(程颐 1033 – 1107) explains that similar to the ordinary man's desire for profits, the gentleman deeply understands what is appropriate and so holds fast to it. ⑤ Cheng's emphasis is on the side of the gentleman. Liu Baonan argues that it is only after satisfying the small man's desire for profits can he be guided to what is appropriate, a responsibility the gentleman is called to assume. ⑥ His concern, too, is on what the gentleman is supposed to do. Thus *li* in this account is employed negatively to illustrate the positive, higher moral ideal *yi*.

9: 1 states that the Master rarely talked about profit. Most commentators

①   Zhu Xi, *Sishu jizhu*, *juan* 2, p. 13.

②   Liu Baonan, *Lunyu zhengyi*, p. 80.

③   Qian Mu, *Lunyu xinjie*, pp. 127 – 128.

④   For an exposition of *yi*, see David L. Hall and Roger T. Ames, *Thinking through Confucius* (Albany: SUNY Press, 1987) , pp. 89 – 110.

⑤   Zhu Xi, *Sishu jizhu*, *juan* 2, p. 14.

⑥   Liu Baonan, *Lunyu zhengyi*, p. 83.

exegete yu 与 in this account as an associative linking *ming* 命 and *ren* 仁. In this understanding, Confucius is reported to have seldom talked not only about profit, but also about destiny and benevolence. [1] I decline this view and agree with Qian Mu who interprets *yu* as "to approve", hence the preferred reading should be that the Master seldom talked about profit but approved of Destiny and benevolence. This is because Confucius talked a lot about benevolence, as evidenced throughout the *Analects*, and he on some occasions expressed his reflections on Destiny as heavenly mandate. [2] But there is no argument that *li* here is held to be negative or at least suspicious, and that is why the Master would refrain from mentioning it often.

13: 17 records that when Zixia, one of Confucius' distinguished disciples, was appointed to be the prefect of the city Jufu, he sought for advice from his Master about the government. Confucius' reply contains two instructionsexpressed negatively: do not be impatient and do not see only petty gains. He immediately complements these two with reasons: being impatient will not reach one's goal, just as seeing only petty gains will not accomplish great tasks. Similar to 9: 1, this account lays out Confucius' saying in the style of parallelism and contrast. *Yu su*(欲速) is juxtaposed or equated with *xiao li*(小利) , and their comparability lies in the same result of their unthoughtfulness. Here Confucius seems not opposed to *li*, profit or gain, per se, but rather concerns himself with the disadvantages that petty gains may engender in the government. Although he does not point out what the "great tasks" are all about, it is safe to assume, as Liu Baonan does, that they refer to *da li* (大利) or great profits that Zixia is expected to bring to the people of Jufu. [3] In this sense, *li* is flexible in meaning, depending upon the degree it points to and the content it is associated with.

---

[1]   Zhu Xi, *Sishu jizhu, juan* 5, p. 1; Legge, *The Chinese Classics*, vol. 1, p. 216; Waley; *The Analects of Confucius*, p. 138; Lau, Confucius: The Analects, p. 96; Dawson, *Confucius: The Analects*, p. 31; Ames/Rosemont, *The Analects of Confucius*, p. 126.

[2]   For the occurrences of *ming*, see particularly 2: 4; 6: 10; 12: 5; 14: 36; 20: 3.

[3]   Liu Baonan, *Lunyu zhengyi*, p. 291.

14: 12 tells of how Confucius answers Zilu's question about what the complete man is. In the mind of the Master, the complete man is the one who possesses such excellent, combined qualities as exemplified by Zang Wuzhong, Gongchuo , Zhuangzi of Bian, and Ran Qiu. And these qualities include wisdom, freedom from desire, courage, and skillfulness. In addition, he should be further refined by ritual propriety and music to reach the consummate standard. Confucius is aware that his ideal personality is too lofty for his contemporaries and therefore reduces it to three basic requirements. Among these three, *jianli siyi* (见 利 思 义), or "remembering what is appropriate at the sight of profit", is directly relevant to our concern. As in 4: 16, *li* and *yi* are here contrasted in juxtaposition, which shows that Confucius conceives them as opposite in meaning. As the complete man should "be ready to lay down his life in face of danger", i. e. , to sacrifice his life for public good when an urgent situation thus demands, so should he be able to distinguish between profit and appropriateness and opt for the latter. Since *yi* is linked to the ideal of being a complete man, *li* is used to designate its negative counterpart.

20: 2 records a conversation between the Master and his disciple, Zizhang, about service in the government. Confucius advises that to be ready to govern, one should honor the *wu mei* (五美) or five virtues and remove the *si e* (四恶) or four vices. Among the five virtues is *hui er bufei*(惠而不费) or to be generous and yet not extravagant. When asked to explain this terse phrase, Confucius replies with an imperative sentence, "Give the common people those benefits that will really be beneficial to them. " The character *li* appears twice here, demonstrating a positive and encouraging sense. To Confucius' mind, *li* itself is not problematic, as long as it is directed to the right dimension. Since it is related to public good, Zizhang or anyone who is prepared to be a government official is urged to implement it.

According to the analysis of *li* in the preceding passages, this character exhibits multiple interpretations and understandings. First, *li* by itself is in general treated negatively or at least suspiciously. As it is commonly related to desire, selfishness, and worldly gains, it occupies a low status in Confucius' moral or ethical system. The Master gives a stern and straightforward warning that if one is dictated by profit in one's actions, one will surely incur much resentment (4: 12). If the gentleman knows and does what is appropriate, then the small man seeks only what is beneficial to himself (4: 16). The standard for an ideal complete man is not too demanding. As long as one "remembers what is appropriate at the sight of profit, " one deserves the title (14: 12). These negative appraisals may account for why Confucius is normally reticent about *li* (9: 1).

Second, *li* is not always harmful, as a matter of fact. It may be negatively evaluated when put on the personal level. But when it is applied to the public sphere, it obtains a positive image. Confucius instructs Zixia not to be blocked by petty gains when serving as the prefect of Jufu. This is because being captivated by small interests is just like being impatient, both of which surely lead to final failure. The other side of the deleterious engagement, however, implies that Zixia should set his eye on "the great tasks, " i. e. , what are beneficial to the people of Jufu (13: 17). This positive encouragement to bring "great profits" to the public is also seen in Confucius' advice to Zizhang. To the latter, the Master opines that to benefit the common people with what they consider advantageous is definitely a political virtue (20: 2).

Third, as *li* may have negative and positive meanings, it is often situated in contrastive statements. This instructional format highlights its importance and subtle implications on the one hand and stimulates the interlocutor to think and make a choice on the other. Thus the gentleman and the small man are paired, just as appropriateness and profit are juxtaposed (4: 16). Impatience parallels petty gains, and their results point to the same end, i. e. , failure to reach the goal (13: 17). To be a complete man, as Confucius advises Zilu, one should at least be able to distinguish between appropriateness and profit, as well as know how to sacrifice oneself in a situation of crisis (14: 12).

Fourth, *li* cannot be an independent virtue; it is person as the moral agent who decides its value. This is evident from some axioms or accounts analyzed where Confucius emphasizes less what *li* is all about than persons who handle it. It is the wise man who knows what kind of benefit he could get from benevolence (4:2). It is also the gentleman who is conversant with what is appropriate, just as it is the small man who by nature leans toward what is profitable (4:16). This also applies to the complete man: it is such an ideal person who is able to consider what is appropriate when confronting profit (14:12).

Last, when*li* is connected to personal interests, it often degenerates into human corruption. But this kind of deplorable cases is used as a foil to reflect the positive side *li* may possibly produce. In ancient China, the chances to turn the "small profit" into "great profit" commonly arose in the political realm. Thus *li*, as seen in the *Analects*, has close relationship with politics. We should be reminded that Confucius gave his advice to Zixia at a time when the latter was about to become prefect of Jufu (13:17), and that the Master did the same thing to Zizhang when this disciple was ready to serve in the government (20:2). In this sense, *li*, the person or moral agent, and politics are intertwined. It is in this intricate network that *li* is either consummated or becomes problematic.

III. Discussion

The preceding analysis of *rang* and *li* makes clear their respective meanings and connotations in the *Analects*. As pointed out, *rang* fundamentally denotes deference or yielding with due respect, emphasizing a person's inner character. In a ritualized context, it facilitates and harmonizes human relationships. *Li*, on the other hand, mostly carries negative meanings, as it usually refers to personal, selfish gain. But it can mean constructively if the profit is obtained for and transferred to the common good. In this regard Confucius considers it crucial that only the well-cultivated gentleman is able to handle it in the right way. It is interesting to observe that persons and politics are two factors both *rang* and *li* are intimately associated with in the *Analects*. It is also these two dimensions that create space within which *rang* and *li* can flexibly extend their applications. When *rang* and *li* are combined into a compound, *rang li*, this flexibility expands even more.

Mencius was one of those early Chinese intellectuals who felt the tension between *rang* and *li* in the political context. In the first place, he upholds that human beings are endowed with fundamental innate feelings, which include those of *ce yin*(恻隐)or commiseration, *xiu e*(羞恶)or shame and dislike, *ci rang*(辞让)or modesty and deference, and *shi fei*(是非)or right and wrong. These *si duan* (四端) or "four germinations," as he calls them, define humans as humans. It is when one nourishes and develops these feelings to the fullest extent that one will have the sufficient power to protect people under the "four seas" (*si hai* 四海). [1] To Mencius, modesty and deference is precisely the beginning as well as the foundation on which a state can be properly governed. This idealist philosophy, however, is often challenged by political hard facts. The first chapter of the *Mencius* opens with the story about his confrontation with King Hui of Liang in this regard:

> "Sir," said the King, "You have come all this distance, thinking nothing of a thousand miles. You must surely have some way of profiting (*li* 利) my state?" "Your Majesty," answered Mencius, "What is the point of mentioning the word ' profit' (*li* 利)? All that matters is that there should be benevolence and appropriateness (*ren yi* 仁义). "[2]

As a ruler, King Hui of Liang is concerned with how to enrich and strengthen his country. His motivation is justified because "profit" in this case is not conducted on the personal level but for the public welfare. But as is

---

[1]   *Mencius*, 2A: 6. I follow D. C. Lau's text and translation with minor modifications; see idem, *Mencius* (Harmondsworth and New York: Penguin Books, 1970), pp. 82 – 83.

[2]   *Mencius*, 1A: 1. Lau, *Mencius*, p. 49.

evident, for a feudal state governed by an autocratic king, it seems hard to talk about his personal profit in distinction from the public interest. Mencius, in line with Confucius' moralist orientation, retorts that not profit but benevolence and appropriateness should be the king's main concern. He argues that if his subjects, from the ministers down to the commoners, are all occupied by the notion of selfish profit in imitation of the King, the society will be fragmented and there will be nothing but chaos in the country. Only when benevolence and appropriateness is inculcated in the people's mind, the state will be brought to order. Mencius held firmly his conviction and tried to persuade not only King Hui of Liang but also other power bidders. [1]

The challenge Mencius encountered was by no means outdated. China and Taiwan are being caught in a comparable circumstance. Especially when Wen Jiabao expressed that China, the much stronger country, was willing to *rang li* or "give up profits", the complexity contained in this phrase has more disputably surfaced. That China consented to give away enormous trade profits to Taiwan is because it considers Taiwanese to be brothers of the same family. In other words, two sides of the Strait are supposed to belong to one country, whatever this country may be defined or understood. If that would be the case, the relation between China and Taiwan is domestic rather than international. And according to one author, traditional Confucianism, synonymous with consanguinitism, regards filiality much more highly than sociality and individuality. In this context, what is valued is a kind of familism which emphasizes hierarchical obedience and situational ethics, and *Ren*(仁) and *li*(礼) or benevolence and ritual propriety as ideal governing principles are easily sacrificed. [2] To be included into China's familial orbit is profitable but risky.

China may argue that it sets peace and harmony as its ultimate pursuit,

---

① See *Mensciu*, 6B: 4; Lau, *Mencius*, pp. 173 – 174.

② Qingping Liu, "Filiality versus Sociality and Individuality: On Confucianism as Consanguinitism," *Philosophy East and West*, 53. 2 (2003), pp. 234 – 250.

so far as the cross-Strait relation is concerned, and the signing of ECFA is precisely aimed at this direction. Besides, "to give the common people those benefits that will really be beneficial to them" (20: 2) is the "great task" that a high-minded statesman should accomplish (13: 17). Indeed, Confucianism treasures harmony and regards it as the highest ideal. [1] But one is reminded that harmony is not equal to sameness. Rather, to achieve harmony, one assumes the existence of differences first, a pluralistic concept yet to be promoted in China. As one scholar asserts, "the requirement of harmony places a constraint on each party in interaction, and, in the meantime, provides a context for each party to have optimal space to flourish."[2] China has not yet convinced Taiwan of being willing to implement such a "beneficial" policy, and thus Taiwanese critics have good reasons to see China's ideal of harmony as a pretext under which it may eliminate differences at all costs.

What pertains to our concern more cogently is that profit as defined by an authoritarian regime like China appears controversial. The huge profits favorable to Taiwan are certainly not private or personal: ECFA was signed between two governments and in public, and it was meant to draw two states closer in the economic terms. But since the Chinese Community Party dominates entire China and decides affairs almost in every respect and down to every level, to pinpoint the criterion to distinguish *xiao li*(小利) or petty gains from *da li*(大利) or great profits is difficult, if not meaningless. What is small and personal profit many turn out to be national in magnitude, and what is great and public benefit may originate from private and individual motivation. China has the sole right to gauge the matter and decide the nature or scale of whatever beneficial to its sovereignty.

In the process of the exchanges of profit between China and Taiwan,

---

[1]   Chenhang Li, "The Confucian Ideal of Harmony," *Philosophy East and West*, 56. 4 (2006), pp. 583-603.

[2]   Ibid. , p. 589.

furthermore, the meaning of *rang* (让) seems to have been treated obliquely. If it means "to give up" and what is given up is material benefit, then it assumes the role of instrumentality employed to finish something the value of which is higher than *rang* itself. The underlying sense of deference or yielding about this character has not come to the front in the political scene. Neither the role of human agency and the importance of human inner quality were advanced. *Rang li* has thus become a convenient term, combing only the surface meanings of two conflictive words to serve a political end that was already suspected and criticized in ancient China. This may partly explain why many people in Taiwan were not overjoyed at the signing of ECFA, as they were sensitive to the absence of the more human and spiritual dimension of *rang* that is essential to mutual trust.

What Taiwan, the much weaker side, really wants is surely a normal international relation in and by which it can negotiate with China. If that would be the case, what are called for are such requisites as equality, freedom of choice, and mutual respect. These principles conform to the spirit of *rang*, as the scene of the two gentlemen competing in a ritualized archery contest demonstrates (3: 7) . It would not bring immediate, big gains to Taiwan in a short term as ECFA would do, but it would promise a more enduring channel by which Taiwanese people could remove their doubts about its strong neighbour's intention and engage in active interaction across the Strait. This scenario, however, may not be acceptable to China which sees the eventual unification of these two sides under "one China" as its uncompromised goal. *Rang* understood as deference or yielding at the expense of this "core interest" proves, as it were, "unprofitable. " *Rang* by itself is purist and even extremist in nature, but *rang li*, although a compromised term, allows a large space for the two sides to negotiate. China opts for this kind of understanding and relegates *rang li* to a level pragmatically manageable.

Impeded by its antagonistic policy against China and constrained by the international power politics in the past decade, Taiwan has been quickly marginalized in East Asia. The recent global economic tsunami has markedly slowed down its development all the more. The ECFA deal is in this context a breakthrough which would open up political and economic opportunities for Taiwan in relation to China and ASEAN. *Rang li* may be far from satisfactory measured by the ideal of the *Analects*, it at least presents a special kind of *li* for people of Taiwan. It depends on how Taiwan would seize it and maximize it to *da li*, i. e., optimal benefit for Taiwan's future. Indeed it would be detrimental for Taiwan to interact with China in fear and out of suspicion. Rather, it is constructive that it does that based upon confidence in its own economic agility, administrative efficiency, cultural diversity, and democratic polity, salient features that China may not all possess. The negotiating process would for certain affect the two parties in reciprocity. *Rang li* may then become a compromised virtue, a positive value that enables two sides of the Taiwan Strait to engage each other in a hopeful and dynamic way.

IV. Concluding Remarks

This paper began with the examination of *rang* and *li* in the *Analects*, detailing their respective meanings and implications. Based upon these discoveries, it proceeded to our contemporary political scene straddling the Taiwan Strait. It is obvious that a huge temporal gap exists between ancient China and modern Chinese communities, and, likewise, Confucius' philosophical idea and ideal may not be always compatible with or applicable to power politics. Yet I found it illuminating to make this kind of cross-reference, as I believe that the wisdom contained in the ancient classic should have important things to say to us. In particular, the signing and impact of ECFA and the pronounced *rang li* as its supporting rationale deserved our effort in such a contrastive study.

No one could predict what will exactly evolve with regard to the relation between China and Taiwan in the future. Pessimists, as many Taiwanese objectors are, perceive China's ambition and interpret ECFA as its political strategy thereby to finally unify Taiwan. Optimists, on the other hand, expect to see an emerging of "Chaiwan" that combines the economic strengths of these two parties into a powerful whole, and thus ascertain a significant role Taiwan would play in the process of formation.[①] Neutralists, however, express that while China and Taiwan may become bed-fellows through ECFA, yet they dream different dreams.[②] Whatever the outcome may be, *rang* as deference or yielding with respect, *li* as the public benefit, and *rang li* as a compromised virtue will test how the two governments perform on the stage of *Realpolitik*.

[①]   Gordon C. K. Cheung, "New Approaches to Cross-Strait Integration and Its Impacts on Taiwan's Domestic Economy: An Emerging ' Chaiwan' ?", *Journal of Current Chinese Affairs*, 1 (2010), pp. 11-36; see also the comments by Ohmae kenich in *United Daily News* 联合报 , reported by Li Chun 李春 (http://udn. com), July 29, 2010.

[②]   This is the common opinion by Charles Freeman III, Terry Cooke, and some others in a open seminar; see the news report "American Specialists: Two Sides of the Taiwan Strait Can Dream Their Respective Dreams, " CNA News 中央社 (http://www. cna. com. tw/ShowNews/Detail. aspx?pNewsID = 201007280142&pType0 = aOPL&), July 28, 2010.

On the Mutually Acceptable Elements between Laozi's Ziran and Confucius's *Ren*

LIU Xiaogan
(The Chinese University of Hong Kong)

Abstract

This paper examines the relationship between Laozi's concept of *ziran* and Confucius's concept of *ren*. Laozi and Confucius are often understood as upholding very different, and at times incompatible views. In brief, Laozi seems to shun the moral and social norms that Confucius advocates. This popular but untested impression of Laozi or Daoism arises mainly because of the lifestyle of some later Daoist figures, especially some historical figures in the Wei-jin period. In order to correct this over-simplified notion of Daoism and develop a more accurate understanding of the relationship of Confucianism and Daoism, this paper attempts to explore the plausibility of finding a common ground between these two thinkers. I will argue that common elements and mutually acceptable ideas between Laozi's *ziran* and Confucius's *ren* can be found in their shared emphases on internal cause of actions, smooth development of things, and harmony of the whole. ①

---

① This project is supported by Hong Kong Government General Research Fund(CUHK447909). The author is heartedly grateful to Dr. Winnie Sung for her efficient assistance in drafting this article.

1. Introduction

This paper examines the relationship between Laozi's concept of*ziran* and Confucius's concept of *ren*. Although Laozi and Confucius have been traditionally viewed as rivals, it is unlikely that there was any serious antagonism between Laozi and Confucius. In the *Laozi*, there is no mentioning of Confucius or the Confucian school. This is probably because there was no clear Confucian school at the time the *Laozi* was composed. Likewise, there was neither institutionalised nor identifiable group of Daoist thinkers with developed doctrines and disciples when the *Lunyu* was composed. It was only until the former Han period that the term "Dao jia" appeared in Sima Qian's *Shiji*. ① Since there was no identifiable Daoist group or Confucian group during Laozi's and Confucius's time, it would be unreasonable to regard the *Lunyu* or the *Laozi* as a text written on behalf of one school with the purpose to criticise its rival school. ② Furthermore, since Laozi's or Daoist philosophies were not yet major trends of thought in their times, it is unlikely that Laozi and Confucius vehemently opposed each other. ③

In view ofthe consideration that Laozi and Confucius do not necessarily oppose each other, my analysis seeks to bring to light certain elements of shared agreement in the two thinkers' thought. In suggesting that there are

---

① The term "Dao jia 道家 (*Dao*-school)" never appeared in any of the pre-Qin texts. Even with the appearance of the term "Dao jia" in *Shiji*, scholars have generally agreed that the referent of the term should be "Huang-Lao. " This is very different from the usage of the term "Dao-school" in modern scholarship, which generally refers the Laozi and Zhuangi traditions. In the *Shiji*, the term "Huang-lao" is apparently used interchangeably with "Dao jia" and "Dao de jia 道德家 (*Dao – de* school). " I also pointed out elsewhere that the term "Lao-Zhuang" first appeared in the "Yaolue (Essentials)" section of the *Huainanzi* (Liu 1987: 299 – 300 and 2006: 368).

② There are many debates concerning the dating of the *Laozi*. I discuss the dating of the *Laozi* in chapters 1 and 2 of my *Laozi niandai xinkao yu sixiang xin quan* (Liu 2005).

③ The opposition between Confucian and Daoist is likely to be deepened by later Confucians' critique of the *Laozi*, especially by Zhu Xi's work. See Sections 78. 1 – 2 in *Laozi Gujin* for my discussions of Zhu Xi's unjustified criticism as well as praise of Laozi.

elements of shared agreement in Laozi's and Confucius's thought, I mean neither that these elements are shared under the same system of thought nor that these elements are merely compatible. I mean that some common points can be found in both Laozi's and Confucius's philosophies and they are mutually acceptable, at least theoretically. Based on these common points, we can try to approximate as much as possible a shared picture that both Laozi and Confucius would find acceptable.

Give the goal of this paper, it is inevitable that the focus of my discussion will be on the commonalities between Laozi's and Confucius's thought. This is not to suggest that the differences between Laozi and Confucius are trivial. Without a deep understanding of their differences, any discussions of their similarities or commonalities will become superficial and meaningless. Any serious comparative studies should avoid abusing the principle of reduction（归约法）and endeavour to develop a sense of appropriateness（分寸感）. The principle of reduction seeks to reduce a possibly rich and complex object of study into a simple and straightforward object. When applied to comparative studies of Laozi and Confucius, for example, such kind of reductive method tends to unjustifiably exaggerate the differences and oppositions between Laozi and Confucius, thus exacerbating the antagonism between the Confucian and Daoist traditions. On the contrary, a sense of appropriateness involves objectivity and truthfulness. It requires one to objectively and honestly reveal what similarities and differences there in fact are. In cases where similarities are hidden in the ostensible differences (or vice versa), or in cases wherein the similarities and differences can only found in just a branch of two thinkers' philosophies, one who is guided by a sense of appropriateness will pay attention to both similarities and differences and seek to bring to light even the subtler points of comparison.

Although my subsequent discussion emphasizes on the commonalities between Laozi and Confucius, it has undergone a careful examination of the differences between their thought. Given the scope of the present paper, I will not be able to rehearse all their differences here. [1] My awareness of their differences, however, will caution me against exaggerating the common ground between Laozi and Confucius.

2. *Ziran* as the Core Value of Laozi's Philosophy

I understand Laozi's philosophy as having an implicit structure that is constructed from a system of concepts. There are many important concepts in the *Laozi*, such as *Dao* (道), *wuwei* (无为), and *ziran* (自然), which Laozi has theorized. The theories behind these concepts are interconnected, giving Laozi's philosophy an overall structure. [2] In my earlier studies, I attempted to dynamically reconstruct this implicit structure of Laozi's philosophy by examining the interconnections among these concepts before. I have concluded that the concept of *ziran* is a core value of Laozi's philosophy. [3] Here, I will focus on the concept of *ziran* and employ it as a new angle to examine the relationship between Daoist and Confucian thought.

The term*ziran* is composed of an adverb "*zi*(自 self)" and an adjective "*ran*(然 so, thus). " The literal meaning of *ziran* is therefore "self – so". It can be used as a predicate to describe the subject or as a noun to denote a concept. [4] The term *ziran* first appeared in the *Laozi*. It is also in the *Laozi* that *ziran* is discussed as a philosophical concept. [5] Although there are extensive mentions of the term *ziran* in scholarly works on Laozi, there is

---

[1]   See, for example, section 38. 5 of *Laozi gujin* for my discussion of the differences between Confucius' and Laozi's view on *wuwei*.

[2]   See preface and introduction of my *Laozi: Niandai xinkao yu sixiang xinquan* for my view on methodology for studying Laozi's thought.

[3]   See Chapter 10 of *Quanshi yu dingxiang* for my discussion of *Dao*, *wuwei*, and *ziran* in Laozi's thought. See also "An Inquiry into the Core Value of Laozi's Philosophy" for my discussion of *ziran* as the core value of Laozi's philosophy.

[4]   See Liu, 2005, pp. 77 – 79.

[5]   None of the relatively early classics such as the *Shjing* 诗经, the *Zuozhuan* 左传, and the *Lunyu* contains the term *ziran*. In other early texts, the term *ziran* never occurred in the *Mencius*. It appears once in the *Mozi*, once in the *Guanzi*, twice in the *Xunzi*, six times in the *Zhaugzi*, five times in the *Lushi chunqiu*, eight times in the *Hanfeizi*, and thirteen times in *Chunqiu fanlu*.

insufficient attention paid to explicate the meaning of *ziran* and its significance in Laozi's thought. Rather, we see a tendency to impose on Laozi's *ziran* the meanings of *ziran* that are only found in modern Chinese. ① As a corollary, scholarly readings of Laozi's *ziran* are laden with a wide range of unjustified assumptions and ambiguities. It has been mistakenly taken to refer to the natural world, biological nature, primitive state, doing nothing to let nature take its course, or even to a state that resembles Hobbes's "state of nature. " In this section, I will propose my own interpretation of Laozi's *ziran*. But before I introduce my interpretation, let us first conduct a textual analysis of Laozi's usages of *ziran*.

2. 1   *Ziran* in the *Laozi*

The last passage of Chapter 25 of the *Laozi* clearly conveys the idea that *ziran* is the core value for Laozi. It is said that:

人法地，地法天，天法道，道法自然。

People model themselves on the earth,

Earth models itself on Heaven,

Heaven models itself on *Dao*,

And *Dao* models itself on *ziran*.

This passage discusses the relationship between people, the earth, Heaven, and *Dao* on one hand, and *ziran* on the other. Laozi seems to be suggesting here that human beings live in the world, between Heaven and earth. Heaven and earth in turn originate from *Dao*. This shows that *Dao* is the ultimate ground and source of all things. Nonetheless, Laozi ends the passage with the line "*Dao* models itself on *ziran*. "This further suggests that even though *Dao* is the most fundamental source and basis of they myriad

---

① Although it is now generally accepted among scholars that Laozi's *ziran* does not mean Nature, Laozi's *ziran* is still taken to refer to the natural world in some recent publications. Yin Zhenhuan, for example, understands Laozi's *ziran* as referring to the various phenomena of the natural world, such as natural disasters and eclipses (Yin, pp. 342 – 344).

things, Dao itself embodies or resides in *ziran*. Hence, we can understand *ziran* as the highest value embodied by the most fundamental source of all things. If we arrange the items mentioned in the above passage, we have: people—earth—Heaven—*Dao*—*ziran*. Although the concepts of earth, Heaven, and *Dao* are clearly important for Laozi, they are only transitional and intermediate concepts in this context. The real emphasis is on the two ends, that is, the relationship between people and *ziran*. To be specific, this passage is saying that human beings, particularly the ruler, should model upon *ziran*. The part that that talks about modelling upon earth, Heaven, and *Dao* are mainly used to reinforce the point that human societies should promote *ziran*. In other words, *ziran* pervades human beings, earth, Heave, and *Dao*. For this reason, we can also regard it as the most basic and core value of Laozi's philosophy.

Since *ziran* is the core value that penetrates all aspects of human life, it will necessarily manifest on the relationship between the ruler and people. Chapter 17 primarily discusses *ziran* in terms of the relationship between the ruler and the people:

大上，下知有之，其次，亲而誉之；其次，畏之，其下，侮之。···悠兮其贵言。功成事遂，百姓皆谓我自然。

The best of all rulers is but a shadowy presence to subjects;

Next comes the ruler they love and praise;

Next comes one they fear;

Next comes one whom they insult.

[...]

Hesitant, [I] do not utter words lightly,

When [I] have accomplished my task and done my work,

Then the common people all say I [practiced] *ziran*. [1]

---

[1] See Liu, 2005, pp. 69 – 70 for my analysis of 百姓皆谓我自然, which is interpreted different from common interpretation.

The above passage expresses Laozi's ideal ruler, who does not force people to do anything and makes no display of his own kindness or merit. He is relaxed and composed and speaks little. The people are aware of his existence but pay no attention to him. All his tasks are accomplished successfully to his satisfaction, and yet the people do not realize that he has done anything, but believe he has practised *ziran*. This is illustrated by the last line, which suggests that the common people cannot feel the ruler's function and his influence on them. This is the "empty throne" ruler idealized by the Daoists. Next comes the ruler who acts in ways that excite people's admiration and affection for him. This is the kind of sage kings idealised by Confucians. An even worse ruler is one who instils fear in people. This is what is commonly called a benighted ruler. The worst kind of ruler is one who inflicts hardships on his subjects and therefore becomes the object of insults and disdain. This is referred to as a violent ruler.

As many scholars have already noted, *ziran* here does not imply that the ruler does nothing. The ideal ruler's power is simply different from the way it is commonly understood. His influence infiltrates his subjects in such a way that they are not aware of his actions and therefore accept his actions as if they have developed of their own accord. This raises the important question of whether the concept of *ziran* allows for the application of external force. It seems that *ziran* can allow for external force as long as the people are not aware of the effect of external force or are willing to accept it. In this sense, *ziran* only precludes the kind of external force that is forcefully imposed on people but not the kind that can be willingly accepted.

A similar aspect of *Dao* is revealed in Chapter 51:

道之尊，德之贵，夫莫之命而常自然

Respect of *Dao* and esteem of *de* are not conferred upon by anyone's command but because it is constantly *ziran*.

Cheng Xuan-ying 成玄英 notes in his commentary on the above line that:

All the honours in this world have to be ranked and hence they are not enduring. Since the prestige and honour of *Dao* and *de* are not related to titles and ranks, they are constantly *ziran*.

If the prestigious status of *Dao* cannot be externally conferred or intentionally pursued, how did it come about then? For Laozi, the greatness of *Dao* does not merely lie in its function of giving life and nurturing things alone; more importantly, its greatness lies in *ziran*. This is manifested in *Dao*'s not taking credit for its generosity and not controlling or possessing its creations. For Laozi, a sage should be someone who should imitate *Dao* and promote *ziran* through giving without expecting anything in return.

Chapter 64 discusses the concept of *ziran* from the perspective of the relationship between the sage and the myriad things. It is said that:

是以圣人欲不欲，不贵难得之货，学不学，复众人之所过，以辅万物之自然而不敢为。

Therefore the sage desires not to desire,

And does not value goods that are hard to come by;

He studies what is not studied,

And makes good the mistakes of the multitude.

He just assists myriad things' *ziran* and dare not to act.

The values uphold by Laozi's sage are considerably different from those of the common because he takes *ziran* to be the ideal conditional for all things. This is encapsulated in the third and fourth lines, on which He Shang-gong (河上公) comments:

The sage learns that others are not able to learn. The commonpeople learn about intelligent deception, whereas the sage learns about *ziran*. The common people learn about ordering the world, the sage learns about ordering the body, holding on to the authentic *Dao*.

The sage takes*ziran* to be the object and content of his learning. In learning to foster *ziran*, the sage avoids using his knowledge, special status, and power to impose on people. It is in this sense that Laozi speaks of the sage "assisting (*fu* 辅)" myriad things' *ziran*. "Assisting" is the special way the sage acts to promote individual well-being. It involves creating a nurturing environment as well as providing care and protection from interference and control. The "myriad things" can be taken as a collective or as individuals-in-the-whole, meaning that the sage's assistance must touch upon every individual within the myriad things. The notion of "assistance" further confirms the point that things do not have to be kept in their status quo. Nevertheless, any changes or development must happen smoothly. Hence, the sage can only assist things to develop themselves but cannot forcefully modify or destroy their courses of development.

As the above analysis shows, *ziran* is the core value that permeates all entities and relationships, including human beings and the cosmos, sages and the people, people and people, and people as individuals in the world. Based on this finding, I will proceed to offer my interpretation of Laozi's *ziran*.

2.2   The Meaning of *Ziran*

I understand Laozi's*ziran* as a clustering concept that has three levels of meanings. It should be noted at the outset that the most basic meaning of *ziran* as "self-so" is found in all three levels.

On the highest level, Laozi's*ziran* expresses a concern for the ultimate state of humanity and the harmonious relationship between humans and the universe. This is akin to what Paul Tilich (1866 – 1965) referred to as "ultimate concern." On the intermediate level, *ziran* can be identified as a concern for the harmony of collective and community groups. On the third level, Laozi's *ziran* conveys a concern for the state of existence and development of individuals. It is noteworthy that individuals on this level are not to be understood as mere atomistic individuals but rather as particular units living in the whole. Underlying these three levels of *ziran* is Laozi's ideal for humanity, that is, harmony in human existence. It is in this sense that I understand *ziran* as the core value in Laozi's thought.

We can derive at least three related implications of *ziran*. First of all, *ziran* places emphasis on the internal cause of things. It does not require external intervention or control because it is able to initiate itself. In this sense, *ziran* requires things to happen as a result of their internal cause. This does not necessarily preclude all kinds of external force, however. To recall, even the ideal ruler has influence and power over people. It is just that the people are not aware of his functions and influence. This implies that external force, if exerted at all, has to be indirect and non-interfering so that one does not feel coerced or oppressed by it. If we extend this implication to moral actions, we learn that moral actions for Laozi have to be internally motivated and caused. Since actions that are caused by external coercion cannot be considered as *ziran*, one must refrain from imposing on others certain moral standards and principles that they are not motivated to accept. The more one respects the internal state of the agent, the more one is fostering *ziran*. Hence, the notion of *ziran* requires one's consideration for the interaction between internal and external causes.

Second, *ziran* implies a tendency for the smooth development of things. Since *ziran* requires one to refrain from coercion and interference, the development of things must proceed smoothly and continuously and should be free of abrupt changes or sharp breaks that result from external intervention. Even if there are any changes in the course of the development of things, the changes should occur gradually. Hence, one should also be able to predict the kind of changes that are likely to occur in the course of development. Thus, *ziran* also allows one to foresee and predict the trend of development. In moral terms, *ziran* calls for a consistent expression of moral character, rather than actions or attitudes that are rapidly or suddenly changed.

Third, *ziran* implies harmony and the absence of conflict. Since both internal and external conflicts are destructive to the smooth development of things, actions that are compatible with *ziran* must be ones that conduce to the actualisation of collective order and harmony rather than ones that incite conflicts and antagonism.

3   A Sense of *ziran* in Confucius's *ren*

The concept of *ren* (仁) is fundamental to Confucius's thought and is commonly considered as the hallmark of Confucius's philosophy. The central importance of *ren* to is palpable in the frequency of its occurrence in the *Lunyu*, in which the word *ren* appears 105 times. [1] Despite different renditions of the term *ren*, which has been variously translated as "benevolence," "goodness," "humanity," "human-heartedness," and "manhood-at-its-best,"[2] the general consensus among scholars remains that *ren* is a central ethical focus of Confucius' teaching.

According to the *Shuowen* Lexicon, a dictionary of classical Chinese terms, the character *ren* is made up of two radicals: the left side-*ren* (人)— refers to human being or person and the right side-*er* (二)—refers to the number "two." Although Confucius is not the first person who uses the term *ren*, *ren* in the classical texts before Confucius is used narrowly to denote particular qualities of the upper class. In Confucius's usage, *ren* has acquired a much broader scope. It is understood both as a particular and general ethical ideal. As Wing-tsit Chan points out, Confucius was the first to regard *ren* as a general ideal that includes all particular ideals. This is supported by several remarks in the *Lunyu* which define *ren* in terms of a range of particular ideals such as filial piety (1.2, 17.21), wisdom (5.19), doing one's utmost (3.19, 5.19, 18.1), firmness, resoluteness, honesty, deliberation, trustworthiness, courage, respectfulness, deference, liberality, diligence, and generosity (13.27, 14.4, 13.19, 17.6). It is clear Confucius also

---

[1] Chan, p. 296.

[2] Ames and Rosemont, p. 49.

understands ren as a particular ideal. For instance, Confucius sometimes places ren above courage (14.4), suggesting that *ren* is a broader ideal than courage. Nonetheless, we also find cases where Confucius lists *ren* alongside with courage as if *ren* runs parallel to courage (9.29). Let us now turn to some elements in Confucius's *ren* that are pertinent to Laozi's *ziran*.

It should be noted that Confucius does not have a concept of *ziran*, as evidenced by the fact that the term *ziran* does not appear in the *Lunyu* at all. At first sight, it is difficult to find any common ground between *ren* and *ziran*. While *ren* is clearly a normative concept that prescribes moral actions, *ziran* is a descriptive concept that objectively describes the state of things, with the consequences of human actions as one of things it describes. Since *ziran* is also a core value, it is possible for us to derive from normative implications from it. Although it does not tell us what actions ought to be taken, it does make us aware of the consequences of our actions. Such kind of awareness can certainly help us to make better decisions about what actions should be taken. In this sense, we can say that the normative aspect of *ziran* is derived and indirect. However, the concept of *ziran* itself is not a normative concept.

Despite the apparent differences, we are still able to draw some linkages between *ren* and *ziran*. It can be observed that both *ren* and *ziran* are concerned with moral actions, human relationship, and the state of society. These common concerns give us a starting point to explore the possible overlaps and connections between *ren* and *ziran*.

3.1   Internally Motivated Expression of *Ren*

Textual evidence shows that *ren*, as an ethical concept and a high level of moral attainment for Confucius, has to be rooted in an agent's feelings and motivation. Hence, *ren* emphasises on the presence of internal reasons and motivation. According to *Lunyu* 4.2:

子曰:「不仁者不可以久处约,不可以长处乐。仁者安仁,知者利仁。」

The Master said, "One who is not *ren* cannot stay long in hardships, nor can he stay long in easy circumstances. A *ren* person finds ease in *ren*. A wise person finds benefits in *ren*.

For Confucius, the most natural expression of *ren* is being at ease in *ren* (*an ren* 安仁). It is when the agent does not have goals other than *ren* itself. Zhu Xi in his commentary on this passage notes that the reason a person is at ease in *ren* is that he keeps his "original heart(本心)" . [1] This further supports the view that *ren* has to come from the inside.

It is interesting to note that Zhu Xi was once being asked of the difference between"being at ease in *ren*" and "taking benefits in *ren*." In reply, Zhu Xi said: "Being at ease in *ren* does not know that there is *ren*, it is as if one wears a belt and forgets that there is waist, walks in shoes and forgets that there are feet."[2] For Zhu Xi, a *ren* person who is at ease in *ren* can leave behind ulterior concerns and worries, thereby focusing her entire attention on *ren* itself. In a similar vein, Cheng Shu-de(程树德) says that, "Doing without a goal is called being at ease in *ren*. If acting because of some other goals, it is for profit, and hence can only be called wise but not *ren*. [3] The main difference between being at ease in *ren* and finding benefits in *ren* is the presence of ulterior motives. One who finds benefits in *ren* (利仁) is motivated by considerations of benefits, rather than by *ren* itself.

Although the agent does not take*ren* to be an end in itself, the actions of a person who finds benefits are still internally motivated. In this regard, it is still better than someone who is forced to abide by *ren*. In the *Liji*, we find a reference to "forcing *ren* (*qiang ren* 强仁)" listed alongside "being at ease in *ren*" and "finding benefits in *ren*." The "Biao ji (表记)" chapter writes:

子曰：「仁有三……仁者安仁，知者利仁，畏罪者强仁。」[4]

---

① *Si shu zhaung ju ji zhu*, p. 69.
② *Yulei*, p. 643.
③ Cheng, p. 229.
④ *Liji*, "Biaoji" chapter.

The Master said, "There are three kinds of*ren*... a ren person is at ease in *ren*, a wise person finds benefits in *ren*, a person who is scared of punishment forces *ren*. "

The reason Confucius disapproves of forcing*ren* is that it is by no means an internally motivated expression of *ren*. In the case of forcing *ren*, not only does the agent fail to take *ren* as an end in itself, she is also not motivated to act in such ways. She abides by *ren* only because she is afraid of punishment or oppression.

Confucius clearly regards being at ease in *ren* as the highest expression of *ren*. Elsewhere, Confucius also speaks highly of someone who finds joy in *ren*.

子曰:「知之者不如好之者，好之者不如乐之者。」

The Master said, "Those who know it are not as good as those who are fond of it; those who are fond of it are not as good as those who find joy in it. " (*Lunyu* 6. 20)

This passage is consistent with the idea in passage 4. 2 because both emphasize on the presence of appropriate inner attitudes and motivations. We do not have to suppose that finding joy in *ren* is another goal separate from that of being at ease in *ren*. Since a person who is at ease in *ren* is motivated to abide by *ren* without ulterior motives, she will automatically find joy in *ren*. Hence, we can understand being at ease in *ren* finding joy in *ren* as two sides of the same coin.

One implication of our observations about different expressions of*ren* is Confucius's emphasis on the presence of appropriate moral attitudes and motivations in moral actions. On this point, Confucius's *ren* echoes Laozi's *ziran*. Recall that Laozi's *ziran* emphasises on the internal cause of things and rejects intrusive external force. Similarly, Confucius's *ren* emphasises on the presence of appropriate moral attitudes and moral motivation in actions.

Although Confucius sees external factors such as education and training as integral to the process of cultivating *ren*, he also thinks that these external factors cannot be forced upon the individual. Actions that merely appear to be in accordance with *ren* but are not moved by the agent's moral motivation fall short of Confucius's idea of "being at ease in *ren*". The element shared between Confucius's *ren* and *Laozi*'s concept of *ziran* lies in their common emphasis on individuals' inner attitudes and motivations.

The basic content of *ren* is encapsulated in the following two quotes:

夫仁者，己欲立而立人，己欲达而达人。

A *ren* person establishes others in wanting to establish himself and helps others to arrive at a goal in wanting to arrive at a goal himself. (*Lunyu* 6. 30)

己所不欲，勿施于人。
Do not impose on others what you do no want. (*Lunyu* 15. 24)

In Confucius's view, these are the two most fundamental principles for governing human relationships. These two principles encompass love and respect towards others and emphasize on the active participation of the agent in the process of realizing *ren*.

However, if there lacks a Laozian sense of *ziran*, there is a danger of one imposing on others her own goals or what she wants. It might be commonsensical that we should not impose bad things on others. But should we impose on others the things we regard as good? Confucius seems to think that we should not impose what we regard as good because it will create tensions in relationships and also defeat the very purpose of *ren*. According to *Lunyu* 5. 12:

子贡曰：「我不欲人之加诸我也，吾亦欲无加诸人。」子曰：「赐也，非尔所及也。」

Zigong said, "I do not want others to impose on me, nor do I want to impose on others either. " Confucius replied, "Zigong, you are not there yet. "

Here, Confucius is not disagreeing with Zigong's ideals as such. What Zigong described requires a high level of moral attainment, which Confucius thinks Zigong is still quite far from it. Zhu Xi notes in his commentary of the above passage that such kind of *ren* acts idealised by Zigong "do not depend on compulsion and therefore is beyond the reach of Zigong. "[①] Zhu Xi's phrase " do not depend on compulsion (不 待 勉 强)" aptly captures Confucius's point that one should not be made to act under compulsion. Like Laozi's *ziran*, Confucius's *ren* also require us to always refrain from imposing and compelling others.

This point that one may not impose on others what she regards as good is further evidenced by Confucius's attitude towards his students. In *Lunyu* 17. 21, Zaiwo expressed disagreement with the three-year mourning period, arguing that one year of mourning is sufficient or else other regular ritual activities will be delayed. Confucius tells Zaiwo that if he would actually feel comfortable eating fine rice and wearing colourful clothes after a year of his parents' death, then there is no need to observe three-year mourning ritual. When Zaiwo is gone, Confucius criticised Zaiwo's attitude for not being in accordance with *ren*. Even though Confucius strongly disapproves of Zaiwo's proposal, he does not directly reproach Zaiwo in his face. Liang Shu-ming (梁漱溟) understands this passage as illustrating the amiability of Confucius. He provides his reasons for why he thinks it is important to mourn for three years but he does not harshly criticise Zaiwo for wanting to mourn for just one year. Instead, he allows Zaiwo to reflect upon and be conscientious about what he learned. [②] Zaiwo is not the only student who challenges Confucius's

---

①   *Jizhu*,

②   Liang, p. 14.

view. On one occasion, Zigong wanted to eliminate the sacrifice of a live sheep at ceremony. Confucius only indirectly pointed out his difference from Zigong by saying that he loves the ritual more than the sheep (*Lunyu* 3. 17). As Liang Shu-ming notes, Confucius merely "points out their difference in opinion but does not make any judgement. "[1] Instead of forcing his students to accept what he regards as right, Confucius allows his students to choose and practice their own views

We can draw two important points from the above stories. First, Confucius has clear and strong moral principles. Second, Confucius does not force his students to act in accordance with his own principles. The reason Confucius does not force his students is certainly not that he lacks authority over his students or that he is not committed to upholding *ren*. Rather, Confucius believes that it is better to allow students to make their own decisions than to impose on them what he regards as right. This kind of attitude and approach are in agreement with the basic spirit of Laozi's *ziran*, that is, the emphasis on the internal cause of things. Confucius made the well-known statement:

不愤不启，不悱不发，举一隅不以三隅反，则不复也。

I do not open the way for those who are not driven with eagerness to learn. I do not supply words to those who are not desperate to put their ideas into words. If I have pointed out one corner of a square but the student does not come back with the other three, I will not repeat. (*Lunyu* 7. 8)

Obviously, Confucius places much emphasis on internal cause. He would like his students to be motivated and driven to learn instead of being forced to learn. To Confucius, a teacher's role is to motivate and guide students to think and make decisions of their own accord. Just as how one can

---

[1]   Liang, p. 14. .

lead a horse to water but cannot make the horse drink, imposing moral principles on others might adversely provoke them to resist. According to Confucius, the presence of moral motivation is fundamental to morality. Those who merely act in accordance with moral principles without being motivated to do can only be regarded as socially obedient but not as moral.

3. 3   Smooth Progression Towards a Goal

In the*Lunyu*, we find description of Confucius's attitude in pursuing his goal:

> 子禽问于子贡曰:「夫子至于是邦也,必闻其政,求之与? 抑与之与?」子贡曰:「夫子温、良、恭、俭、让以得之。夫子之求之也,其诸異乎人之求之与?」

> Ziqin asked Zigong, "When the Master arrives in a state, he invariably gets to knowabout its government. Does he seek this information? Or is it given to him?"

> Zigong said, "The Master gets it through being cordial, well-behaved, respectful, frugal and deferential. The way the Master seeks (*qiu*) it is, perhaps, different from the way other men seek it." (*Lunyu* 1. 10; trans. Lau, p. 5)

*Qiu*can be loosely translated as "seeking" or "pursuing." As a concept, it presupposes a goal and an orientation towards the goal. In the context of the *Analects*, *qiu* can refer to material gain, political influence, or understanding from others. Confucius's goals primarily involve the latter two. The above passage shows that Confucius is willing to take part in politics in order to make his own proposals known to others. Through abiding by *ren* and associating with those who are willing to learn from him, Confucius eventually gained the trust of feudal lords with his own moral character. It is in this sense we say that Confucius progresses towards his goal in a smooth and gradual manner. Although he has expectations for himself, he did not forcefully push himself to obtain political recognition or positions.

Aside from political recognition, Confucius does not forcefully seek understanding from others. When Confucius was alive, his teachings did not receive wide attention. His students were often left feeling not being understood or even misunderstood. In view of this, Confucius repeatedly addresses the problem of "not knowing oneself" and emphasizes the importance of peacefully accepting others' attitude towards oneself. Confucius famously said:

学而时习之，不亦说乎？有朋自远方来，不亦乐乎？人不知而不愠，不亦君子乎？

Having learned something, to then practise it at the right time, is this not a joy? Having those whom you study with come from afar, is this not a joy? Not feeling unsettled (*bu wen*) by when others fail to understand you, is this not how a superior is? (*Lunyu* 1. 1)

The first part of the passage describes apositive situation wherein people easily share similar feelings such as instances where one can practice what is learned and gather with like-minded friends. The second part describes a negative situation, in which one is not being understood or appreciated by others. In such situation, many people will feel frustrated and offended. But for Confucius, one should not even feel a slight disturbance (*bu wen* 不愠) in such situation. As Zhu Xi notes, *bu wen* does not mean extreme anger; it is only a slight feeling that something is not fair. ① This puts an even higher requirement on the individual. Not only should one not be offended by a lack of understanding from others, she should not even feel that she is not being treated correctly.

Moreover, Confucius maintains that one should continuously seek to cultivate the self and understand. Confucius says:

---

①　*Yulei*, p. 454.

不患人之不己知，患不知人也。

Do not worry about not being understood; worry about not understanding others. (*Lunyu* 1.16) [1]

不患人之不己知,患其不能也。

Do not worry about not being understood; worry about not their having reason not to understand you. (*Lunyu* 14.30)

君子病无能焉，不病人之不己知也。

The superior person is troubled byhis own lack of ability, not by the failure of others to understand him. (*Lunyu* 15.19)

In Confucius's view, trying to improve oneself and to understand others are what one can do and should do. The requirement is on the self rather than others. This is likely to by why Confucius does not complain against Heaven nor blame people (*Lunyu* 14.35). Hence, in seeking understanding from others, Confucius's approach is again gradual and relaxed.

In sum, Confucius advocates gradual and smooth progression towards a goal. Since Laozi's *ziran* also implies a tendency for the smooth development of things, it is conceivable that Confucius would agree with Laozi on this point. Although Confucius has a very different conception of moral cultivation and moral attainment from that of Laozi, they at least share the agreement that things should progress in a smooth and gradual manner.

3.3　Absence of Conflict and Harmony

The traditional impression of Confucius is that he is a sombre and industrious teacher. This impression is reinforced by the passage that describes Confucius as someone who keeps trying to achieve his goals even though he knows his efforts are futile (*Lunyu* 14.38). Nonetheless, the life of Confucius is not without Laozi's sense of *ziran*. Confucius once said:

---

[1]　*Lunyu* 1.16.

Inthe eating of coarse rice and the drinking of water, the using of one's elbow of a pillow, joy is to be found. Wealth and rank attained through immoral means have as much to do with me as passing clouds. (*Lunyu* 7. 16; trans. Lau, p. 60)

This passage expresses Confucius's yearning for harmony between the internal and the external. Confucius once asked his students, Zi Lu, Zeng Dian, Ran You and Gong-xi Hua what they would do if their abilities are recognized. Zi Lu said he wanted to administer a state of thousand chariots and believed he can give people courage and direction within three years. Ran You would like to administer an area of sixty to seventy *li* square and believed that he could make people live in abundance. Gong-xi Hua said he would like to help officiating ritual ceremonies. Zeng Dian's answer is markedly different from the others in that he wants to detach himself from worldly concerns. Zeng Dian said:

莫春者，春服既成。冠者五六人，童子六七人，浴乎沂，风乎舞雩，詠而归。

In late spring, after the spring clothes have been newly made, I should like, together with five or six adults or six or seven boys, to go bathing in the River Yi and enjoy the breeze on the Rain Altar, and then to go home chanting poetry. (*Lunyu* 11. 26; trans. D. C. Lau, p. 105, 107)

Confucius later said he is in favour of Zeng Dian's vision. Why does Confucius agree with Zeng Dian the most then? In Huang Kan's explanation, this question was asked at a time of social unrest when many people are competing to be government officials. Only Zheng Dian knows his own dispositions and limitations. Instead of forcing himself to be someone he does not want to be, he chooses to live a kind of lifestyle that can provide him with equanimity. [1]

The above passage is strikingly different from the tenets of Confucian teachings. In fact, it is much close to Laozi's *ziran*. Even if we understand this conversation between Confucius and Zeng Dian as an exception, it is reasonable to regard what is represented in this conversation as a component of Confucius's thought. It reveals to us another side of Confucius. We see that Confucius also appreciates the kind of peaceful and harmonious lifestyle. Although the concrete feelings and spiritual attainment of Confucius do not necessarily coincide with that of Laozi, the kind of lifestyle idealized by Confucius is obviously pertinent to the state of *ziran* idealized by Laozi.

Laozi advocates the harmony of society as a whole. The rulers should make should not directly interfere with the life of the people, to the extent that the people do not even feel their presence and effects. The concept of *ziran* implies the harmonious and comfortable living of all people. It is conceivable that Confucius will also appreciate this as a high level of spiritual attainment of the ruler. According to Confucius:

为政以德, 譬如北辰, 居其所而众星共之。

The rule of virtue (*de*) can be compared to the North Pole Star. It remains in its place while the multitude of stars pay tribute to it. (*Lunyu* 2. 1)

He also says:

无为而治者, 其舜也与? 夫何为哉, 恭己正南面而已矣。

If there is a ruler who is*wuwei* but gives order to things, is he not Shun? He holds himself in a respectful posture and faces due south (*Lunyu* 15. 5)

---

[1] *Jishi*, p. 811.

Although the concept of *wuwei* originates in Laozi's thought, Confucius's praise of Shun in terms of *wuwei* shows that Confucius is familiar with the concept of *wuwei* and that accords a positive meaning to it. While the specific political measures and theories promoted by Confucius may be different from Laozi, Confucius is likely to accept the call for harmony derived from *ziran*.

4. Shared Elements in Confucius' and Laozi's Thought

Since Laozi and Confucius shared the same social and historical background, they were confronted with similar issues. They differ in their beliefs and ways in achieving it. While Confucius hopes to reconstruct moral and political order on the basis of *ren*, Laozi hopes to eliminate rulers' imposition on and control over the people. Nonetheless, they share a common goal, that is, to lead the society from disorder to order and harmony. They both seek to improve the situation through spiritual values rather than military, politics, or legal measures. In doing so, they have both constructed their own enduring moral systems.

Based on the above discussion, we can draw out some shared elements in Laozi's and Confucius's teachings. First, both Laozi and Confucius emphasize on internal cause and reject coercion. Just as Laozi's *ziran* requires things to be internally caused, Confucius's *ren* requires moral actions to be caused by appropriate inner attitudes and motivations. Although they are not completely against the use of external force, they both think that external force should not be used coercively and directly. Hence, the Laozi's sage has minimal presence; the Confucius's *ren* person does not impose on others. Second, both Laozi and Confucius favour a gradual and smooth development of things. Ethical ideals for them can only be obtained through one's own self-motivated effort, instead of through forcing oneself or others. Hence, the process of obtaining ethical goals should be a gradual and smooth one. Third, both thinkers underscore the importance of harmony within and without. While Confucius's focus is more on harmony in the society, Laozi yearns for harmony in the universe at large.

It is true that the two thinkers the foci of Laozi's and Confucius's philosophies are considerably different. The former emphasizes on a holistic order, whereas the latter emphasizes on the role of moral standards in governing individuals and social relationships. Nevertheless, by bringing these shared elements between Laozi and Confucius, we can better appreciate their differences. Laozi's philosophy could be in agreement with Confucian moral standards and other socio-political systems as long as they are not imposed on the people. Under certain circumstances, it is even possible that Laozi's *ziran* and Confucius's *ren* can collaborate and mutually facilitate the realization of each other.

Work Cited

Ames, Roger and Rosemont, Henry Jr. 1998. *The Analects of Confucius: A Philosophical Translation.* New York: Ballantine Publishing Group.

Chan, Wing-tsit. 1955. "The Evolution of the Confucian Concept *Jên*," *Philosophy East and West* 4. 4: 295 – 319.

Chen, Shude 程树德. 1990. *Luyu jishi* 论语集释. Beijing: zhonghua shuju.

Lau, D. C. trans. 2002 [1979]. *Confucius: The Analects.* Hong Kong: The Chinese University Press.

Liji 礼记. All references are to the volume, page, and line numbers in the *Sibu chongkan* 四部丛刊 edition.

Liang, shuming 梁漱溟. 1987. *Kongzi yanjiu lunwen ji* 孔子研究论文集. Beijing: Jiaoyu kexue chubanshe.

Liu, Xiaogan 刘笑敢. 1999. "An Inquiry into the Core Value of Laozi's Philosophy." In Mark Csikszentmihalyi and Philip J. Ivanhoe. eds. *Religious and Philosophical Aspects of the Laozi.* Albany: SUNY Press.

——. 2005 [1997]. *Laozi: niandai xinkao yu sixiang xinquan* 老子:年代新考与思想新诠. Taibei: Dongda tongshu.

——. 2006. *Laozi gujin: wuzhong duikan yu xiping yinlun* 老子古今:

五种对勘与析评引论 . Beijing: Zhongguo shehui kexue chubanshe.

Yin, Zhenhuan 尹振环 . 1998. *Boshu Laozi shixi* 帛书老子试析 . Guizhou: Guizhou Renmin chubanshe.

Zhu, Xi 朱熹 . 1983. *Si shu zhang ju ji zhu* 四书章句集注 . Beijing: Zhonghua shuju.

——. 1986. *Zhuzi yulei* 朱子语类 . Beijing: Zhonghua shuju.

Ren(仁) in the *Analects (Lunyu)* : sceptical prolegomena

R. A. H. King(University of Glasgow)

In the following pages I will try to articulate some of the problems I have with some remarks made by western commentators on 仁 rén in the *Lúnyŭ*. The problems I will consider cluster around the concept of virtue, and the way we may talk about it, or talk about it generally. Progress can only be hoped for when one realises the magnitude of the problem. The great temptation is for us to assimilate talk of rén to talk of virtue; the fascinating thing is that rén in *Lúnyŭ* resists this treatment.

One thing I wish to do is to point to some ways in which virtue, arêtê, is understood by Plato. Why not appeal to more modern conceptions? First a general point. I would claim that the term *virtue* (as opposed to terms for individual virtues such as *courage, wisdom, self-control*) is used extremely rarely in modern arguments about ethics, outside the classroom, and outside learned writing, and those influenced by it. Whilst we have a concept of virtue, it is not used to structure either education or laws, for example. Secondly, Aristotle is often used in discussions of virtue, as though his teacher had nothing worthwhile to say on the subject. But he is less suited to my present purposes, because although he does give general definitions of virtue and of the virtues, the use of general statements in Aristotle's *Ethics* is fundamentally a question of philosophical reflection on an ethic which has already been internalised. Their use in Plato is much more varied.

My strategy is to point very simple mindedly to the assumptions made in accounts of the *Lúnyǔ*, and to suggest that a) it is very implausible to make these assumptions b) what exactly we are to understand these concepts is not clear.

Consider the following remark by Kwong-loi Shun towards the beginning of his article on *rén* and lǐ in the *Analects*:

...in the Analects "*rén*" is used both more narrowly to refer to one desirable quality among others, and more broadly to refer to an all-encompassing ethical ideal that includes all the desirable qualities (2002: 53).

He then goes on to give some passages where *rén* occurs as one "desirable quality" among others, such as wisdom and courage (IX 29, XIV 28), and those passages where it "includes other desirable qualities such as courage (XIV 4) . " He then conducts his discussion in terms of the *rén* "in the broader sense of an all encompassing ethical ideal. " (2002: 53)

Clearly, *desirable quality* is here doing duty for *virtue*. What is to be gained by avoiding the term *virtue*? Well, there is no easy term for it in the Chinese of the *Lúnyǔ*. Yet *Lúnyǔ* contains, as far as I know, no term for *quality*, nor indeed *attribute*. So we cannot take the text to be *saying* rén is a quality, let alone a desirable one. So the interpreter chooses a term like *quality*, because, say, they think any ethical system, or this one in particular, is best understood in terms of a quality. Now this requires arguing. What a quality is, and more especially what an ethical quality is, is not something one can take simply as read. Similarly, too for "ideal": If one is interested in the shape of the thought under consideration, the presence or absence of ideals, as opposed, say, to historical models, or figures in traditional narratives, is of some import.

So we have here the central problem with the term rén: it is ambiguous.

This is widely perceived to be a problem. I am merely noting this problem here, and just make one comment. It is, of course, possible that these are uses that are conceptually related-for example benevolence, the narrow sense of rén, could in fact be the whole of virtue, if only one understood *virtue* aright; it could be a determining element in all other virtues, it could be the end or aim of all other virtues, or it could be a precondition for all virtue.

Brooks and Brooks use the idea of layers of composition of the text to deal with theproblem of the ambiguity of rén:

> The "profit" value scorned in LY 4 seems to be typical of the "little people". Confucius's counterpart value, the mysterious [rén], is translated by Waley as "Goodness" (with an intentional capital "G") . This interpretation owes much more to 04c reformulations (see, for example, 12: 22) than to LY 4. The sense of "good" that fits the military ethos is being "good at" the warrior's specific skills. Brooks & Brooks 1998: 19.

Their reading of rén in the *Lúnyǔ* is thus very simple, although they do not say how they take Waley's "goodness". Their own reading is a version of the functional reading of virtue: being good is being good at performing some function. The function they choose, for historical reasons, is that of waging war. I find this puzzling, since the text they place such emphasis on, Book IV, has much to say about rén, but none of it is, at first blush, about warriors.

Let us turn to the use of rén to speak of the whole of virtue. Others are less wary of the term *virtue* than Kwong-loi Shun. Benjamin Schwartz (1985: 75 – 6) remarks on Confucius' use of *rén*, it is

> an attainment of human excellence which-where it exists-is a whole embracing all the separate virtues. Thus it certainly embraces all the

social virtues and the capacity to perform the li in the proper spirit. ①

Here we have a play on the connection between virtue, and the more general idea of an excellence. Apparently, rén itself is not*a* virtue, but is a whole embracing the virtues. It includes, besides the "social virtues" an ability to perform the rites. The way Schwartz fits the rites in *alongside* "social virtues" is telling. Rites are a major stumbling block for the introduction of the talk of virtue into the *Lúnyǔ* : they do not attach easily to one individual alone. While they prescribe and proscribe actions, a rite or a body of rites is, categorically, not an attribute of a person. (Of more interest is the connection between lǐ and nomos.)

Ivanhoe and van Norden in the section "Important Terms" (2001: 391) give the following account of rén:

For Kongzi, this term [ren] refers to the sum total of virtuous qualities, or the perfection of human character. (It is etymologically related to the character for " human ", and thus has been previously rendered as "manhood-at-its-best".)

Here we are being offered several entirely distinct conceptions. On the one hand, this would seem to imply that there is a complete list of virtues ("the sum total") ②, and a person may or may not have all of them. On the other hand, we have the idea that human character can be perfected. Perhaps these two phrases are meant to be different formulations for the same conception. (I ignore the red herring of etymology, a commonplace in

---

① Similarly Dawson: "The graph consists of "man" plus "two" and the word summarizes how a human being should ideally behave towards other human beings, i. e. it embraces all the social virtues. Although it does refer to the individual's attainment of ideal human qualities, it is important not to think of it as merely indicating the psychology of the human being such as a translation as "magnanimity" or "compassion" would suggest. It rather refers to the practical manifestations of being humane. " Dawson 2000: xxi

② Similarly van Norden 2007: 117 – 8 "the summation of all human virtue. "

discussions of rén.)

One version of how the virtuerén relates to other virtues is that offered by Yearley (2002: 245):

> The quality noted as rén, at least as discussed in Book 4, is a general one that is instantiated or specified, in different ways in different contexts. Always rendering rén as benevolence [sic!] (as for example Lau does) is therefore problematic, because it leads us to think that one instantiation is the whole. The difference we see between the general concept and its specific instantiations, that is resembles the common distinction we make between "virtue" and "virtues".

Here there is a suggestion of a series of distinctions deeply embedded in western metaphysics-between the general, the specific, and instances. The instances in question here would appear to be*actions*, and the point is being made, perhaps, that virtue can lead to actions that are just or brave, and not merely benevolent. This mighty apparatus would need much elaboration before one could see how a virtue can be instantiated in actions (rather than say in an individual character). In his footnote to this passage (fn. 12, p. 267 – 8), Yearley explains in brief what he means by *virtue*:

> A virtue is a disposition to act, desire and feel that involves the exercise of judgement. The judgement may not be clearly present to my consciousness, much less the result of sustained reflection. At minimum, I must be able to explain (at some point, in some fashion) to myself or another person why I did something: e. g. why I was generous...Virtuous activity also involves choosing virtue for itself. I possess not the virtue of generosity, but a semblance-or even a counterfeit-if I act because of some ulterior motive such as helping specific people so they will think well of me. Finally, virtuous activity involves choosing specific virtues in light of some justifiable life plan.

A few remarks on this summary of Yearley's view will have to suffice here. Now, if we are to see this conception of virtue at work, however far beneath the surface, in*Lúnyǔ*, we have to suppose that disposition, action, and feelings are categories at work here. The supposition merely needs to be stated for its problematic nature to be clear. The same applies to the idea of justifying action, that most crucial of Socrates' legacies to us.

Take the sentence:

Rén is virtue.

This might appear on the surface to be something readers of the *Lúnyǔ* could agree on as being a doctrine in that work. Clearly, it is not a sentence that could serve as a translation of any of the many sentences containing the character 仁 in *Lúnyǔ*. Interpretation has to be done to arrive at such a formulation. *Virtue* seems to work as a general term in this sentence. What use are sentences containing a term for virtue?

Take some examples from Plato. One common use is perhaps to form general premises in an argument. Now an argument is usually not merely an argument. The status of arguments bears thinking about-the combative refutation of competitors, leading on compliant listeners, proving something to be the case. The two texts I discuss illustrate respectively each of the former uses, but not the third one. Of course, it may be the case that these arguments could be used to prove something; but that is not what Plato is doing.

In *Republic* I 353B2 – C7 Socrates is trying to persuade Thrasymachus that it is better to live justly than unjustly. He is using a conception of an end or function (ergon) as that which something either does alone, or does better than other things (353A9 – 11) (I have added "S" for "Socrates", and "T" for "Thrasymachus" to make reading easier; the whole dialogue is of course a narrative by Socrates:

S: And that to which an end is appointed has also an excellence? NeedI ask again whether the eye has an end?

T: It has.

S: And has not the eye an excellence?

T: Yes.

S: And the ear has an end and an excellence also?

T: True.

S: And the same is true of all other things; they have each of them an end and a special excellence?

T: That is so.

S: Well, and can the eyes fulfil their end if they are wanting in their own proper excellence and have a defect instead?

T: How can they, he said, if they are blind and cannot see?

S: You mean to say, if they have lost their proper excellence, which is sight; but I have not arrived at that point yet. I would rather ask the question more generally, and only enquire whether the things which fulfil their ends fulfil them by their own proper excellence, and fail of fulfilling them by their own defect?

T: Certainly, he replied.

(Trans. Jowett)

The English word *excellence* is being used here as a translation for the Greek word arêtê. The Greek word is much more general than the English word *virtue*, as it is currently used (if it is used at all). In a Greek context, arêtê, often translated *excellence*, is a general term applying to artefacts and animals as well as humans, and in humans to moral, intellectual and other skills. It thus applies to any thing a) which has a function (ergon, Jowett translates *end*) and b) where this function can be performed well or badly. So we have here a use of a general term *virtue*, which is used to make a general connection between virtue and function. This strategy for understanding *virtue* has great advantages. Use of the term with reference to humans is analogous to the use of the term with reference to other things. The use of the concept function (ergon) grounds the talk of virtues in a systematic view of what there is. Now it may be that these are both disadvantages: one may want to do ethics without metaphysics. After all, most people have an interest in ethics, very few in metaphysics. It may seem an intolerable burden to require that all should agree about metaphysics before agreeing on ethics. And one may object that the talk of means and ends (cf. e. g. the classification of goods by Glaucon at the start of *Republic* Book II 357C6 – D2) in fact misses the point about virtue: virtue is not functional. The advantage of conceiving of virtue in terms of a function may, however, lie in the fact that humans, whether good or not, are bound to fulfil functions (be useful) in a polity. ① But connecting virtue and function is not a move that goes without saying.

So what is the general talk of *virtue* doing here? We have here a very general use of the term, in order to connect excellence with the notion of function or end. The general statement at 353C5-7 (highlighted above) forms a premise in the argument to show that a soul can only perform its function well when it possesses its excellence, justice (353E, cf. 350CD) . The generality of the statement about virtue and excellence is necessary so that it can serve as premise in an argument.

In the *Laws*, the Athenian argues against the Cretan and Spartan that laws (nomoi) are not (should not be) designed to produce courage in the citizens, but "the whole of virtue". In the discussion of laws, the question arises what end they serve. In Crete, we are told, they serve the end of producing courage. The Athenian Stranger ("Ath. "), in contrast to the Cretan Cleinias ("Cle. "), wishes laws to serve the end of producing the whole of virtue. For only then will the city they regulate be good.

> Ath. Nay, I think that we degrade not him [the Lawgiver] but ourselves, if we imagine that Lycurgus and Minos laid down laws both in Lacedaemon and Crete mainly with a view to war.

---

① One then may seek a way in which virtuous people have a disposition to do things, not merely because these things are useful but because they are noble (kalon). This is Aristotle's solution.

Cle. What ought we to say then?

Ath. What truth and what justice require of us, if I am not mistaken, when speaking on behalf of divine excellence; -at the legislator when making his laws had in view not a part only, and this the lowest part of virtue, but all virtue, and that he devised classes of laws answering to the kinds of virtue; not in the way in which modern inventors of laws make the classes, for they only investigate and offer laws whenever a want is felt, and one man has a class of laws about allotments and heiresses, another about assaults; others about ten thousand other such matters. But we maintain that the right way of examining into laws is to proceed as we have now done, and I admired the spirit of your exposition; for you were quite right in beginning with virtue, and saying that this was the aim of the giver of the law, but I thought that you went wrong when you added that all his legislation had a view only to a part, and the least part of virtue, and this called forth my subsequent remarks. (630DE)

The point here is that Plato thinks that humans should possess a variety of virtues, and that these together make up the whole of virtue, that is, excellence for humans. The purpose of laws is to make the citizens good, not to just give them a part of virtue. This is a statement which requires in Plato's view that there is a complete list of virtues which are provided for by the laws. In this way, the phrase, *the whole of virtue* has meaning. Plato apparently assumes here that the four ' cardinal' virtues of the *Republic*, -courage, self-control, wisdom and justice-constitute the whole of virtue.

Another way which Plato expresses the same thought is by talk of the*greatest* (megistê) *virtue*, which is then identified with *complete justice*:

In laying down his laws every legislator who is any use at all ... will never have anything in view except the greatest virtue ... complete justice. 630C

Perhaps the thought is that the greatest virtue is that virtue which contains the whole of virtue. But there are puzzles about this last formulation: what is the relation between part and whole in the case of the virtues? How is it possible to identify the whole (virtue) with a part (justice)? Plato's solution to this problem in the *Laws* is far from clear; at one point he makes the claim, not argued for, that justice and happiness (*eudaimonia*) coincide (661 BC). Elsewhere, he ranks justice third among the virtues (631 BD). ① We do not need to go into this here, ② but merely note that the part -whole relation in the case of *virtue* is a complicated issue.

So Plato in fact has two formulations for the way one can talk about the whole of virtue. He uses this conception to specify the end laws (should) serve. The first formulation suggests we pick all the elements in virtue, the second that we pick the greatest virtue. Plato would appear to think that he can equate these two formulations. Perhaps the thought is that if one has the greatest virtue, the highest in rank, then all the others will follow.

Talk of *excellence*, and perhaps of *virtue* suggests ranking, and ranking is something of an obsession with Plato. The *Philebus* is devoted to ranking human lives as to their goodness. In the *Laws*, he is clearly interested in ranking both people and goods. Virtues are said to be divine goods, superior to human ones: Human goods look towards divine goods, and all look to nous, reason, which is supreme (*Laws* 631E). Furthermore, there is a correlation between the ranking of people and their virtue-most notoriously in the *Republic* Books VI and VII where above all the elaborate philosophico-mathematical training of the guards fits them to rule.

Clearly, there is a great interest in ranking in early Chinese thought as well-beginning from the fundamental distinction between junzi, the nobleman, and xiaoren, the common man, which occurs in many variants (for example

---

① Aristotle solves this problem by saying that *justice* is ambiguous (*Nicomachean Ethics* V 1 - 2) - either the term refers to the whole of virtue relative to others, or else to a particular virtue concerned with motivation due to the idea of a proper share (Actually, Aristotle has great difficulty is finding a formulation to fit all the various kinds of justice as a particular virtue.)

② For discussion, see Stalley 1991.

Lúnyǔ IV 16). But clearly there is also ranking between the virtues (rén above courage XIV 4) ① and among people (Yan Hui is put before the other followers in his love of learning in VI 3, the number of rows of dancers permitted in rites is mentioned in III 1).

This raises the question how these rankings are structured, and the purpose they serve. Here we may ask how these rankings are related to rén in *Lúnyǔ*. In fact, none of the rankings among people I cited above mention rén. Still, one simple model would be that rén is the attribute which is used to pick out the highest rank. There does seem to be a particularly close connection in some texts between the junzi and rén (for example, IV 5). But in one text (VI 30) there is something above rén, in another someone who loves rén "would put nothing above it":

> IV, 6   子曰:" 我未见好仁者, 恶不仁者。好仁者, 无以尚之; 恶
> 不仁者, 其为仁矣, 不使不仁者加乎其身。有能一日用其
> 力于仁矣乎? 我未见力不足者。盖有之矣, 我未之 见也。"
> The Master said, For my part, I have never seen anyone who loved [rén] and hated the not – [rén]. One who loved [rén] would put nothing else above it. One who hated the not – [rén] would himself be [rén]; he would not let the not-[rén] come near his person. Is there anyone who for a single day has put forth all his strength on [rén]? For my part, I have never seen anyone whose strength was not sufficient for it. There may be some, but, for my part, I have never seen one. (Trans. Brookes and Brookes)

Here there is clearly from the point of view of the agent (or ruler) a

---

① XIV 4: 子曰:[...] 仁者,必有勇。勇者,不必有仁。The Master said, ... A Good man will certainly also possess courage; but a brave man is not necessarily Good. (trans. by Waley as XIV 5).

priority torén. In fact, as in many of the sayings, there is a complicated structure, leading perhaps to a climax at the end: what is really being said here is not so much that rén comes before all else, but that rén is accessible to all, since Confucius is said to say that he has never seen anyone without the strength (lì, not brawn here, I take it) , for rén.

Heiner Roetz (1992: 196) makes the following judgement about rén in theLúnyǔ. I translate

The original reads: " Es [die *Lúnyǔ*] macht zur Menschlichkeit zahlreiche unzusammenhängende Aussagen, von denen ein großer Teil aus„ performativen Sprechakten " [...] wie Lobsprüchen oder Anempfehlungen besteht und die ferner oft nur sekund„ re Implikationen eines " menschlichen " Verhaltens berühren oder nur indirekt aussagekräftig sind. Nur wenigen Stellen sind Wesensbestimmungen der Menschlichkeit entnehmbar, wenngleich nicht auf einem analytischen Niveau, auf dem das ethische System des *Lunyu* selber und der Stellenwert der Menschlichkeit in ihm mitreflektiert würden. Beides liegt unter der bruchstückhaften Oberfläche des Werkes verborgen. ":
The *Lúnyǔ* makes numerous disconnected statements about humaneness, of which a large part consist of "performative speech acts", such as praise or recommendation, and which only touch secondary implications of " humane " behaviour, or which are only indirectly informative. There are few texts which can give us definitions of humaneness, even if not at an analytical level, on which the ethical system of the *Lúnyǔ* and the position of humaneness within is are reflected. Both lie hidden under the fragmentary surface of the work.

This seems to me to be a counsel of despair. Before we rush into following Roetz, there are a few remarks to be made, especially on the subject of "performative speech acts". For the fact that I use a term, such as good, or brave when making a recommendation, does not mean that, in principle, the content of the recommendation is especially opaque. On the contrary, *Be brave* is a perfectly clear recommendation or even command. Its content may be understood from the context. But any obscurity it is prey to does not lie in the nature of performative speech acts. Indeed, Suppose it is true that most of the uses of rén in the *Lúnyǔ* occur in performative speech acts, such as acts of praise, or recommendations: there must still be something that is being recommended or praised, however difficult it is to reconstruct this content. The purpose of the saying may not be to give a definition, but there should be some semantic content, however elastic that one can recover.

When we come to early Chinese ethics from a Greek background, we may indeed bemoan, as Roetz does, thelack of single authoritative, or argued definitions of terms. But, actually, I think things are rather worse than this. It may be true that the Platonic Socrates demands, and never gets, definitions of virtues from his interlocutors. There is a presumption in the early to middle dialogues of Plato that one cannot defend ones way of life (bios) unless one can give an account of virtues. For Socratic virtue is knowledge (for example in the *Meno* and the *Protagoras*), and knowledge is of definitions. Thus you can only subsume an action under a virtue, and so justify it, if you can, when called on, define the virtue in question. Yet this view arguably does not survive into Plato's later period; the function of definitions in ethics may no longer be a matter of actually living by them, but the work of reflection. (This view of universal statements in Greek ethics generally is argued for by Christopher Gill 2005.) In other words, we are brought back to the question of what work general statements about virtue perform in the ethical system.

Even Roetz' talk about the fragmentary nature of the work is problematic. For a fragment implies a whole that went before. And while we may think there were versions of Lúnyǔ prior to and unlike the one we have, there is no call tothink of such a version as the whole of which we have fragments. Clearly, there is a problem with context and arrangement of the sayings (I return in a moment to the question of their function). These are deep waters for a non-Sinologist. But one comment is perhaps allowed. Too much concentration on the arrangement of the sayings in extracting meaning from them in fact places great emphasis on the work of compilation, rather than on the content of the sayings themselves. However artful the arrangement of the sayings, I take it no one would claim that Confucius himself arranged them. And some of the sayings themselves, of course, are quite artful enough to require a mass of interpretation.

Now it may be that I am requiring talk in ethics to conform to inappropriate standards. For example, I am assuming here that the way we talk in ethics should be assessed, quite straightforwardly, as to truth or falsity (For a defence of this view, see Wiggins 2006: Chapter 12). Now assessing the truth of what people say requires, among other things, that it is clear what they are saying. Talking about the "elusiveness" of *Lúnyǔ*, and connecting this to its two main themes, "virtues" and the figure of Confucius, Lee Yearley writes:

> Neither virtues nor significant people, when well treated lend themselves to clear, much less static pictures. Real virtues, that is, display themselves differently depending on the situation in which they manifest themselves. Yearley 2002: 236

Now, the limited exactness of ethics is a standard toposin Aristotelian ethics (*Nicomachean Ethics* I 3), and Yearley belongs to the Aristotelian tradition via St. Thomas Aquinas. But one may wonder what the use of virtue is, if it is not stable. Is there then *no* saying what a good person is? One function of virtue is to be a stable feature of a world in change. Plato was impressed by Socrates' imperturbable nature, as well as by the unchanging nature of definitions. Now Yearley thinks that virtues express a conception of the good life; but he does not see a simple correlation, let alone a necessary one, between actions and character. But the point is surely that one cannot simply assume that this connection-more generally that between a disposition and its exercise-is not amenable to general description. Surely such a general description is a standard task for philosophical ethics. One problem that arises is how one chooses a virtue for its own sake, which is standard Aristotelian doctrine, and which Yearley follows. Just what does one need to know to do this? Some, for example the Socrates of the *Meno* might contend that one needs to define the virtue concerned, even: virtue in general. Others, such as Aristotle, would see no problem in an action being chosen for the sake its being noble, with no definition of any virtue, let alone virtue as such, in the offing.

Work Cited

BROOKS, Bruce E. und A. Taeko Brooks (1998): The Original Analects: Sayings of Confucius and His Successors. New York: Columbia University Press.

DAWSON, Raymond (2000): The Analects. Oxford: Oxford University Press. [1st ed. 1993]

Gill, Christopher (2005): Are Ancient Ethical Norms Universal? In: ibid. ed. *Virtue, Norms and Objectivity. Issues in Ancient and Modern Ethics*, Oxford, 15 – 40.

IVANHOE, Philip J. and Bryan W. Van Norden (ed). (2001): *Readings in Classical Chinese Philosophy*. New York: Seven Bridges Press.

ROETZ, Heiner (1992): Die chinesische Ethik der Achsenzeit: Eine Rekonstruktion unter dem Aspekt des Durchbruchs zu postkonventionellem Denken. Frankfurt a. M.: Suhrkamp.

SHUN, Kwong-loi (2002): „Rén 仁 and Lǐ 礼 in the Analects.. In: Bryan W. van Norden (ed.).

SCHWARTZ, Benjamin I. (1985): The World of Thought in Ancient China. Cambridge, Massachusetts: The Belknap Press of Harvard University Press.

Stalley, Richard. (2003). Justice in Plato's Laws. In: Plato's Laws.

From theory to practice. International Plato Studies, Volume 15, ed. Luc Brisson, Christopher Rowe et al. Sankt Augustin.

Bryan W. van Norden (ed.) (2002) : Confucius and the Analects: New Essays. Oxford: Oxford UniversityPress.

VAN NORDEN, Bryan William (2007): Virtue Ethics and Consequentialism in Early Chinese Philosophy. Cambridge (u. a.): Cambridge University Press.

WALEY, Arthur [1938]: The Analects of Confucius. [= Everyman's Library Classics & Contemporary Classics, vol. 184]. New York (u. a) : Alfred A. Knopf 2000. 1st ed: London: George Allen & Unwin Ltd. 1938.

Wiggins, David. (2006). Ethics. Harmondsworth

Yearley, Lee. (2002). An existentialist reading of *Lunyu* Book IV, In Van Norden ed.

The Forum on New Interpretation of Classics:
the English version If *Lunyu*

Morality and Re-interpretation of Belief

From the Universal to the Particular

——Way, Virtue and Practical Skills in the Analects

Xinzhong Yao

(King's College London)

Dao is primarily a path, but often extended as the way. According to *Shuowen jiezi zhu*, it is the path along which one walks (*Dao*, *suo xing dao ye*) and by which one reaches one's destination (*yi da wei zhi dao*) [1]. An earlier form of this character in bronze inscriptions appears to be composed of three parts: *jie* (street), *shou* (head) and *zu* (foot), which manifests several significant characteristics of a philosophical or religious school: the leader (head) as a pathfinder or a pioneer takes his followers to walk along the path to their destination. Since the ' head' also denotes a self-conscious person, the character of ' *dao*' refers to the way in which an individual follows his or her own path of life.

Perhaps the best-known usage of the way is in Daoist texts, and this has given an impression that *dao* is unique to Daoist philosophy. In fact, the way is common to all philosophical and religious systems in China, for each of them claims the way as the foundation of their theory and practice. Mozi, for

---

[1] Duan Yucai: *Shuowen jiezi zhu*, 1998, p. 75. From the primary meaning of ' path', *dao* is extended to refer to other things such as methods, arts, the essence or original status of the universe, principles or laws, doctrines, ethical principles, speaking etc. (see *Hanyu da zidian*, 1993, pp. 1608 – 09).

example, argues for his principle of ' universal love and mutual benefit' as ' the way of the sage-kings' (*sheng wang zhi dao*) and ' the principle of governing the empire' (*zhi guo zhi li*) [1]. The teaching of Confucius is said to be ' *fuzi zhi dao*' or ' *zi zhi dao*' (the Way of the Master, 6: 12[2]) and Neo-Confucians name their doctrines ' *dao xue*', the learning of the Way. After being introduced to China, Buddhism is also taken as a form of *Dao*, and the Eightfold Path to the Buddhahood is translated as the Eightfold Orthodox Way (*ba zheng dao*). Even for the imported religions such as Christianity, the way is also used to render their key terms; for example, ' In the beginning the Word (*Logos*)' (John 1. 1) is often translated as *tai chu you dao*, In the beginning there was the *Dao*'. As the way is commonly used in different philosophical and religious traditions, modern scholars have suggested that it be seen as a shared concept that has an intrinsic meaning and understanding for Chinese society and that defeats any in-depth translation[3].

This article is concerned with the intrinsic meaning of the way in its association with other key concepts such as *tian* (Heaven), *de* (virtue) and *ji* (practical skills) as elaborated in the *Analects of Confucius* together with a couple of other texts that are contributed to Confucius and his followers in pre-Qin China[4]. It is aimed to examine how the universal way is particularised through virtues and practical skills to become the way of humans in the

---

[1]   Mozi, Chapter 15, see Wing-tsit Chan (ed.): *A Source Book in Chinese Philosophy*, Princeton University Press, 1963, p. 217.

[2]   Except otherwise given, all in-text references to books and chapters are for *the Analects* and translations are based on D. C. Lau: *Confucius—The Analects*, Penguin Classcs, 1970.

[3]   Da Liu: *The Tao and Chinese Culture*, London: Routledge and Kegan Paul, 1981, p. 1.

[4]   *The Analects of Confucius* is a collection of the thought recorded and collected by the followers of Confucius in the 5th century BCE, although the extant version of the book did not come into being till the 2nd century BCE. In this article ' Confucius' really refers to the groups of the people who took Confucius as their master. Further, Confucius' teaching is not confined to *the Analects*; it is also preserved or further illustrated in other texts, particularly in Zhong Yong (*The Doctrine of the Mean*) and Da Xue (*The Great Learning*), two short texts that are generally agreed to have been produced not earlier than the 1st century BCE. Despite this, at least some of what is said to have come from Confucius in these texts had their origins in Confucius or his immediate followers.

teaching of Confucius.

Metaphysical and Ethical Approaches

Modern scholars have employed various means to introduce different definitions or interpretations of the way. In general two types of meanings have been ascribed to it; one referring to the universal and therefore sublime law of the cosmos (Heaven and Earth), which transcends the will and action of an individual, the other referring to the practical way of life which is individual, personal and practical. In most of Chinese philosophical classics these two meanings are interrelated and interdependent, knowing the one often depending on the appreciation of the other. On occasions, however, there is also tension or even opposition between them, when accepting one is said to imply the rejecting of the other[1].

Early Daoist philosophers place an emphasis on its metaphysical aspect where the way is primarily referred to as the law of the universe[2], or the origin of the world (*gen*, the root), to grasp which one must give up at least some of personal qualities, such as desiring and preferences, or practical tools such as language. No obvious intention is, for example, observed in the *Daode jing* to strike a balance between the universal and the particular as far as the concept of the way is concerned, as 'The way that can be spoken of is not the constant way' (Chapter 1). The due worth of the 'inferior' or particular ways is recognised only through the concept of *de* where the universal is individualised as personal virtue.

While the metaphysical approach to the Way in Daoist philosophy may be the best known, scholars have pointed out that in terms of an historical order, Daoists might have transformed the Confucian interpretation of the Way as

---

[1]   For example, in the *Daode jing* it is said that ordinary people often mock at the universal Dao.

[2]   The Daoist *dao* is, primarily, 'the way in which the universe work[s]' (Joseph Needham: *Science and Civilization in China: volume 2: History of Scientific Thought*, Cambridge: Cambridge University Press, 1956, p. 36).

' moral doctrine' to a notion as a ' metaphysical monistic absolute' . ① Like that in the *Daode jing*, the Way in the *Analects* is also used as a philosophised term referring to the truth or principle sustaining the metaphysical, physical and social worlds, or the universal Way, the highest level of cosmic reality as well as the most comprehensive view of the world that humans are possibly capable of. It seems that Confucius sufficiently noted the ineffable character of the universal truth, which as the Way of Heaven (*tian dao*) seems to have transcended human language. As a consequence, Confucius seemed not to have often talked about it (5: 13), probably because of its subtlety and profoundness that is beyond what an ordinary language could describe. However, in contrast to Daoists who tend to magnify the tension between the universal and the particular, Confucius and his followers tend to reconcile them, insisting that the way must not be separated from the way of individuals' life: ' The Way cannot be separated from [humans] for a moment. What can be separated [from humans] is not the Way' (Zhongyong, 1) . ② It is clear that this issue is approached from an ethical perspective. According to this perspective, the Way and human life should have been integrated, and the reason why the Way is part of human life but is often beyond human grasp is said to be due to the fact that humans are often deviated from the Middle Way (*zhong dao*), which is said in the mouth of Confucius that ' I know why the Way is not understood. The Worthy go beyond it and the unworthy do not come up to it' (Zhongyong, 4) . ③

Compared with the use of the Way in *Daode jing* that primarily refers to the ultimate truth or supreme reality, the ethical approach of the *Analects* has substantially particularised it as ways, particular and specific paths and methods by which a thing manifests itself and a person makes his/her own life. In this sense, everything and everybody has its/his own way. For

---

① Chad Hansen: *A Daoist Theory of Chinese Thought: A Philosophical Interpretation*, Oxford and New York: Oxford University Press, 1992: p. 13.

② *A Source Book in Chinese Philosophy*, p. 98.

③ Ibid. , p. 99.

example, there is the way of the great learning (da xue zhi dao) ①; a father
has the way of a father (*fu zhi dao*, 1: 11); the former kings had their way
(*xian wang zhi dao*, 1: 12); a gentleman has a gentleman's way (*jun zi zhi*
dao, 5: 16); and a good man is defined by the way of a good man (*shan ren*
zhi dao, 11: 20).

Diversified and particularised, the way provides criterion for human
living. It can be taken but can also be abandoned. In an ideal society, those
who follow the way are promoted to the position of ruling, while those who
abuse or depart from the way are demoted or even executed (*Analects*, 12:
19). Here the way is considered to be the moral standard of life, and those
who have followed it should be regarded as a model by which we rectify
ourselves (1: 14). However, from the universal principle that all humans
must abide by to a particular goal for each individual to realise, the way
cannot be internalised except through practising what is right (16: 11).

Any particular contains elements of the universal. However distinctive as
different ways are from each other, they seem to partake, one way or another,
of the universal way which is so highly regarded that Confucius even said
'When hearing the Way in the morning, die content in the evening' (4: 8).
Because of this universality, the way carries with it in most cases a laudatory
meaning of righteousness and truth. It has an intrinsic moral value and does
not need an ethical adjective if it is used for a desirable quality②. The value
of the way in a Confucian context is fully manifested in the contrast between
those who possess the Way (*you dao*) (1. 14) and those who 'do not possess
the Way' (*wu dao*) (3. 24) or those who 'have lost the Way' (*shi dao*, 19:
19), referring to a variety of people who do not seek the truth or who violate

---

① *The Great Learning*, The Text, see *A Source Book in Chinese Philosophy*, p. 86.

② In the *Analects*, we can read the expression of small ways (*xiao dao*). However, here the
'small' is not contrasted with the great way in a moral sense; rather it is meant practical arts that have
something whorthwile (19: 4).

the moral standard, behaving in an unjust, immoral and unrighteous way[1]. It can also be observed in the contrast between the highly valued way of ancient times (*gu zhi dao*, 3: 16) and the devalued way of contemporary times (*jin zhi dao*[2]), which is in fact a contrast between the ancients and Confucius' fellowmen. As the ideal for life and the root of virtues, the Way must be sought after (*mou*), and humans should be really concerned (*you*) if they cannot attain to the Way (15: 32). For Confucius it is worrisome and even dangerous if the Way is not carried out in the state or does not prevail in the world (*dao bu xing*, or *tianxia wu dao*, 3: 24). It is even more so for the state if those in authority do not follow the Way, because Confucius believes that ' If those in authority have lost the Way, the common people will become rootless' (19: 19).

Although the Confucian way is used most frequently to refer to the right course of life or action, this does not exempt it from being abused or distorted by those whose morality is low. Although the ways are the same, different people may well aim at different achievements by practising it: ' A gentleman learn the way in order to love people, while an inferior man learns the way in order to be easily employed' (17: 4). From this there comes a contrast between the way of a superior person (*jun zi zhi dao*) and the way of an inferior person (*xiao ren zhi dao*) which is spelled out in the *Doctrine of the Mean*. However, the contrast of two different demonstrations of the way does not necessarily negate its intrinsic righteous nature; rather it describes how the superior or inferior feature of the Way is added by the ways it is used or applied: different people take the way differently and therefore manifest their ways differently. On the other hand, however, this statement can also be led to a different conclusion where the metaphysical or universal feature is

---

[1]   A similar meaning is also expressed in the Doctrine of the Mean, Chapter 33, see *A Source Book in Chinese Philosophy*, pp. 112-1113.

[2]   There is no exact phrase of *jin zhi dao* in the *Analects*. However, the frequent uses of *jin zhi* (today's) study (14: 24), politicians (13: 20), and filial piety (2: 7) demonstrate the contrast between the way of the ancients and the way of his contemporary fellowmen.

minimized and even denied. If the way can be bended to one's preference as said in the following statement: the way can be straightforwardly followed but can also be bended in a crooked way (18:2), then there is a real risk that the way can be differentiated into different categories, in which the metaphysical way is completely replaced by particular ways. As far as the nature of the way is concerned, not only a difference of quantity but also a difference of quality can be indeed brought out. Confucius insists, for example, that people must not take counsel together if their ways depart from one another (*dao bu tong*, 15:40). However, in general this risk does not run high in *the Analects*. Interpretatively the Confucian Way is the same but its manifestations differ, and the differentiation comes from humans who pursue the way rather than from the way itself. Confucius is concerned about how to maintain the integrity of the way, calling for people to cultivate it (*xiu dao*; Zhongyong, 1) or study it (*xue dao*, 17:4), in order to fully understand it or to be part of it. Cultivating or studying the way does not mean that the Way can be modified or transformed; rather it is a moral requirement that humans must ' believe in the Way' with all our heart (19: 2), because if not, humans cannot achieve anything important: there is no much value for a person who believes in the way but without firm sincerity (19:2). This is essentially a moral argument that the universal way must not be altered to one's own benefits, and the value of the way cannot be appreciated except through an ethical perspective.

Way, Virtue and Human Efforts

Underlying the connection between the universal and the particular is the unity between the metaphysical and the ethical, a metaphysical-ethical oneness that sustains the Confucius' world and is therefore central to his teaching. Thus in seemingly secular applications of the way we have found a spiritual meaning, while speculations on Heaven are rooted in moral considerations. Virtue is not simply a matter of an ethical concern; it is based on the understanding of Heaven and is dictated by the Way of Heaven. Without a full understanding of the Way or the Mandate of Heaven, Confucius insists, it is not possible for us to establish a particular way of life and make a wise choice in human living. While acknowledging the ethical perspective of *the Analects* is tied to a religious destiny, we must reiterate that the Way in Confucius is not independent of humans; it can be known or learned only through its particularisation in personal life. This is an underlying reason why Confucius is said to have distanced himself from an abstract discourse on the metaphysical way, and consequently his disciples seldom heard about their master's words on the Way of Heaven.

Since the metaphysical way and the ethical way are taken as two in one, the interconnection between the universal and the particular is naturally emphasised: while the Way of Heaven determines what we should pursue in life, its value and importance cannot be fulfilled unless through a virtuous life. This has made the Confucian discourse fundamentally ethical and practically political. The primary concern of Confucius is how to govern the state in righteous way, and to him the ruling of the state requires, not a balanced structure of administration but reverence in dealing with business, beholding to sincerity, being economic in expenditure, and employing people at the proper seasons' (1:5).

Confucius does not go any further in his deliberation on the integrating function of the way. Unlike his followers, he does not explore how the way is related to the heart/mind (*xin*) or human nature (*xing*). This is done in the *Doctrine of the Mean* where the first sentence states: ' What Heaven imparts to humans is called human nature. To follow this nature is called the Way. Cultivating the Way is called education' (Zhongyong, 1)[1]. Due to the interrelatedness, the universal way must be cultivated in the heart and

---

[1] *A Source Book in Chinese Philosophy*, p. 98. Zhu Xi (1120 – 1200), the greatest representative of Neo-Confucianism in the 12th century, comments on this sentence that it is intended to illustrate that the roots of the Way are originally from Heaven and they will not therefore subject to change (Zhu Xi: *Sishu zhangju jizhu*, Beijing: Zhonghua shuju, 1983, p. 17).

personal life, which is called ' education' or ' self-cultivation' in which human apprehension grows and leads to the right path of life. Through internal cultivation the way that seems to be outside of humans becomes internalised as human consciousness, or the way as the potential in human nature becomes illustrious virtues. This way, the universal has fully particularised as psychological, social, moral and spiritual ways that are the necessary elements for individuals to lead a virtuous life. Having said this, we must make it clear that this new perspective is not totally different from Confucius's perspective. One point that Confucius makes very clearly is that the universal way cannot automatically enhance humans' intellectual and moral worth; the way requires to be extended or enlarged by individual will and action, and its value can be manifested to its maximum only through human efforts: "It is humans who can make the Way great. It is not the Way that can make humans great' (15: 29).

The ethical nature of thediscourse on the way in *the Analects* determines that the statement that humans can make the Way great is not all what Confucius wants to make; rather he must engage in a multidimensional discussion of how humans can make the Way great. This multidimensional discussion is the core of Confucius' discourse which focuses on how to lead a virtuous life, and how to enhance the quality of one's life. For Confucius, the way is to be lived rather than simply followed, because only through living by it can the universal be particularised and become part of everyone's own life. Virtue thus stands at the core of Confucius' reflection on the Way.

In *the Analects* virtue is not an abstract concept; it is associated with the meaning and worth of life. It requires to have a firm will on the way (*zhi yu dao*, 4: 9; 7: 6) that one can gain a meaning in one's daily life. To lead a virtuous life, one of the effective ways is to rectify one's own behaviour in light of those who possess the way: *jiu you dao* (1: 14). There is little in *the Analects* suggesting that the way must be comprehended by deliberating on its subtle meanings or as the ultimate truth or reality—this has differentiated him not only from Greek philosophers but also from Daoist authors of important texts such as *Daode jing* and *Zhuangzi*. For him, the pursuit of the way is primarily to practise virtues, a course of life that carries with it significant ethical value.

Confucius is keen to explore the reasons why ' the way does not prevail' . On occasions he seems to suggest that this is the function of Destiny (14: 36). However, more subsequently he seeks reasons for this failure in the lack of human effort. In this sense the way cannot prevail unless people have virtues or live by virtues. Virtue is thus likened as the root while the Way the trunk that grows up naturally if the root is established: ' when the root is established, then the Way can spring up' (1: 2) . As the root, virtue is composed of all good qualities of human living; in particular those of the family such as filial piety and brotherly respect (*xiao* and *ti*) . In a more abstract sense, however, virtue is not simply a good habit or correct attitude; rather it is believed to have been generated by Heaven. Confucius has proudly announced that the source of his virtue is in Heaven. When he was confronted with life threats he braved himself and his disciples that he had no fear at all because Heaven had produced virtue in him (7: 23) . Hence virtue in *the Analects* has two connotations. On the one hand, virtue is an excellent character demonstrated in such qualities as loyalty (*zhong*), trustworthiness (*xin*), courage (*yong*), respectfulness (*gong*), generosity (*kuan*), particular qualities which require intensive cultivation[①]. On the other hand, for Confucius virtue has a meaning of charismatic excellence that is associated with the mission from Heaven and with the fulfilling of this mission. The belief in the association of Heaven and virtue has given an added value to the ethical discourse of the way in Confucius. With his trust in Heaven, for example, Confucius dismisses the relevance of the fact that nobody understands him; rather he confirms again and again that he does not complain against Heaven, nor against other humans, claiming that he can be fully understood by Heaven (14: 35) .

---

① ' Not cultivating virtue' (*de zhi bu xiu*) is one of Confucius's four worries (7: 3) .

In Confucianism the way, virtue and Heaven are the three pillars supporting its moral universe, and their relations are central to all discourses on the way. In the later Zi Si-Mengzi strand of Confucian texts, the way is internalised as theheart/mind (*xin*) and is enriched through the concept of human nature (*xing*). The discourse on the way is therefore expanded through an outwardly movement from the internal to the external, from the low to the high and from the moral to the spiritual. For example, in the *Doctrine of the Mean* we find the starting point for the Way in the cultivation of one's person, which enables one to serve one's parents; sincere service of one's parents will enable one to understand other people; finally when one understands other people one is able to know Heaven[1]. It seems apparent for the author(s) of this text that knowing Heaven is the ultimate end of one's cultivation, namely, the source and guarantee of the value and noble meaning of life, and that Heaven is reached through overt activities of serving parents and understanding other people. This process can be illustrated ain the following linear movement:

Personal Cultivating → *serving parents* → *understanding others* → *knowing Heaven*

In the *Book of Mengzi* we have also found a linear movement for the Way. For Mengzi, the value of the Way lies in the expansion of one's *apriori* potentials: the nature of humans is rooted in the heart/mind, and to know humans truly we must not go to external events or phenomena, but look into our own heart/mind. Therefore, by extending our heart would we have good knowledge of our own nature. Because our heart/mind is the same as the hearts/minds of all other people, and our own nature is the same as the nature of all other people, then if we truly know our own hear/mind and

---

[1] ' A noble person cannot but cultivate his person. As he thinks about cultivating his person, he cannot but serve his parents. As he thinks about serving his parents, he cannot but know other human beings. As he thinks about knowing other human beings, he cannot but know Heaven' (Zhongyong, 20) *Sources of Chinese Tradition*, second edition, volume one, compiled by Wm. Theodore de Bary & Irene Bloom, New York: Columbia University Press, 1999, p. 336.

nature, we would be able to know the hearts/minds and nature of other people. By this knowledge we would be able to grasp what is universal to human existence and to serve the Way of Heaven. This movement can be illustrated as follows:

Extending one's heart/mind → understanding one's nature → understanding the nature of other people → knowing and Serving Heaven

In the discourse of the *Analects*, there is also an aspiration for the high. For example, Confucius strives for the progress from what is below to what is above by which he is understood by Heaven (14: 35). However, this kind of movement is not central to his discourse of the way. It seems that his focus is not on an outward movement. Rather he tries to construct an interconnected circle of the Way, Virtue and Heaven, which are not arranged in a linear progress, but as a circular movement. In contrast with the idealistic perspectives on human-Heaven relations, Confucius establishes in *the Analects* a moralistic approach to a realistic human-Heaven relationship by inserting virtue and human efforts between them, engaging in a discourse that involves the three aspects of a moral life: Virtue-the Way-Heaven, in which the way grows through virtue, while virtue is central to all elements of life. This can be illustrated in the following diagramme:

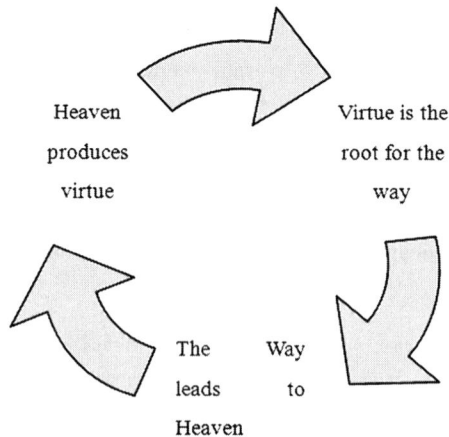

Heaven produces virtue

Virtue is the root for the way

The Way leads to Heaven

Because of the circular nature, there is no absolute starting or ending point in this discourse. As far as the relation between the way and virtue is concerned, noevidence suggests that Confucius takes the way that is rooted in virtue and the way that cultivates virtue as two separate or contrasting entities. For him the way cannot arise unless humans consciously cultivate it in their personal and family life or ' hao it', which is what he really meant by ' when the root is established, there comes the arising of the Way' (1:2).

How to establish the root is thus of significance for Confucius's discourse. There is a tension between the universal and the particular. To overcome the tension, rationalistic Confucians resort to the interaction between individuals and their communities and between a human person and the external world, while idealistic Confucians call for the cultivation of human heart/mind and for the development of moral and spiritual qualities that are believed to be innate to human existence. This is possible because for them one's innate quality and the virtuous quality of Heaven are of the same origin, as said in the *Doctrine of the Mean* we read that humans reflect on the Way of Heaven by cultivating ' sincerity' : ' Sincerity is the Way of Heaven. To think how to be sincere is the way of humans. One who is sincere attains centrality without striving, apprehends without thinking' (Zhongyong, 22) ①.

Confucius is also fully aware of the tension between the upward tendency of the universal Way and the downward forces that has dragged it to particulars, and is therefore concerned about the incomprehensibility of the destiny of the way in the human world. He is worried about the human inability to reverse the trend that the way fails to prevail in the world. While admitting the real risk of human failure, however, Confucius is not totally pessimistic about the future. He is a person who persists in doing what he knows clearly as impossible to realise (14:38), and therefore tends to believe that humans are capable of overcoming the gap between human efforts and the fulfilment of the Way. Any failure in carrying out the universal way is not the

---

① *Sources of Chinese Tradition*, second edition, volume one, p. 338.

failure of the Way itself, but a failure in human efforts. He is deeply concerned that failure to cultivate virtue and to practise what is right makes one's life less valuable and meaningful. However, he does not in general attribute the failure totally to the nature of humans, nor to the limitations Heaven has placed on human beings; rather he says that this happens because of a moral shortcoming or the weakness of one's will: some of us are too lazy and tend to set limits for ourselves before we even start (Analects, 6: 12). Since the reason for humans to fail to be with the way is one's moral weakness, then it is natural for Confucius to believe that by overcoming it and by addressing the shortcomings are all humans able to make a change to the course of an unsuccessful life, and that the way can be prevailing only through the process of making efforts. In this sense, Confucius considers the way is a personal choice: you can choose to be with it or you can choose to you're your back on it. It seems that Confucius believes in a natural difference of personal qualities such as intelligence and moral excellence. But equally true is that he emphasises humans make them worthy by learning and training, which enable an ordinary person to become an ideal person, a *junzi* (gentleman or superior person) whose way is threefold: ' virtuous he is free from anxieties; wise he is free from perplexities; courageous he is free from fear' (14: 28).

Way as Practical Skills

The way and virtue are unified through moral efforts; this implies that the way and virtue are not only universal principles or values, but also are practical to provide skills to solve problems and difficulties people are faced with in their daily life. In the context of the *Analects*, practical skills have a moral nature and are to be defined by their moral quality. The best skills for Confucius are not technological by nature; rather they are moral virtues such as benevolence and trustfulness, fidelity, kindness and honest, which enable the ruler to rule the world peacefully (2: 1), to live a happy and long life (6:

20). On the other hand, there are a good number of skills whose moral qualities are not as obvious as these virtues. These are referred to as minor arts (*xiao dao*) that also have their worthwhile usefulness in human life (19:4).

Practical skills demonstrate an important virtue: wisdom. As an individual, each human being has to explore his/her own way of life, and to find meaning in it. To lead a meaningful life, we need not only moral cultivation and virtues; we are also required to solve day-to-day problems by employing certain skills and abilities by which life difficulties can be dealt with and complicated situations can be resolved. A person follows the Way, not only because he/she has faith or is engaged in moral cultivation, but also because he/she has skilfully followed the right course of action that makes life secure and safe, while a foolish person does the contrary. On many occasions, the way is upheld and virtue is gained not only by one's knowledge and understanding, but also by one's practical skills.

Confucius associates the way with skill and ability, and considers Heaven to be the source of abilities only in a metaphorical sense, taking Heaven as an inspiring power while regarding practical skills and abilities as coming from people's learning, practice and effort. One of Confucius's contemporaries commented that Confucius was surely a sage sent by Heaven; otherwise why should he be skilled in so many things? For this Confucius did not go to Heaven or Heaven's mission to give an account of his skill and ability; rather he described himself as someone who grew up in humble conditions and became therefore skilled in many menial things, and this enabled him to have had many practical accomplishments in regard to everyday matters (9:6). For him, the way grows up in personal experience, and is associated with wisdom, reason and passion. For example, Confucius admits that he does not possess knowledge, but by using proper methods (skills) he can answer various questions (9:8).

Skills and abilities as emphasised in *the Analects* can be roughly classified into two categories, ' hard' or specific, and ' soft' or general.

'Hard' and specific skills and abilities refer to those that enable us to be capable of a particular task, while 'soft' and general skills and abilities refer to those that enable us to be respected in community and therefore to lead a successful career. Although a competent person is likely able to complete all his tasks more easily, general abilities cannot replace specific skills, and labour division requires each of us to be skilled in a limited number of areas. Both specific and general skills and abilities are equally important in Confucius' consideration of the way of life. Therefore talking in a practical sense, Confucians take the view that how to pursue a meaningful life depends to a great extent what skills and abilities one has possessed. For him it is apparent that a skilful person copes with life more easily and more successfully, while an incapable person is always frustrated with failure to solve his own problems. Confucius taught his students that lack of skill and ability would lead to disappointment in life and therefore ' It is not the failure of others to appreciate your abilities that should trouble you, but rather your own lack of them' (14: 30).

In many contexts, practical skills seem to be dealing only with one's particular job and with other people one happens to be associated with. In this kind of dealings, the rites (li) are the guidelines for people to follow. In many others, however, we find Confucius is also deeply concerned with the skill and ability in how to deal with oneself, particularly for those who bear a wide range of ethical, legal and political responsibilities. In dealing with the self, Confucius emphasises the self-cultivation and take cultivating the self as the path to personal virtue, to peaceful relations with others, and even as the administrative skills to bring peace to the people (14: 42) . Whether in dealing with others or with one's self, the key is the exercising of what is right, because this is the only guarantee for one to reach the Way (16: 11) . This exercise can be of different kinds. For instance, for an artisan in any of the hundred crafts he must master his trade by staying in his workshop, while for a gentleman the only means by which he can reach the way is through learning (19: 7). To illustrate the importance of practising a variety of skills for completing tasks, for example, Confucius compares the cultivation of political skills to the sharpening of tools of a craftsman. ' A craftsman who wishes to practise his craft well must first sharpen his tools' . Likewise, a gentleman who wishes to be capable of governing the world must skilfully ' seek the patronage of the most distinguished Counsellors', and to ' make friends with the most benevolent gentlemen' (15: 10). Skilfully dealing with others and with oneself requires a balanced attitude and manner. Therefore the mean or the Middle Way is important, as both going beyond and falling short are equally wrong (11: 16).

Practical skills are also concerned about how to use language. The way is the meaning of practical life but this meaning is not readily there for humans to speak out. In fact the right way of living must be ensured by speaking less than speaking more. In Daoism there is a strong disdain towards the talkative, and the *Daode jing* points out, ' The one who knows does not speak; the one who speaks does not know' (*Daode jing*, 56). A similar attitude is also shared by Confucius, who does not think that wisdom comes from one's manipulating words[1]. Confucius describes himself in learning as ' quietly storing up knowledge in my mind' (7: 2), and praises those who do not have a big mouth as virtuous, because ' A person of benevolence loathes to speak' (12: 3).

Confucius' caution over using language and words arises from both theoretical and practical considerations. First, it is related to his understanding of the metaphysical universe. For Confucius, the Way of

[1]   Although both praise silence and disregard speech, the difference between Confucius and Daoists should not be overlooked. Neo-Daoists such as Wang Bi (226-249) attempted to blur the line and regarded Confucius as a more sublime sage than Laozi, the supposed author of the Daode jing, as he transmitted wisdom without writing anything and devoted his life to 'remembering silently (Liu, I-ching (1976) *Shih-shuo hsin-yu: A new account of tales of the world*, tr. by Richard B. Mather, Minneapolis: University of Minesota Press, p. 96). This is a misinterpretation of Confucius, because Confucius' silence is praised in a moral sense, intended to emphasise that inner cultivation is more important than seeking external reputation, and to shun off damages caused by imprudent comments, while for Daoists, silence is the nature of Dao and is therefore the metaphysical source of wisdom.

Heaven guides humans but does not tell them what they should do. ' What does Heaven ever say? Yet there are the four seasons going round and there are the hundred things coming into being' (17: 19). Since he believes that humans must follow the way of Heaven, then it is natural for him to refrain from talking and to tell his students not to be talkative. Secondly, the preference for silence over speaking is due to their perception of the gap between the universal way and the particular language. The way is universal as can be appreciated only through a deeper understanding of, and insight into, the overall situation and the cause of things, while particular language is an artificial means by which we represent what has happened and makes connections between things. What we say therefore is not necessarily what really happens, and when we try to describe something it does not necessarily mean that we have understood it or properly described it. True knowledge of the way therefore lies in the quality of words, not in their quantity. Thirdly, that Confucius' giving priority to silence rather than speaking reflects his view of virtue. For him, virtue is doing and is cultivated through doing rather than speech. However beautiful, words coming out before action would bring undesirable effects; while speaking after action will prove effective. Therefore Confucius sets it as one of the necessary qualities of a gentleman that he is ' quick in action but cautious in speech' (1: 14). Considering the strong effect of bad words, Confucius even tends to agree that ' a saying can lead the state to ruin' (13: 15).

More obviously associated with the way and virtue are the skills of how to deal with riches and poverty. We live both in a natural environment and in a social context, and the quality of our life depends, at least partially, on what we can employ to satisfy our needs and what kinds of people we come to be associated with. Human needs are manifested through multi-facets and are satisfied at various levels. In terms of material prosperity, we need a certain amount of goods to lead a decent life, without suffering the terrible hardship of hunger and cold, and in terms of inter-personal relationship, we need to be associated closely with some people while distancing ourselves from others.

Therefore, how to deal with the issues of poverty and wealth, and how to make right people our friends have naturally become an important part of Confucius' discourse of the way.

Contrary to later Confucians, for Confucius, there is nonatural contradiction between the way, virtue and wealth. In fact wealth and striving for wealth are taken as an integral part of the right way of life in *the Analects*. Confucius was quoted as saying that the head of the state should not worry about poverty but about instability (16:1), and has repeatedly said that being rich and being morally good do not necessarily contradict each other and that being poor does not necessarily lead to good, for poverty would prevent people from being virtuous: ' It is more difficult not to complain of injustice when poor than not to behave with arrogance when rich' (14:10). Therefore one of the key policies Confucius promoted is ' to make the people rich' (13:9).

Pursuing wealth is not only socially sound but also morallyjustifiable. Confucius once said that ' If wealth were a permissible pursuit, then I would be willing even to act as a guard holding a whip outside the market place' (7:12). The moral problem with pursuing wealth does not lie in wealth itself, but is tangled with the means by which one gets rich. While highlighting the moral value of wealth, Confucius strongly opposes the pursuit of wealth by an immoral or unjust means: ' Wealth and rank attained through immoral means have as much to do with me as passing clouds' (7:16). Although he admits that ' wealth and high station are what all people desire', and that ' poverty and low station are what all people dislike', he declares that unless he becomes rich and reaches the high rank in the right way he would not remain in them, and if he does not become poor and low ranked in the right way he would never try to escape from them (4:5). Morally permissible means for wealth was more likely to have existed in a well-governed society, while in a chaotic society people more frequently go for wealth through unjust ways. It is in this sense that Confucius comments that ' It is a shameful matter to be poor and humble when the Way prevails in the state. Equally, it is a shameful matter to be rich and noble when the Way falls into disuse in the state' (8:13).

Not only must wealth be acquired through virtuous action, but Confucius also demands that it must be used according to the way. Where does poverty or wealth come from? Why have some people become rich while others poor? Confucius answers these questions from a practical account of the means one happens to be able to employ, and takes a humanistic view of the rich and the poor. Due to the complexity of social conditions and personal circumstances, it is possible that whatever one does, one may still remain poor. However, there is a sharp contrast between a person of virtue and a person that lacks virtue in their attitude towards poverty. A virtuous person accepts poverty easily while a mean person would be overwhelmed by a dire life situation. Confucius compares a gentleman who in poverty acts as a gentleman (*jun zi*), with a mean person (*xiao ren*) who in extreme straits would throw over all restraint (15:2).

The way and virtue are also associated with the skills of how to makefriends and how to avoid certain kinds of people who will affect one's moral integrity. It is therefore important for the people to hold on their own way to have good people as friends. Confucians take the principle for the intercourse between friends as one of the five universal ways (*da dao*, Zhongyong, 20). Highly valuing the importance of friendship for the way of life, Confucius does not recommend one to be in company with every sort of people; rather, he asks students to choose carefully the people they are to be associated with. How to keep a distance from the unworthy, and how to be a friend with the virtuous are not only an important part of the Way, a demonstration of one's virtue, but also an art of life. Primary concern in Confucius about friends is given to one's personality and moral virtues. Confucius taught his students that in order to benefit from friendship, they must carefully choose their companions, who must be morally good and be more advanced in moral cultivation (9: 25). The reason why Confucius advises his audience to ' make friends with the most benevolent gentlemen in a state' (15:10) is that they would benefit from these benevolent gentlemen. He goes even further to define three kinds of people as beneficial, and another three as harmful: ' To make friends with the straight, the trustworthy in word and the well-informed is to benefit. To make friends with the ingratiating in action, the pleasant in appearance and the plausible in speech is to lose' (16:4).

True friendship not only enriches the way and virtue, but also can make our life more pleasant. The first sentence of the *Analects* records Confucius as saying that ' Is it not a joy to have friends come from afar?' (1:1) However, a joyful thing can easily be turned into distress if we do not cultivate friendship in a right way. It is important for Confucius to establish trust between friends, because without trustfulness they would easily lose confidence in each other. Many of the close disciples of Confucius defined ' trustfulness' (*xin*) as the criterion for maintaining friendship (1:4; 1:7).

Conclusion

The way in *the Analects* is one of the most important concepts for Confucius' teaching, and is elaborated as the path by which the universal and the particular are interrelated. In the concept of the way Confucius and his disciples have successfully constructed a Confucian world that is sustained by virtue on the one hand and by practical skills on the other. Associated with virtue and practical skills a particular way does not negate its universal nature; rather it seeks to particularise the universal into concrete ways of life for individuals. Through virtue and moral efforts an individual gains moral qualities that the way itself embodies, while through practical skills an individual opens up his/her own way of life, leading a career that does not deviate from universal principles and virtues. In mutually supplementing, the way, virtue and practical skills have thus formed the three pillars in an ethical discourse as presented in *the Analects*.

A Spiritual Turn in Philosophy: Rethinking the Global Significance of Confucian Humanism

Tu Weiming

Contemporary philosophy, as an academic discipline, has been shaped by two significant turns in its methodological orientations: epistemological and linguistic. With a view toward the future, it is likely that a new turn which I deliberately choose to characterize as the "spiritual" is in the offing. There are clear signs of this development. An obvious one is the return of philosophy to its original source of inspiration, namely "the love of wisdom."The relevance of Aristotelian ethics, the Stoic discipline, and other forms of self-knowledge in the Greek heritage to the current modes of philosophizing is obvious.

In a broader context, virtually all Axial civilizations—Hindu, Buddhist, Daoist, Confucian, and Judaic (and by implication, Christian and Islamic) have become fields of inquiry for professional philosophers. This does not mean that philosophers have chosen to be "religious. " The central concerns of philosophical analysis, such as epistemology, logic, philosophy of mind, linguistic philosophy, and ontology remain dominant in philosophy departments all over the world. By and large, philosophy teachers self-consciously distance themselves from their colleagues in religious studies by insisting that free, disinterested, rational, and systematic exploration is significantly different from faith-centered or commitment-motivated studies.

The re-presentations of the thoughts of paradigmatic personalities, notably Buddha, Confucius, Laozi, Mencius, Xunzi, Zhuangzi, Shankara, Maimonides, and Ibn Arabi in philosophical studies show the authentic possibility of a new mode of thinking as exemplified by the works of some of the most brilliant living philosophers. Confucian humanism like Buddhism and Daoism, is both philosophical and spiritual. It is a source of inspiration in our joint venture to rethink Asian philosophy as an integral part of current global reflections on the meaning of being human in the 21st century.

Historically, none of the major Axial-age civilizations in Asia-Hinduism, Buddhism, Confucianism, and Daoism made a clear distinction between philosophy and religion. Virtually all philosophical contemplation is embedded in spiritual insight and cultivation. Indeed, without spiritual disciplines, sophisticated intellectual reflection is impoverished. The confluence of disinterested analysis and experiential understanding, is a defining characteristic of the Axial modes of thinking. Actually, as philosophically seasoned historians, such as the French academician, Pierre Hadot, have convincingly demonstrated that, to some Greek thinkers, philosophy is a way of life exemplified by spiritual exercises. This is also the Harvard professor, Hilary Putman, approaches Maimonides, Rosenweig, Buber, and Levinas in his lecture course on the "Four Jewish Thinkers. " It seems obvious that philosophers in close collaboration or friendly competition with colleagues in other disciplines, such as religion can be a highly productive way of thinking in the 21st century. Needless to say, this is also a wholesome practice of returning to the core and source of the philosophical enterprise: self-knowledge.

Confucian humanism, unlike the secular humanism characteristic of the European Enlightenment, is a comprehensive and integrated vision on the human condition.

Traditionally, ideal Confucians assumed a variety of roles throughout their lives. As scholar-officials, they shouldered political responsibilities and performed their educational functions in society. Like Indian gurus, they were teachers; like Buddhist monks, they were ethical exemplars; like Jewish rabbis, they were learned scholars; like Greek thinkers, they were wise men; like Christian priests, they were spiritual leaders, and like Islamic mullahs, they were community leaders. However, in the final analysis, their commitment to the improvement of the human condition, rather than to a reality outside or beyond this world compelled them to take on social responsibilities as their calling. Yet, their intellectual horizons and spiritual concerns were broader and deeper than academic disciplines such as ethics, political philosophy and social philosophy.

Confucian humanism seeks to integratefour dimensions of human experience: self, community, nature, and Heaven. It is not a form of secular humanism, but a humanism that entails both naturalist and spiritual dimensions. As a holistic humanistic way of life it proposes that the agenda of human flourishing involves (1) sustained integration of the body and mind, (2) fruitful interaction between the self and community, (3) harmonious relationship between human species and nature, and (4) mutual responsiveness between the human hearts and minds and the Way of Heaven. A person so conceived is an observer, appreciator, participant and co-creator of the evolutionary, indeed the cosmic, process. Human consciousness must be expanded from the self, family, community, nation, world, earth and ultimately, to the "great transformation" of the cosmos.

I would like to present a focused investigation of the Analects, the most celebrated and influential core text in the so-called Confucian cultural area— China, Korea, Japan, and Vietnam. My purpose is not to givea Sinological reading of the classic but to ground my "personal" reflection on it. It is an attempt to think philosophically from Confucian roots. By the way, when I said "personal, " I do not mean private or idiosyncratic. It is intended to be an " embodied" knowing that, hopefully, is transparent and publicly accountable for comments and criticisms. In other words, it is my desire to offer a "local knowledge" that hopefully is also globally significant.

TheAnalects is, I believe, the distillation of what must have been a series of rich, varied, spontaneous, timely, dynamic, memorable, and thought-provoking interchanges between Confucius and his disciples over the stretch of several decades. It may have taken more than two generations for the most intimate and knowledgeable followers of Confucius to compile the "book. " It seems that they did not intend it to be a finished product. Rather, they may have deliberately chosen to make it open and receptive to new contributions, but it is obvious that they were cautious and judicious in their choice of each entry. The reason for this strategy is not difficult to imagine. Assuming that the purpose of the compilation was to keep a memory of their Master, the paradigmatic personality, whom they missed, adored, and respected, there were several ways to complete such a task. They could have chronicled the Master's most important activities, jointly authored an appreciative biography, or systematically recorded his core ideas. Instead, they opted for a highly personal style, recording authentically how he talked, acted, thought, and, most vividly, responded to specific questions. It works brilliantly.

As a classic, the *Analects* is open-ended. It lends it self to new additions as well as to divergent glosses, different commentaries, and novel interpretations. Its text, by nature, is receptive to an even-expanding network of contributors. It seems to be a vast public space with ample room to accommodate a variety of insights attributable to the Master.

Like the *New Testament* and the Socratic dialogues, the *Analects* is a source of inspiration for those who cherish the experience of directly seeing and hearing the Master's teaching. As several scholars have pointed out, Chapter X offers a subtle and nuanced depiction of Confucius' manner of dressing, walking, approaching superiors, meeting strangers, and receiving friends. Indeed, his facial expressions, his body language, and above all his ritual performance are vividly portrayed. This contextualized daily routine discloses his appropriateness in specific situations. In the eyes of his students, what he did evoked an aesthetic sense of elegance. He comes alive in lived concreteness rather than in abstract universalism. Even with the lapse of more that twenty-five centuries, an attuned ear can still hear his inner voice and sense his presence. Confucius' vibrant personality, indeed his humanness, is vividly revealed.

As digested conversations and condensed discourses, a dialogical mode pervades the Analects. This hasprofound implications for intercivilizational dialogue today.

The Golden rule in Confucian ethics is "Do not do to others what you would not want others to do to you". This statement is intentionally presented in the negative to emphasize the virtue of reciprocity. Theassumption is that what is best for me may not be the best for my conversation partner. Edifying conversation begins with sympathetic resonance. However this passive statement must be guided by the principle of humanity: "In order to establish myself, I help other to establish themselves, in order to enlarge myself, I help others to enlarge themselves. "

Therefore, tolerance of difference is a prerequisite for any fruitful dialogue. Yet, merely being tolerant is too passive to go beyond the self-indulged egoism. We need to be acutely aware of the presence of the other before we can actually begin communicating. Awareness of the presence of the other as a potential conversation partner compels us to accept our co-existence, with an even-expanding network of human relationships as an undeniable fact. This leads to the recognition that the other's role (belief, attitude, and behavior) is relevant and significant to us. In other words, there is an intersection where the two of us are likely to meet to resolve divisive tension or to explore a joint venture. As the two sides have built enough trust to see each other face-to-face with reciprocal respect, a meeting of the hearts and minds becomes possible. Only then can a productive dialogue begin. Through dialogue, we can appreciate the value of learning from the other in the spirit of mutual reference. We may even celebrate the difference between us as the reason for expanding both of our horizons.

Dialogue, so conceived, is neither a tactic of persuasion nor a strategy of conversion, but a way of generating mutual understanding through sharing common values and creating a new meaning of life together. As we approach civilizational dialogues, we need to suspend our desires to sell our ideas, to persuade others to accept our beliefs, to seek their approval of our opinions, to evaluate our course of action in order to gain agreement on what we cherish as true, or to justify our deeply held convictions. Rather, the purpose is to learn what we do not know, to open ourselves up to multiple perspectives, to reflect on our own assumptions, to share insights, to discover tacit agreements, to explore best practices for human flourishing and above all, to cultivate the art of listening.

The art of listening, essential for personal knowledge, is cultivated as a precondition for elegance in verbal expression. The Confucian style of teaching, contrasted with the Socratic method, underscores experiential understanding and silent appreciation.

Learning, which features prominently in the *Analects*, involves practice as well as cognition. It is a spiritual exercise. One learns not only with the heart-and-mind but also with the body. Learning so conceived entails transforming the body as well as enlightening the mind. As the practice of the " six arts " (ritual, music, archery, charioteering, calligraphy, and arithmetic) clearly indicates, both physical and mental disciplines are required and learning and thinking ought to complement each other.

Implicit in this style of education is the existence of a fiduciary community, a community of trust. The fellowship of the like-minded that Confucius formed with his disciples was a voluntary association dedicated to improving the human condition through education. Modern historians interpret the traditional description of Confucius as the "First Teacher" in terms of his social role, namely, he was the first scholar to establish private schools in China. The students who gathered around Confucius, like Jesus' disciples, were not children but adults who were truth seekers, passionately engaged in the quest for the meaning of life. They were attracted to him by his great vision and profound sense of mission. His radiant and yet unassuming personality must have been a source of inspiration for them: "To store up knowledge in silence, to remain forever hungry for learning, to teach others without tiring—all this comes to me naturally. "

Confucius may not have had a set curriculum, but the *Analects* offers sufficient evidence to support the view that his educational purpose was no less that learning to be human. The primary aim of education is character-building. What does this mean? Neo-Confucian thinkers interpreted this to mean " learning for the sake of the self (quoting Confucius directly) , " "learning of the body and the heart-and-mind, " "learning of the heart-and-mind and human nature, " "learning of the sage, " "learning of the profound person, " and "learning of human nature and destiny. "

Self, body, heart-and-mind, human nature, sage, profound person, and destiny suggest that learning to be human covers the whole spectrum of our lifeworld. The assertion that Confucius was exclusively concerned about life and human affairs without being deeply immersed in the discourse on death and the spirit is untenable.

Surely he focuses his attention on life rather than death and in serving the human rather than the spirits. The implication is obvious: he considers understanding life is a precondition for understanding death, and serving the living is a precondition for serving the spirits. But this implies that a full understanding of life necessitates any appreciation of death and serving the live man well requires the ability to serve the spirits well.

Undeniably there is a transcendent dimension in the Confucian form of life. He also claims that only Heaven knows him. He strongly believes that his mission of cultural transmission is not only a human endeavor but also a fulfillment of the Mandate of Heaven. He is in awe of Heaven and he seems to have a tacit understanding of Heaven's creativity in the cosmic process.

What is Heaven then? A general observation based on the teaching of his most prominent follower: Mencius is in order. The uniqueness of being human is our inner ability to learn to become worthy partners of the cosmic process. This is predicated on the assumptive reason that we are empowered to apprehend Heaven through our self-knowledge.

As Mencius avows, if we can realize the full measure of our heart-and-mind, we will know our nature; if we know our nature, we will know Heaven. Surely existentially, we cannot fully realize our heart-and-mind, thus, in practical terms, it is unlikely that we will ever know our nature in itself and, by implication, it is unlikely that we will ever know Heaven in its entirety. But in theory and to a certain extent in practice, we can be attuned to the Way of Heaven; specifically, through our persistent moral endeavor, we can realize a sympathetic resonance with Heaven.

Understandably, the highest manifestation of self-realization is the "unity of Heaven and humanity". This is the reason underlying the idea of "immanent transcendence" in Confucian humanism.

Confucius lived during a period of political disorder and social disintegration. The elaborate ritual tradition, refined bythe Duke of Zhou, one of the most influential statesmen in pre-Confucian times, became dysfunctional. Internecine warfare flared up between rival states. Several hermits tempted Confucius to withdraw from the world to enjoy a peaceful and tranquil life in communion with nature. The Master, though respectful of such an existential preference, was determined to pursue his own course of action: "I cannot associate with birds and beasts. Am I not a member of this human race? Who, then, is there for me to associate with? If the world were following the Way, I would not have to reform it. " [18:6] It is not surprising that among the historical religions (Judaism, Buddhism, Jainism, Daoism, Christianity, and Islam), Confucianism is unique in refusing to make a difference between the sacred and the secular and regarding the secular as sacred. Confucius did not posit a spiritual sanctuary (church, temple, synagogue, monastery, or ashram) as a sacred place for contemplation, meditation, prayer, and worship. Nor did he envisage a holy land or the other shore as ultimately real and radically different from our lifeworld here and now. By committing himself to transforming the human condition from within, he was inevitably intertwined with the political affairs of the time. However, in regarding the secular as the sacred, he envisions the ultimate meaning of life is realizable and indeed ought to be realized in ordinary human existence.

He maintains that in thinking about the world, we should always take as the point of departure our existence as concrete living persons here and now. Thus, reflection on things at hand is the basis for ultimate self-realization. In his view, the political process begins at home. It is inseparable from one's way of living. What happens in the privacy of one's home is socially, anthropologically, and even cosmically significant. Implicit in this style of Confucian praxis is the creation of a discourse community through self-understanding and mutual learning. The Group solidarity was not an imposition by the Master according to a preconceived pedagogical model. Nor was it forged by a firm resolve to perform a clearly defined political and ethical function. Rather the disciples gathered around Confucius were encouraged to develop their own potential as knowledgeable, cultured, ethical, and tasteful contributors to the public good. This constructive mode enabled them to practice their own paths of self-cultivation through reciprocal respect and mutual appreciation. Confucius urged them not to become utensils defined in terms of their functional utility but all-round profound persons capable of political action at different levels under all circumstances.

This is relevant to the contemporary situation. In a comparative civilizational perspective, this seemingly unique Confucian spiritual orientation—regarding the secular as sacred, or, more appropriately, rejecting the separation between the defiled earth and the sublime Heaven—has been embraced by most, if not all, major spiritual traditions in our age. Virtually all Axial-Age civilizations have undergone substantial transformations so that they can respond meaningfully to the crises of the modern world. No mainstream ethical or religious belief can afford to ignore environmental degradation, abject poverty, social disintegration, violence, crime, drugs, or terrorism as worldly affairs beneath the purview of their God-centered spirituality. Without a doubt, a defining characteristic of religion is its avowed compassion and love for humanity; thus, all forms of suffering, from brutal torture to routine boredom, are worries of spiritual leaders. However, since the "ultimate concern" is often directed otherwise, salvation is seldom to be found in the world here and now. Those who have identified themselves with the things that are God's rather than the things that are Caesar's would not consider politics as a calling, let alone accepting the bureaucracy as the proper domain for spiritual commitment. However, nowadays spiritual and religious leaders are duty-bound to be politically concerned, socially engaged, and culturally sensitive.

The human condition today dictates that spiritual and religious leaders become proficient in two languages: one specific to their faith communities and one for global citizenship. Similarly, experts and professionals should also feel obligated to become bilingual. They must be able to address themselves to two overlapping linguistic communities. One is the expert language relevant to their profession and the other is the language of the public intellectual. Unless they are capable of rising beyond their own interest groups, they cannot properly situate their expertise or professionalism in an increasingly complex and interconnected global village.

What kind of a society, or moreappropriately community, did Confucius actually create to facilitate his vision of transforming our world from within? Since Confucius regarded himself as the guardian of the Way of human survival and flourishing, he appealed to the sages and worthies who were the architects of the cumulative tradition rather than a transcendent reality alone beyond human comprehension or a natural evolution without human participation. Although Confucius was never entrusted with a territory to put his idea of the model government into practice, the social reality that he actually constructed turned out to be profoundly meaningful. The fellowship, as the result of his collaborative effort with his disciples, was open, flexible, communicative, interactive, inclusive, and mutually beneficial. He engaged his students not as a philosopher who methodically led them to see the essence of things step by step. There is nothing in the *Analects* that resembles the elaborate reasoning in the Socratic dialogue. Indeed, Confucius distrusted mere verbal persuasiveness, he despised glibness, and he resented clever expressions. Although he highly valued eloquence in diplomacy, lucidity in thought, and articulateness in literature, he preferred tacit understanding to effective argumentation. The latter reminded him of the trickery in legal disputes, even litigiousness. In civil cases, he favored negotiation, mediation, or out of court settlements, rather than formalistic, arbitrary, and coercive mechanisms of control.

The ideal society that Confucius envisioned and the discourse community he created through exemplary teaching was a voluntary association. The primary purpose of such an association was to help facilitate the self-realization of each of its members. A polity based on such a social vision involves a reflectivity of both the political and intellectual elite and an effective procedure by which humane government is set in motion.

Confucius' determination to transform politics through moral strength, cultural values, social cohesiveness, and historical consciousness, is often misunderstood as his naive enthusiasm in the primacy of the political order. Rather, it is predicated on the perception that the ultimate purpose of politics is human flourishing. Surely, politics is intertwined with power, influence, and authority, but the purpose of politics is ethics through education. The maintenance of security and the sustenance of livelihood are not ends in themselves but rather they are conditions for human flourishing. The Confucian instruction that "from the ruler to the commoner all should regard self-cultivation as the root" is supposed to provide the basis for a fiduciary community, rather than to inculcate a mechanism of social control. To use Emile Durkheim's terminology, Confucius, through mutual understanding and corporate self-consciousness, brought about an organic solidarity. Among Confucius' disciples there were literati, farmers, artisans, soldiers, merchants, and practitioners of a variety of other occupations. The division of labor enriched the Confucian fellowship through its diversity of backgrounds and plurality of life-orientations.

Again, an issue of contemporary relevance looms large. How can the Confucian perception of fiduciary community and social solidarity account for political legitimacy and democratic participation? Indeed, how can the

Confucian style of governance accommodate human rights? Max Weber's critique of universal brotherhood as a premodern ideal incompatible with modern society defined in terms of secularization, professionalization and rationalization is also pertinent here. More seriously, if the Confucian self were perceived as an inclusive individuality fixed in birth, rank and status, it is definitely incapable of responding to the highly differentiated social roles that a modern person habitually assumes to lead in a normal life in a post-industrial, if not postmodern, society. Certainly the idea of the self as a specific un-destructive and non-changeable identity is outmoded. But these charges against the Confucian tradition are one-sided. In a deeper sense, the real issue at stake is not only how to judge Confucian humanism can respond to modernist critique, but also to explore the possibility of critiquing these modernist presuppositions from Confucian insights in rethinking the the human. In the Twenty-first century, a broad humanist vision embodying both Heaven (the ultimate source of meaning of life) and earth (nature) is necessary. Human interconnectedness and mutual dependence have forged and wired all members of the human species into one economic and scientific world. In this new reality or virtual reality the need for universal ethics to nurture the awareness of co-existence is obvious. Governance so conceived cannot work without a strong sense of responsibility of the elite. The idea of rights is based on individuality. It is imperative that, in addition to dignity, independence, autonomy, and freedom of the individual, a sense of responsibility, especially, especially of the elite, is required. Since the quest for personal integration and authenticity has emerged as a crucial concern of the elite, can a functional equivalent of rights, especially economic and social rights, of the marginalized and underprivileged be derived from the responsibility of the elite? A society governed by responsible leaders committed to the wellbeing of the people is definitely more humane than a society dictated by the freedom, rationality and self-interest of the elite. To respect human rights of all people does not automatically lead to a polity that care for their security, livelihood, and self-development.

Confucians believe that Liberty without justice, rationality without sympathy, legality without civility, rights without responsibility, and individual dignity without social solidarity cannot bring about an enduring world order nurtured by a richly textured culture of peace. All five core values in the Confucian tradition—humanity, rightness, civility, wisdom, and trust are not merely local values but universal values rooted in the East Asian theory and practice.

Let's return to the *Analects*. Confucius' charisma lay in his magnetic power to draw a divergent group of energetic men to share his vision and mission to transform the world from within by tapping the mental and physical resources of each one of them through the art of self-cultivation.

It may not be farfetched to suggest that what Confucius with his disciples created was more than a community of the like-minded. It was a cultural movement that engendered a learning civilization based on the philosophy of self-cultivation. Confucian self-cultivation, far more complex than the personal quest for inner spirituality, is multi-dimensional. It involves not only the body and mind but also the total environment of one's existence. Confucius' own depiction of his spiritual journey is a case in point:

At fifteen, I set my heart upon learning. At thirty, I took my stand. At forty, I had no delusions. At fifty, I knew the Mandate of Heaven. At sixty, my ear was attuned. At seventy, I could follow the desires of my heart without transgressing any rule. [2:4]

This pithy autobiographic note has inspired numerous interpretations. Obviously, Confucius lived up to his self-understanding that he was primarily a learner: "In a hamlet of ten houses, you will certainly find people as loyal and faithful as I, but you will not find one man who loves learning as much as I do. "

Throughout his life Confucius persistently tried to improve himself. He fully acknowledged that sagehood or moral perfection was beyond his reach and that he learned without flagging and taught without growing weary. Indeed, he sought every opportunity to learn: "Put me in the company of any two people at random—they will invariably have something to teach me. I can take their qualities as a model and their defects as a warning. " He frankly admitted that he had to acquire the cumulative wisdom of the past to make him wise: "I was not born of knowledge, but, being fond of antiquity, I am quick to seek it. "

Furthermore, he was deeply concerned that he might lapse in his self-cultivation: "Failure to cultivate moral power, failure to explore what I have learned, incapacity to stand by what I know to be right, incapacity to reform what is not good—these are my worries. " In short, he was the sort of learner "who, in his enthusiasm, forgets to eat, in his joy forgets to worry, and who ignores the approach of old age. "

Underlying Confucian education is the firm conviction that human beings are multifaceted. The reductionist mode of thinking is not only simplistic but also misleading. We are not merely rational animals, tool users, or linguistic beings because we are at the same time and under all circumstances, aesthetic, social, ethical, and spiritual. We can fully realize ourselves only if we care for our body, heart, mind, soul, and spirit. As we move from the center of our existence to meet ever-expanding and increasingly complex relationships, we embody home, community, nation, world, earth, and the cosmos in our sensitivity and consciousness. This is why true humanity is relational and dialogical as well as psychological and spiritual. Education must take as its point of departure the concrete, living person here and now, a person embedded in primordial ties, especially the affective bonds within the family.

By implication, in a modernist perspective, those ties, such as race, language, gender, status, age, and faith, are also relevant here. In a way, each of us is fated to be that unique person, situated in a particular time and space, who has never existed before and will never appear again. Indeed, we are as different as our faces. Yet, Confucians also believe that the commonality and communicability of our heart-and-mind is such that our natures, in essence, are the same and that we can share our sight, sound, emotion, will, sense, taste, and experience. This confluence of difference and similarity enables us to become what we ought to be not by severing the primordial ties that have made it possible for us to be concrete and living persons. Rather, we transform them into vehicles for self-realization. That is the reason why, as learners, our lives are enriched by encountering a variety of humans who are individually unique and who communally share a great deal of information, knowledge, and wisdom. Furthermore, our feelings, desires, motivations, and aspirations are personal but not necessarily private. We often reveal our intensely personal concerns to relatives, friends, colleagues, associates, and even strangers. Their sympathetic understanding of our inner worlds is profoundly meaningful to us.

Any attempt to reduce the variety of living experience to merely the physical, mental, or spiritual is counter-productive. Human beings are by nature psychological, economical, social, political, historical, aesthetic, linguistic, cultural, and metaphysical animals. The full realization of the human potential is never one-sided. Confucius believed that an enabling environment for human flourishing is "harmony without uniformity. "A respect for difference is vitally important for the development of a wholesome community.

When Confucius was asked about the virtue of repaying maliciousness with kindness, he retorted: how will you repay kindness? Then he suggested, repay kindness with kindness and repay maliciousness with justice. The Confucian ethic implicit in this line of thinking is an ethic of situational appropriateness, political engagement, social responsibility and care. It covers the whole range of our lived world. I would like to draw a few implications from the humanistic vision in the *Analects*. These are not evident in the text. They are my interpretations and elaborations of the Confucian project.

My intention is make these observations in the Confucian spirit but they can also be judged to be misreadings. I would like to show that, as a source of inspiration, the fruitful ambiguities in the *Analects* offer rich food for thought.

1. The idea of the "continuity of being." In this view the human is connected with all modalities of being: minerals, plants, and animals. If we probe deeply to find some linkages, the human is part of a continuum. But the uniqueness of being human is qualitatively different from all other modalities of being. The defining characteristics of the human are not reducible to any of the properties that have become constitutive parts of the human condition. For example, Xunzi observed:

Fire and water possess energy but are without life. Grass and treeshave life but no consciousness and feeling. Birds and beasts have consciousness and feeling but no sense of rightness. The human possesses energy, life, consciousness, and feeling, and in addition, a sense of rightness.

This idea of the human is predicated on two principles: interconnectedness and uniqueness. In short, the distinctiveness of the human is based not on separation but connection. The reason is that although an emergent property is not reducible to its constitutive parts, genetically and structurally it is always intertwined with all the elements that have contributed to the particular form of its existence.

2. Creationism or evolutionism may make a profoundly significant difference in understanding the origins of human nature, but for the Confucians, it is the structure of the human here and now rather than the genetic reasons that have made it, so that is the focus of their attention. The uniqueness of the human, whether created or evolved, is intimately connected with Heaven, Earth, and the myriad things. In other words, the human body is a microcosm of the cosmos. Its wellbeing is intimately united with the macrocosmic ecology.

3. The primary concern of human flourishing is to discover and recover the rich resources for self-knowledge, especially those that seem not to have been derived from social conditioning. We should try to understand and

appreciate the depth and breadth of the innate capacities possessed by all humans. Admittedly this is Mencius' rather than Xunzi's position, but it is noteworthy that even for Xunzi, although virtues will have to be internalized, a vitally important, indeed the most significant inherent quality of the human mind, is intelligence.

4. The innate capacity for the human to develop a moral sense or the learned capacity to internalize virtues is part of a much more elaborate and complicated picture. It is unlikely that reductionist definitions, such as the human being as a rational animal, tool user, or endowed with linguistic ability, will capture the full measure of the way of being human. Human beings are by nature, aesthetic, social, political, historical, and cosmological beings. They become fully human by bringing to fruition all dimensions that constitute concrete and living persons here and now.

5. Although ethics deals with the relationship between individuality and sociality, morality, as Confucians understand it, must be conceived in cosmological as well as anthropological terms. The full manifestation of humanity must transcend anthropocentrism. The tripartite division of aesthetics, ethics, and religion under the influence of Kierkegaard must be perceived in a new configuration. To use the same vocabulary to illustrate the point: feelings, such as commiseration, sympathy, or compassion, are the basis of morality. Aesthetics is not opposed to ethics. Ethics is not only rule-governed. It is also a manifestation of harmonized emotions. Religion does not require "a leap of faith." It is the result of the necessity of the expansion of the ethical realm. If ethics does not raise the question of ultimate concern, it falls short of its full expression.

6. The "anthropocosmic" idea is predicated on a holistic and integrated humanism, substantially different from secular humanism. Morality, the way to learn to be human, must be rooted in nature and extended to Heaven.

7. Heaven features prominently in this discourse. Morality as an innate quality is inconceivable without constant reference to Heaven. Heaven is creativity in itself, but the advent of the human hasmade a difference. The

human as a co-creator imitates but also participates in Heaven's cosmic transformation.

8. Heaven cannot be conceived merely in naturalistic terms. As the Heavenly Way is encoded in human nature, what the human does affects Heaven as well. Morality conceived as a defining characteristic of learning to be human must be extended beyond individuality and sociality to embody a larger universe.

This " anthropocosmic " vision presupposes a unity between anthropological and cosmological perceptions on the human condition. In the language of the *Book of Change*, the cosmos is never a static structure but rather it is a dynamic process. In its constant unfolding, it always generates new realities by creatively transforming the existing order.

Learning to be human in the cosmic sense is to learn to emulate Heaven's creativity which is open, dynamic, transformative, and unceasing. Whether we came into being by the mysterious design of a transcendent reality or through a persistent evolutionary process, we find an intimate niche in the cosmos as our ultimate source and meaning of life.

This sense of wholeness and connectedness is captured by the opening lines of the so-called *Western Inscription* by Zhang Zai, an eleventh century Confucian thinker:

> Heaven is my father and Earth is my mother, and even such a small being as I finds an intimate place in their midst. Therefore, that which fills the universe I regard as my body and that which directs the universe I regard as my nature. All people are my brothers and sisters, and all things are my companions.

Finally, a short concluding remark: Economic globalization is characterized by instrumental rationality, science, technology (especially information and communications technologies), professionalism, materialism, liberalization, technocratic management, legitimization of desires, and individual choice. The "economic man" is a rational animal conscious of his self-interest, motivated to increase his wealth, power, and influence by maximizing his profit in a relatively free market adjudicated by the law. He embodies a host of modernistic values, such as freedom, rationality, rights consciousness, work ethic, knowledge, technical competence, cognitive intelligence, legality, and motivation. Yet, other essential values requisite for social solidarity are either relegated to the background or are totally ignored, notably justice, sympathy, responsibility, civility, and ethical intelligence.

In a world characterized by materialistic and egocentric tendencies, the thirst for spiritual gratification often takes the form of fundamentalist extremism and exclusive particularism. Confucian humanism, as expressed in the *Analects*, is a balanced and open approach to the purpose of life. It offers a spiritual exercise essential for self-knowledge and it is a primordial wisdom that deserves our understanding and appreciation. Thank you for listening!

Confucian Co-creative Ethics:
Self and Family

Haiming Wen

(School of Philosophy, Renmin University of China)

Introduction

Considering Chinese accounts of subjectivity/selfhood to be either collectivist or relational is a popular view in western scholarship, and it is true that Confucius was most concerned with relationships. [1] This kind of general account of the Confucian self requires careful examination. In recent years, Chinese ethics has attracted global attention as research on moral philosophy rises to the height of an "ethics boom" in philosophy and politics. [2] Confucian self-cultivation has long been one of the central topics in Western scholarship concerning Chinese ethics. As Wing-tsit Chan points out, the Confucians were the first in ancient China to propagate the doctrine of the fulfillment of

---

[1] *Individual Self, Relational Self, Collective Self*, ed. by Constantine Sedikides and Marilynn B. Brewer, Psychology Press, 2001, p. 270. Karyn L. Lai, regards a dynamic and realistic picture of the self as the centre of ethical decisions in Chinese philosophy. See Lai, *An Introduction to Chinese Philosophy*, Cambridge University Press, 2008, p. 273.

[2] Karl-Heinz Pohl, "Introduction: Chinese Ethics in a Global Context," in *Chinese Ethics in a Global Context: Moral Bases of Contemporary Societies*, edited by Karl-Heinz Pohl and Anselm W. Muller, Leiden, Boston: Brill, 2002.

human nature. [1] However, with the exception of research on the circles of self-expansion in the *Great Learning*, [2] little scholarship has been done on how Confucians expand their selves to the larger world in which they live.

This article begins with the major textual resources in the Confucian tradition and then compares this idea of self-expansion with that of the Deweyan self and community. Confucian ethics has often been misread as a communal or communitarian ethics, especially when contrasted with western theories of individual and state. However, it is very important to start with the Confucian self and individual[3] and examine how a Confucian project could be carried out through one's lived experience. Human beings deal with ordinary affairs of the day: they relate to others and form families, communities, and societies. This demonstrates the fundamental character of the contextually creative self, and is representative of the way one person creates via relations with others; the self and the other are co-creative. [4]

Confucian ethics has long beenconsidered as either deontic ethics, [5]

---

[1]   Wing-Tsit Chan, "The Individual in Chinese Religions, " in *The Status of the Individual in East and West*, ed. by Charles A. Moore, Honolulu: University of Hawaii Press, 1968, p. 185.

[2]   Tu Wei-ming mentiones this expanding circle in the *Great Learning* many times in his writings and speeches. For example, Tu Wei-ming, "Heart, Human Nature, and Feeling: Implications for the Neo-Confucian Idea of Civil Society, " Reischauer Lecture, Harvard University. Paper presented at the Ethikon Conference, Redondo Beach, CA, July 10-12, 1998, p. 27.

[3]   As Hsieh Yu-wei points out, " Confucian ethics regarded individuals as roots, and communities as leaves-or individual as foundations and communities as roofs. " See Shieh, "The Status of the Individual in Chinese Ethics, " in *The Status of the Individual in East and West*, ed. by Charles A. Moore, Honolulu: University of Hawaii Press, 1968, p. 116.

[4]   Many scholars have noticed that the Confucian self is relational to others and its context. For example, Wm. Theodore de Bary comments that the Confucian person defines one's "self" in relation to others, and constructs a web of reciprocal obligations or moral relations in which one finds oneself and defines oneself. See de Bary, *Learning for One's Self, Essays on the Individual in Neo-Confucian Thought*, New York: Columbia University Press, 1991, p. 3.

[5]   Li Ruiquan considers Confucian ethics as similar to Kantian "rule deontology" because for both of them, being moral is not judged by calculation of the effect of action, but with regard to the public mind, being freed from selfish desires, as the right path for communal good. See Li, *Confucian Life Ethics*, E' hu Press, 1999, pp. 16-29. Much research has been done on the comparison of Confucian ethics and John Rawls "theory of justice. "

virtue or role ethics①. However, I argue that Confucian ethics is better regarded as co-creative ethics②, which can be rooted in a group of key terms available to the Chinese philosophical vocabulary that allow for the development of a robust theory of self and other. Analysis of these terms is especially fruitful when they are reinterpreted through the ethics of John Dewey. ③ In other words, from the perspective of how a self creates and is created through family or communual relationships, Confucian co-creative ethics can be structured as self-other relationality. ④ In comparing them with Deweyan arguments about the self, Confucian ideal selves—sages—are strongly based on a co-creative sense of relationships. ⑤

Experience: Confucian and Pragmatism

For Deweyan ethics, people are mutually penetrating and continuous with each other and their environments. It is through everyday interactions

---

① See Yu Jiyuan, *The Ethics of Confucius and Aristotle: Mirrors of Virtues*, New York/London: Routledge, 2007. Similarly, some scholars like Gregor Paul argue that *from a Chinese perspective and in a Chinese manner*, Chinese philosophy provides all the doctrines and arguments one needs to argue for the realization of universally valid ethical norms. See Paul, "Global Ethics and Chinese Resources" in *Chinese Ethics in a Global Context: Moral Bases of Contemporary Societies*, edited by Karl-Heinz Pohl and Anselm W. Muller, Leiden, Boston: Brill, 2002, p. 87. As for role ethics, please refer to Roger T. Ames, *Confucian Role Ethics: A Vocabulary*, University of Hawaii Press, forthcoming.

② Tu Wei-ming realizes that there is a creative dimension between *ren* and *li*. See "The Creative Tension between Ren and Li, " in *Philosophy East and West*, XVII: 1-2 (January-April 1968) , 29-39.

③ As Abraham Edel points out, Dewey's emphasis on change is a methodological reorientation of ethical theory. See "Pragmatic Tests and Ethical Insights, " in Edel, *In Search of the Ethical: Moral Theory in Twentieth Century America*, vol. 5, New Brunswick and London: Transaction Publishers, 1993, p. 27.

④ On-Cho Ng has summarized the scores of scholars such as Tu Wei-ming, Wm. Theodore de Bary, Chung-ying Cheng, Roger Ames, and Henry Rosemont, who have claimed that the Confucian self is a "relational self" (Rosemont, 1998, 54-66; Tu, 1985, 7-16, de Bary, 1991, 1 – 41, Cheng, 1989, 167 – 208, and Ames, 1994, 187 – 212). See Ng, "The Confucian Ethics of Being and Non-Being, " in *Deconstruction and the Ethical in Asian Thought*, ed. by Youru Wang, London and New York: Routledge, 2007, p. 109.

⑤ Tu Wei-ming regards Confucian self-cultivation as a process of self transformation which is also a communal activity. See Tu, "Ultimate Self-transformation as a Communal Act: Comments on Models of Self-Cultivation, " in *Journal of Chinese Philosophy*, Vol. 6,1979, pp. 237 – 246.

and communications that people derive their constitutive identities. Confucian ethics also develops a notion of relationality, in which the ideal person is the sage who can handle with virtuosity her co-creative relationships. The sages are not transcendent, but rather are considered exceptional people who live in ordinary circumstances. The exemplary persons (*junzi*) are "exemplary" not because they transcend this world, but because they are examples or models for others to follow in the present. This reveals how the notion of self can emerge from relational creativity in a communicating community. Thus, Confucian ethics should be considered as co-creative ethics since the co-creative extension of relationality is helpful in constituting human selves based on a co-arising sense self and family, society and community.

Deweyinfuses new meanings into the common word "experience" throughout his writings. ① By parsing the word "*jingyan* 经验 ," the Chinese counterpart of experience, we can expand to other related terms that justify this new perspective of the co-creative nature of the Confucian self and other. What is the Confucian vocabulary that expresses the notion of "co-creativity?" The Chinese term for experience is *jingyan*, where the original meaning of *jing* 经 means to "go through" or "pass. " It also stands for the vertical lines in woven textiles, and denotes a warp in the *Shuowen Lexicon*. The common meaning of *yan* 验 is to "examine, check, test. " In other words, *jingyan* means a particular path or course (*jing* 径) that one chooses to go through, and to make the subject of one's examination. The English word "experience" originally means "to try, " implying that people partake of events personally, living through events via this participation.

The Confucian co-creative nature of self and other can be elaborated

---

① For example, Joseph Grange starts his project of comparing John Dewey and Confucius by first discussing Dewey's novel insight into "experience". See Grange, *John Dewey, Confucius and Global Philosophy*, Sate University of New York Press, 2004, p. 1.

upon through a comparison with William James and John Dewey's notion of experience. ① In *A World of Pure Experience*, James offers a threefold categorization of what he calls the cognitive relation, or the relation between the knower and the known. In James's view, epistemology is to know a *relationality* subsumed under the factual thesis of his radical empiricism. James also holds that experience is relational, as he writes in 1904: "The relations that connect experiences must themselves be experienced relations, and any kind of relation experienced must be accounted as 'real' as anything else in the system." ② In short, in James's pragmatic theory, the static relation of "correspondence" between our minds and reality is converted into a rich and active commerce between our particular thoughts and the greater universe.

James's idea that pure experience is more original than mind and matter resonates with the Deweyan idea of experience as "the manifestation of interactions of organism and environment." ③ For Dewey, experience happens in continual interactions: "The organism is a part of the natural world; its interactions with it are genuine additive phenomena." ④ Hence, James's and Dewey's original constitutive field of experience is the interaction of a reflexive, mutually creative field. Experience "arising out of the state of tension" is a constitutive field of creativity. Only the world that functions and enters into one's experience can be called an "environment." Through the interactive *environment* one's "*experience*" is active, rhythmic, and

---

① Joseph Grange starts his comparison between John Dewey and Confucius by discussing the meaning of Deweyan experience, which for him bears novel insights such as "happens within a context or situation," "every experience is individual," "doing and undergoing," "medium within which we act," "experience is always cadenced," "builds upon itself," "cumulative" etc. See Grange, *John Dewey, Confucius, and Global Philosophy*, State University of New York, 2004, p. 1 – 15.

② James, William (1912). *Essays in Radical Empiricism (ERE)*, New York: Longmans, Green and Co. Reprinted in Lincoln and London: University of Nebraska Press, 1996, 22.

③ Schilpp Paul Arthur, ed. (1939). *The Philosophy of John Dewey. The Library of Living Philosophers, Vol. I.* Evanston IL: Northwestern University, 531.

④ LW4.

consummatory. This *"experience"* is lively and creative because an organism is fully continuous with its environment and participates in each moment. Interaction as a reflexive process can be viewed from both active and passive perspectives: for Dewey, doing and undergoing are two sides of an experiential continuum. Hence, Deweyan experience is reflexive and happens prior to any distinction between subject and object.

The Confucian Co-creative Nature of Self

Acomparison between Confucian relationality and Deweyan social philosophy reveals that Confucius and Dewey's philosophies share a comparable understanding of human natural tendencies. [1] The Confucian sense of self and other is expressed through a series of terms that contain the connotation of co-creativity. In the following discussions, the Chinese terms that contain the meaning of "being together with each other" or "mutual association," such as *he* 合, *yu* 与, *tong* 同, *tong* 通, *he* 和, *cheng* 成, *ren* 仁, etc. are analyzed.

He 合: Confucian cosmology is characterized by the continuity of *tian* and human making (*tianren heyi* 天人合一). In the phase *tianren heyi*, the word *he* 合 indicates a continuity. [2] The original meaning of *he* 合 is "to close" or "to shut," but later it comes to mean "together" and "unite." Thus, the expression *heyi* 合一 means to "be harmonious," not in the sense of static oneness, but in the sense of continual creative togetherness.

Tong 同: This is a Chinese term that is very close to *he* 合, which literally means "to be alike, to be the same, to have in common, to be together." Its original meaning in the *Shuowen Lexicon* is "to converge." In

---

[1]   Joseph Grange states that Dewey and Confucius agree that human beings are primarily social. See Grange, *John Dewey, Confucius, and Global Philosophy*, State University of New York, 2004, p. 15.

[2]   According to Donald J. Munro, it is highly probable for both Confucian and Daoist thought the belief of the union of self and other stems from the early notion that certain men are able to act as "counterpart to heaven (*pei tian*)." See Munro, *The Concept of Man in Early China*, Stanford, California: Stanford University Press, 1969, p. 155.

the *Mozi*, *tong* 同 is associated with "combination" (*he* 合) and "similarity" (*lei* 类) . Therefore, *tong* acquires the meaning of duplicating and accumulating. Also, Hexagram # 13 *tongren* 同人 in *The Book of Changes* is a hexagram that is composed of *tian* and fire, indicating the relationship between self and others should be "affinity," and the related commentary states that all things and events return to the same place though traveling on different roads.

Tong 通: Phonetically similar to *tong* 同, the original meaning of *tong* 通 is "to open; through; to penetrate." In the *Shuowen Lexicon* it is defined as penetrating or reaching (*da* 达), and in the *Analects* it means "getting the point across." The *Book of Changes* characterizes it as coming and going without stopping; also, it means to carry out a practice smoothly. The hexagram #29 *Kan* 坎 is portrayed as penetrating in *shuogua*. *Tong* 通 can thus be understood to mean that interacting with people is to communicate with them effectively. This implies that people's will can "interpenetrate" and be "agreeable with one another," so *tong* 通 in different situations can be correlated with being receptive (*shou* 受), following (*sui* 随), and agreeing with (*cong* 从) in Hexagram #31 *Xian* 咸 .

Peng 朋: The famous first line of the *Analects* indicates that having friends coming from distant quarters should be a source of enjoyment[1] because this is a demonstration that one attracts friends through one's excellence (*de* 德).[2] *De* in this sense is an active "aggregating (*de* 得)" situation involving communication among friends. *De* is manifest through the excellence that is happening and extending one's relations. According to Zhu Xi, *peng* 朋 means "the same in kind." Its classic meaning is "classmate," as Hexagram #58 *dui* 兑 states: "Friends should discuss and help each other." According to Kong Yingda's commentary on this line, "*peng* 朋 is a

---

①   Ames, Roger T. and Henry Rosemont, Jr. , trans. (1998). *The Analects of Confucius: A Philosophical Translation* (*Analects*). New York: Ballantine Books, 1. 1.

②   *Analects* 4. 25.

classmate studying under the same door; and *you* 友 is a friend sharing the same purposes. " Now, people tend to interpret *peng* by reference to the modern meaning of *pengyou* 朋友 that normally means "friend. "

Ren 仁: In Confucian ethics, humanity/benevolence (*ren*) is a co-creative relationship between self and other. The Confucian notion of *ren* 仁 is constituted by "person" and the number "two" and connotes two people being together, so *ren* can be interpreted as a kind of conduct open to multiple people who are co-creative to one another. In this sense, Confucian *ren* is formative of self-other relationality. The other common Confucian ideas such as "appropriateness" (*yi*) , "ritual" (*li*) , "wisdom" (*zhi*) , and "living up to one's words" (*xin*) all carry the sense of making one's relationships with others bloom. According to Li Zehou, Confucius uses *ren* to formulate his understanding of mind-heart (*xin*), which he indicates is a foundation for Confucian "cultural-psychological formation. "[1]

The Confucian Co-creative Nature of Family Relationships

The Confucian sense of family is akin to the idea that everyone in the world is an extension of oneself, so the family covers and extends to all under heaven. [2] Zhang Zai points this out in his *Western Inscription* (*ximing* 西铭), in which he coins the term *minbao wuyu* 民胞物与, which is short for "treating all your people as one's family" and "being together with all things that are happening. "[3] From this point of view, an analysis of *yu* 与 and related terms will help us understand more clearly the Confucian idea of "being together with. "

Yu 与: *Yu* means "and, association, participation, to get along with, to

---

[1] See Li, Zehou (1998). 论语今读 [Reading The Analects Today]. Hefei: Anhui Art Press, 29 – 30.

[2] Fei Xiaotong discusses how the Confucian self-cultivation project is actualized and systematic in common Chinese people's life like the expansion of a wave on the surface of a lake. See Fei, *Countryside China* (*Xiangtu Zhongguo*), Beijing: Peking University Press, 1998, p. 27.

[3] "民吾同胞,物吾与也. " Zhang, Zai (1978). 张载集 [The Whole Collection of Zhang Zai], Zhonghua Shuju 中华书局, "Ximing 西铭".

take part in, with and so on. " The original meaning of *yu* derives from the action of giving a spoon to others, which is also associated with "to raise together with. " Thus, it is extended to mean "being together with" and "giving to friends. " In the *Shuowen*, friends being together are defined as a "fellowship. " *Yu* has the meaning of "to get along with; to be friendly with" in *Zhuangzi*. ① In *Analects* 17. 1, it says: "The days and months are passing; the years will not wait for us. "② Here, *yu* is translated as "wait," but it can be interpreted as "together" in the cosmological meaning of being together with time.

In *Analects* 18. 6, Confucius states, "We cannot run with the birds and beasts. Am I not one among the people of this world? If not them, with whom should I associate? If the way (*dao*) prevailed in the world, I wouldn't need to change it. "③ Here, both *yu* 与 and *tong* 同 have the meaning to "be together with. " *Yu* 与 is a verb which means "to participate" or "to be involved in," while *tong* 同 is "inside" and "already in. " Here, Confucius refuses to be a member of a group of which he does approve. Specifically, he means that he refuses to join those groups of people who would not pursue *dao* as assiduously as he does.

Being a verb denoting to get involved in a group, *yu* 与 also means "resonance" in Hexagram #61, *zhongfu* 中孚: "The crane is singing in the shade of the tree, its baby crane is resonating with it. I have good wine. I will share with you. " Here, *yu* 与 means "to share with you" because of resonance (*he* 和). The sentence following this line in the "Great Appendix" cites Confucius' words: "The exemplary person sits in his room; his honest and sincere words will get responses from a thousand miles away, never mind from those close by. " People associate with one another because of a degree of resonance between them.

---

① "孰能相与无相与。" 释文:"犹亲也。" *Zhuangzi* 6, "Dazhongshi 大宗师 . " *Zhuangzi* 庄子 . *A Concordance to Chuang Tzu* (1956). *Harvard-Yenching Institute Sinological Index Series: Supplement no.* 20. Cambridge, MA: Harvard University Press.

② *Analects* 17. 1.

③ *Analects* 18. 6.

Zhi 至: For Confucius, both *ming* 命 and *ren* 仁 are constitutive terms whose meanings are continuously developing and co-creative with the different contexts in which Confucius and his disciples are situated. In *Analects* 9. 1, it says, "The Master only rarely spoke about personal advantage, but he advocated addressing the propensity of circumstance (*ming*) and authoritative co-humanity (*ren*) . "① Confucius himself clearly claims that *ren* is not something concrete or far away, but something in the making that can be constituted by oneself right away: "No sooner do I seek it than it has arrived. "② The word *zhi* 至 here means to "reach" and "arriving at" which means our thoughts and feelings always participate in the process of becoming one together in the field of co-humanity (*ren*) .

He 和: *He* is defined as being "harmonious, coordinated" in the *Shuowen*. *Analects* 13. 23 says: "Exemplary persons (*junzi*) seek harmony not sameness; petty persons, then, are the opposite. " *He* indicates the Confucian way of understanding individuality, which is to acknowledge the unique existence of each particular; rather than disciplining them into uniformity, it is to harmonize their diversity. ③ Thus, the exemplary person seeks and values the whole context, while the petty person seeks sameness (*tong*) and values only his or her unique situation, showing no respect for the experience of others. Metaphorically, Confucius compares the character of exemplary people to wind, and the character of petty people to grass. ④ The wind reveals the ethical context as a whole, penetrating to every corner of the world, while the grass only bends according the wind overhead. Thus, the context of the grass includes merely what is nearby. Exemplary persons extend themselves to

---

① Li Zehou reads *yu* 与 as "to be in agreement with, to be happy with, " which is consistent with the idea that 与 is actually a word that suggests the constituting of one within one's field of relations.

② *Analects* 7. 30.

③ As Thome H. Fang points out, the Confucian individual aims to participate in the cosmic creation through the process of transformation and become a co-creator with heaven-and-earth. See his "The World and the individual in Chinese metaphysics, " in *The Status of the Individual in East and West*, ed. by Charles A. Moore, Honolulu: University of Hawaii Press, 1968, p. 26.

④ *Analects* 12. 19.

the context as a whole and understand the force of circumstance and the words of previous sages that petty persons totally disregard, suggesting that petty persons are limited by their particular situations. ①

Cheng 成: Basically, exemplary persons can grow within their context, while petty person are confined to their own world and cannot grow. The word that denotes growth is *cheng* 成, which literally means to become fully grown, or to succeed. The meaning of *cheng* in the *Shuowen* is to "complete, accomplish; succeed." The *Analects* 14.12 says: "Zilu inquired about consummate persons." Here, *chengren* 成人 refers to an integrated, complete person. ② *Cheng* as a verb indicates the importance of context in one's accomplishment. For example, in *Analects* 12.16, Confucius says: "The exemplary person (*junzi*) helps to bring out the best in others, but does not help to bring out the worst." ③ Zengzi indicates that friends should communicate through *wen* (文) (refinement, scholarships); and through this kind of scholarship one can foster authoritative co-humanity based on friendship with others. ④

An(安): To be peaceful in relationships in entailed by the term *an* 安, which originally means "safe, set, peaceful, tranquil, satisfaction." When using it as a verb it means bringing peace to others. *Analects* 14.42 says: "They cultivate themselves by bringing accord to their peers." ⑤ Here, *an* 安 is interpreted as "bringing accord to," which reveals the Confucian notion that one can bring harmony to others by harmonizing one's own mind. In *The Book of Changes*, it is said that human beings can bring peace to others when there is a good understanding about relationships with others. Hence it is very

---

①   *Analects* 16.8.

②   Confucian rationale of human greatness is to develop from the natural capacity to the ideal perfection. See Thome H. Fang, "The World and the individual in Chinese metaphysics," in *The Status of the Individual in East and West*, ed. by Charles A. Moore, Honolulu: University of Hawaii Press, 1968, p. 28.

③   *Analects* 12.16.

④   *Analects* 12.24.

⑤   *Analects* 14.42.

reasonable for *The Book of Changes* to claim in this Confucian way, "before reaching for help, make sure your relationship with others is peaceful."

Shu(恕): For Confucius, the way to achieve harmonious relationships is through *shu*(恕): "do not impose on others what you yourself do not want." This sentence has been taken as analogous to the Golden Rule and analyzed extensively from different angles. *Shu* usually means to "excuse someone, forgive." It actually comes from *ren* 仁, defined as "kind-heartedness" in *Shuowen. Shu* (恕) is a way of handling relationships such that whatever one does, one bears in mind the concerns of others. Thus, as "putting oneself in the others' place"[1] it means caring for others in a way that recognizes the other as a similar human being, co-creative with oneself in the same context of the world. Tu Wei-ming writes, "The Confucian Golden Rule, ' Do not do unto others what you would not want others to unto you' does not simply mean that one should be considerate to others; it also means that one must be honest with oneself."[2] In what you think, feel, and do, you should be aware that others are able to be affected just as you are, and you too share in the effects of your impact on others. For Confucius, knowing others is the beginning of being together with others: "Don't worry about not being acknowledged by others; worry about failing to acknowledge them."[3]

Confucius's statements display his belief that human beings are embedded in a dynamic pattern of ongoing relationships with others. Confucius himself needed company on his journey of pursuing *dao*. At times we can tell that Confucius had a strong urge to find someone who could share his goal. As *Analects* 13. 21 records, "The Master said, ' If one cannot find the company of temperate colleagues, one has no choice but to turn to the more rash and the more timid. ' "[4] Though Confucius constantly evaluates his

---

①   *Analects* 4. 15.

②   Tu, Wei-ming (1985). *Confucian Thought: Selfhood as Creative Transformation.* Albany: State University of New York Press, 56.

③   *Analects* 1. 15.

④   *Analects* 13. 21.

followers in the *Analects*, he could not find a satisfactory peer. One reason might be Confucius himself, who always felt lonely because no one could share the *dao* in which he participated. He did consider one of his disciples, Yan Yuan, to be a good candidate to succeed him in his teachings, but Yan Yuan most regrettably died young. ①

The way to understand that one's intentions are always correlated with others is to realize oneself and to rid oneself of "speculation, demands for certainty, inflexibility, and self-absorption. "② Such a posture of one's person opens up one's intentions and allows one to communicate freely with things that are happening. This "co-creating with others" as the basic meaning of *ren* contains the original creative inspiration for Confucian thought about self and other.

Deweyan Self As Together with Others

Relatively few Western philosophers mention family. When they do, however, as in Aristotle and Hegel, their views are based upon the notion of the autonomous individual. The classical liberal concept of the individual joining a community③ is difficult to find in the Confucian tradition, because Confucian philosophers think that one belongs to a family or a state in the first place, so the relationship among group members is more important than individual identity. In the Confucian tradition, the world of a baby starts from its familial relationships. The relationship between a baby and its family members is an extending phenomenon of "living creativity. "

Although Dewey does not have the Confucian focus on family, for him, the self is "essentially social, being constituted not by isolated capacity, but

---

①   *Analects* 6. 3.

②   *Analects* 9. 4.

③   Liberal myth narrates the modernization of western culture in terms of liberation of individuals from rigid primordial loyalties, represented by the feudal family system buttressed by dogmatic religious institutions. See Richard Madsen, "Ethics and the Family: China/West, " in *Chinese Ethics in a Global Context: Moral Bases of Contemporary Societies*, edited by Karl-Heinz Pohl and Anselm W. Muller, Leiden, Boston: Brill, 2002, p. 280.

by capacity acting in response to the needs of an environment-an environment which, when taken in its fullness, is a community of persons. "① Thus, Dewey understands human groups as organizational, whether that group is the family or the state, and reconstructs the term "individual" to mean the active participation of individuals within a community, wherein shared, consummated experiences evolve. For him, the identity of an individual is formed through communication with the community. ② This consummation reaches a level of complexity and dynamism with full communication, and opens opportunities for the full growth of each individual. At the same time, "a progressive society counts individual variations as precious since it finds in them the means of its own growth. "③

According to Dewey, the concept of society is not one dimensional: "There is no single thing denominated ' society'; there are many societies, many forms of association. "④ The Deweyan view of society is "individuals-in-their-relations" in which "individuals develop not in a remote entity called ' society' at large but in connection *with one another*. "⑤ In this sense, society is closer to the notion of community which is "a sharing whereby the meanings are enhanced, deepened and solidified in the sense of communion. "⑥ Dewey considers communication as the way in which people who live in community come to possess things in common, such as aims, beliefs, aspirations, knowledge. ⑦

---

①　EW3: 335.

②　As John Rawls points out, in a democratic society, it is a political convention to appeal to the common good, but it is not necessary for the well-intention policy to benefit the least advantaged class. So some policies aim at justice but might not fulfill its goal. See John Rawls, "Distributive Justice, " in *John Rawls: Collected Papers*, ed. by Samual Freeman, Cambridge, Massachusetts & London, England: Harvard University Press, 1999, p. 153.

③　MW9: 315.

④　LW7: 324.

⑤　LW8: 80.

⑥　LW1: 159.

⑦　MW9: 7.

Confucian Selves Becoming Moral Through the Co-Creativity of Family Relations

Inthe Confucian classics, the family is the basic structure of human existence. The Confucian concept of family follows the natural order that invokes the image of a human society whose natural endowment is from *tian* (天 the heavens) or ancient ancestors. ① The Confucian sense of family concerns human beings not only in the private sense of family, but also in public sense of community. In the ancient oracle bones, the word *jia* (家) refers to a pig in one's house. Its original meaning is "home; domicile; dwelling place" in the *Shuowen Lexicon*. In *The Book of Changes*, the Hexagram #37 Family (家人) is composed of wind and fire, indicating that family is about affairs within the walls of the home. *The Book of Changes* also connects family with state in the sense that succeeding in a state begins with sustaining a family. In addition, *Shijing* defines family according to what is inside a door. More specifically, the *Book of Rituals* (*Liji*) reveals that family comes after a husband and a wife have been together.

Throughout history, most Confucian teachings have been concerned with how to become amorally good person in one's own family and community. These teachings have been used to persuade common people to remain in their social status, which is the extention of family status. In a family, the son becomes the father when he establishes his own family, but in a society, common people are rarely able to become rulers. Since the Han Dynasty, Confucian social theories have been famous for their insistence on the "three Guidelines (*san'gang* 三纲)," which were regarded as permanent principles for ruling society and making sure that all members of the family and society play their roles properly. In these circumstances, the co-creative relations between self and other are generally confined to family members. Put in

---

① Confucius does not think that people who walk different paths should plan and do things together. Basically, those people do not have a common shared future shouldn't associate. As he states, "People who have chosen different ways (*dao*) cannot make plans together." See *Analects* 15. 40.

another way, the Confucian sense of otherness does not go much outside family relationships. Confucian moral cultivation does not include co-creating with enemies or strangers. In other words, persons grow exclusively through family relationships.

In theDeweyan fashion, people prefer to live in a constantly creative society, and they are a dynamic part of societal integrity. When the society lacks freedom and the principle of society hurts individuals, then "an identity crisis is a social crisis. "[1] The Confucian view about the relationship between one's identity and community is built on the idea that a person derives her individuality first through being a family member, and then through the proper performance of social roles. According to Kwong-loi Shun, Confucian thinkers advocate the ideal that people are shaped by virtue of the social positions they occupy, or in recurring social interactions, as well as through the embodiment of certain attitudes appropriate to such behavior. Confucian self-cultivation also involves the cultivation of desirable qualities within various social contexts. It is through participating in this social order and letting oneself be shaped by it that one becomes fully human. [2]

Confucius argues that exemplary persons and sages—those who are fully human—can save the world from moral decay. Sages, by virtue of their penetrating insight into the creativity of heaven and earth, have realized and embodied their wisdom in morality. Confucius's sense of morality "is a continuing process, not a fixed achievement. "[3] Moral growth is an "ever-enduring process of perfecting, maturing, refining" our habits. [4]

---

[1] Solomon (1999). This is different from self-determining freedom as Rousseau proposes, which demands a self to break from all external impositions and decide for oneself alone. See Charles Taylor, *The Ethics of Authenticity*, Cambridge, Massachusetts and London, England: Harvard University Press, 1992, p. 27.

[2] Kwong-loi Shun, "The Person in Confucian Thought," in *Confucian Ethics: A Comparative Study of Self, Autonomy, and Community*, ed. by Kwong-loi Shun and David B. Wong, Cambridge University Press, 204, p. 140.

[3] MW14: 194.

[4] MW12: 181.

From this perspective, for Dewey, "The bad man is the man who no matter how good he*has* been is beginning to deteriorate, to grow less good; the good man is the man who no matter how morally unworthy he *has* been is moving to become better. "① Comparably, the distinction between *junzi* and *xiaoren* is one of the distinguishing features of Confucianism. However, as Confucius indicates in the *Analects*, *junzi* as exemplary persons and *xiaoren* as petty persons represent extreme categories rather than the common "citizen" as some contemporary scholars suggest. Under this trend, too little attention has been paid to the identity of the majority, those referred to as "*zhongren* 中人", "*min* 民"or "*shuren* 庶人" in the Confucian classics.

Confuciusbelieves that people share their lives with the social environments around them, through which people can affect the state. Dewey prefers people to participate in society as a focus for expression. For both of them, being alive is a continuing process and an ongoing extension of relating to society: "The facts that constrain personal identity are neither given nor determined by the subject. They are a matter of social construal, dependent upon the context as well as the (often malevolent) motives of others. "② In this process we come and go, and accomplish what we aspire to. For example, Dewey's "philosophical care of the self seems to be expressed so completely in care for the community. "③ This community, using Confucian terms, starts from family and extends from there to the state and "all under heaven (*tianxia*). "

Another way of interpreting the Confucian doctrine of family isthrough its hierarchical structure: Confucius emphasizes social communication between the ruler and the common people, while Dewey advocates a communicating community. Under this interpretation, Confucius identifies not the source of power and how common people can become rulers, but the enculturation

---

① MW12: 180-1.

② Ibid. 182.

③ Shusterman (1997): 54.

(*wenhua* 文化) of human relationships. Specifically, the ritual system is a process of enculturation. Also, the relations of filial piety (*xiao* 孝) and brotherhood (*ti* 悌) are turned into social foundations. In this way, generations of Confucians have focused on how to become human beings, which strongly implies that playing a positive role inside one's family leads to an important social status outside the family.

From theConfucian social perspective, self-cultivation is the process of expanding the self to include one's family and one's state. Confucianism advocates the achievement of individuality through relationships and contextual creativity. However, Confucian forms of association, especially family and clan, may become oppressive. In response to such problems, Confucian "individuals" cultivate their continuity with "society" and try to be harmonious with it. ①

Deweyan Communicating community

The Deweyan idea of continuity between people and society starts from his idea that social institutions are "means of *creating* individuals. "② Human nature is developed only when people share things in common, such as families, industrial companies, governments, churches, and scientific associations. ③ Thus, humans create through their being-together in groups, and develop their freedom in a co-creative society. In Dewey's words, "the self is a connecting, relating activity. "④ In addition, Dewey claims that there is "no ready-made and antecedent conception of ' the individual man' "⑤In a

---

① Wm. Theorore de Bary prefers " presonalism " to " individualism " because " Confucian individualism" shares some common ground with forms of personalism in Western tradition as it discint from a modern liberationist "individualism. " See de Bary, "Individualism and Personhood, " in *Asian Values and Human Rights: A Confucian Communitarian Perspective*, Cambridge Massachusetts, London, England: Harvard University Press, 1998, p. 25.

② M12. 191.

③ MW12: 199.

④ EW2: 210, 216.

⑤ Dewey (1916): 69.

similar fashion, George Herbert Mead conceives the mind not in terms of individual consciousness, but in terms of social acts. The self, in this view, is an aggregate of temporal perspectives or "situations."[1]Societal creativity is the mediated product of the interaction of human beings and society through human practice.

The harmony ofthe continual context of experience and society involves living peacefully with the socio-political dynamics of becoming a person in an ideal flourishing community. The important point is to let the community be balanced but flexible, which means not having an assertive will, but a will that is the confluence of the community's context and that harmonizes possible tendencies. The leader of a community should consider the intentions of the group, harmonizing them rather than suppressing them. A community leader should appreciate the holistic context of individuals, not just reflect on small groups of people.

Dewey counters the notion of society that sets community interests over its members. He uses the examples of a marriage and of stockholders in a joint-stock company. [2] Participants in one association have characteristics, such as powers, rights, and responsibilities, which are different from the characteristics the participant has in other associations. Nonetheless, "an individual cannot be opposed to the association of which he is an integral part nor can the association be set against its integrated members."[3] For Dewey, democracy is the only form of "moral and social faith" that does not "rest upon the idea that experience must be subjected at some point or other to some form of external control; to some 'authority' alleged to exist outside the processes of experience."[4]

---

[1]　Schneider (1963): 470.

[2]　Emerson has a similar metaphor: "Society is a join-stock company, in which the members agree, for the better securing of his bread to each shareholder, to surrender the liberty and culture of the eater." See Emerson (1981).

[3]　Dewey (1998).

[4]　LW14: 229.

Dewey agreeswith the concept of collective human experience because he thinks individuals are unique by virtue of their participation and communication with others. Dewey admits that the American community relies primarily on individualism, but he strongly disagrees with the individualist perspective because he thinks human beings are naturally social, live in communities, and communicate with others in context. ① Dewey states, "liberty does not mean the removal of the checks which nature and man impose on the life of every individual in the community, so that no one individual may indulge impulses which go against his own welfare as a member of society. "②The idea that association with a community diminishes personal liberty is not evident in Dewey's thoughts.

TheDeweyan idea of democracy is the other aspect of establishing a communicating community where people co-create each other. As Dewey puts it: "Democracy is neither a form of government nor a social expediency, but a metaphysic of the relation of man and his experience in nature. "③ Thus, democracy can be regarded as a value that humans co-create with others and society in general. In this way, democracy is a way of balancing the movements of community members as a whole. Dewey remarks: " Clear consciousness of a communal life, in all its implications, constitutes the idea of democracy. "④ Put it another way, the idea of democracy is a manifestation of a cherished community values. Accordingly, democracy is a " social idea, "⑤ and a "mode of associated living. "⑥

The idea of democracy entails the awarenessof the communicating community, because self-realization is always social and communal: "The idea of democracy is a wider and fuller idea than can be exemplified in the

---

① Dewey (1998): 16.

② MW8: 297.

③ MW6.

④ LW2: 328.

⑤ LW2: 325.

⑥ MW9: 93.

state even at its best. To be realized it must affect all modes of human association, the family, the school, industry, religion. "① For Dewey, a progressive community is helpful for one's realization because it widens the area of shared concerns, and it liberates personal capacities. ②

From the perspective of the members of the whole society, democracy should "be the contribution they make to the all-around growth of every member of society. "③ Democracy penetrates into human relationships and helps them grow. For every member of the society, the way to enrich one's community is to have a free and safe environment in which people gather and discuss freely about whatever they want. ④ Humans gather, come what may, but only certain social values lead to meaningful and valuable gatherings. Thus, freedom serves as a prerequisite for a democratic environment, since democracy requires that people prefer to persuade and be persuaded by reason. From this perspective, democracy requires "the improvement of the methods and conditions of debate, discussion and persuasion. "⑤ Dewey also states that democracy is "essentially a cooperative undertaking, one which rests upon persuasion, upon an ability to convince and be convinced by reason. "⑥ In short, the "democratic road is the hard one to take" because it "places the greatest burden of responsibility upon the greatest number of human beings. "⑦ Thus, democracy means people should learn to live every moment in co-creative relationships in order to enhance the value of the relationship in an ethical and moral way.

From the perspective that philosophy adds value to our lives, Dewey

---

① LW2: 325.

② MW9: 93. Dewey uses the term "self-realization" to cover both the activity of and the object of realization of meaning. See Jenifer Welchman, *Dewey's Ethical Thought*, Ithaca and London: Cornell University Press, 96.

③ MW12: 186.

④ LW14: 227.

⑤ LW2: 365.

⑥ MW10: 404.

⑦ LW13: 154.

agrees that there are different perspectives. ① It is the confluence of every individual's behavior that forms the direction of the group. Dewey also indicates that evaluation is an accumulating process, "In any case, so far as judgment takes place … all valuation is in some degree a revaluation. "② Dewey tends to criticize classical individualist analyses of personality and society as undermining the values a prescriptive individualism would require. ③ Dewey holds that human value and significance come from practical experience, and the "deepest problem of modern life" is "the problem of restoring integration and cooperation between man's beliefs about the world in which he lives and his beliefs about the values and purposes that should direct his conduct. "④ Human belief and conduct are co-creative with the environment, and the reflexive co-creative process is extended by the values that human beings add to it.

Conclusion: Confucian Co-creative Ethics

Both Confucian and Deweyan ethics evaluate the values and effects of people's practices and cherish these as the enhancement of a kind of co-creativity. Like the Confucian idea that self-cultivation should be practiced via "regulating one's family (qijia 齐家) ," Dewey's idea of democracy "must begin at home, and its home is the neighborly community. "⑤ Therefore, Confucian ethics is co-creative because it is the philosophical point of view that human beings are able to create valuable relationships through a better understanding

---

① LW2: 327 – 8.

② Dewey (1916) : 386.

③ This process of self-cultivation is a process of creativity under context, which is close to Hegel: "individuals can attain their ends only in so far as they themselves determine their knowing, willing, and acting in a universal way and make themselves links in this chain of social connexions. " Hegel finds the unity of individual satisfaction and freedom in conformity with the organic community. But his notion of community is different from Confucian notion of family. The difference is that there is no Hegelian sense of individual in Confucianism. See Knox (1952) : 187.

④ LW4: 204.

⑤ LW2: 368.

of the nature of co-creativity. This philosophical point has the potential to revive the untimely decline of the Confucian philosophical tradition, and points to a new direction for the emerging cross-currents of American and Confucian philosophies. Confucian co-creative ethics can thus serve as a potent resource out of which China can develop a family centered conception of democracy. In the future we can evaluate Confucian ethics based on whether or not a family-centered democracy is able to emerge from it.

The Construct of Heavenly Principle and the Faith in Heavenly Principle in the Analects

Wang Jun

(Southeast University)

Confucian culture is the typical ethical culture of which morality is the essence and prop. The utmost essence of an ethical culture is the construct of a moral world view, and the first problem for an ethical culture to think over and solve is how to transform a natural world view which is innate for everybody into a moral world view.

Founded by Confucius, the ethical construct of heavenly principle and the faith in heavenly principle have become the foundation for people to transcend their secwlar and enter into a non-utilitarian moral world and to achieve the ideal state. As Mencius pointed out, "I like life, and I also like righteousness. If I cannot keep the two together, I will let life go, and choose righteousness. "(*Mencius*, 11. 10) and "to be above the power of riches and honours to make dissipated, of poverty and mean condition to make swerve from principle, and of power and force to make bend. " (*Mencius*, 6. 2) Otherwise, people will submit to desires and inexorably sink into a completely utilitarian world view.

How is this kind of moral world view established in Confucian culture?

By investigating into *The Analects*-the most important book of

Confucianism, this article will expound the above-mentioned problem from the perspectives of the ethical construct of heavenly principle and the faith in heavenly principle built by Confucius.

I. "The Gentleman Stands In Awe Of Three Things" And Confucian Construct Of Heavenly Principle

Confucius establishes the heavenly principle by distinguishing the ordinances of Heaven, great men and sages, together with his conception of "golden age" of Yao, Shun and Yu. The typical proposition is "The Gentleman stands in awe of three things", from which we can discern how Confucius sets up the ethical heavenly principle.

Confucius said, "The Gentleman stands in awe of three things. He stands in awe of the ordinances of Heaven. He stands in awe of great men. He stands in awe of the words of sages. (*The Analects*, 16:8)

In my opinion, the so-called ordinances of Heaven is actually the heavenly principle with ethical meaning. The great man, according to Confucius, is the person who acts according to the heavenly principle, exemplified in Yao, Shun and Yu who realized the Golden Age. as Confucius said, "Great indeed was Yao as a sovereign! How majestic was he! It is only Heaven that is grand, and only Yao corresponded to it. " (The Analects, 8. 19)

And the sages conceived by Confucius are the persons like King Wen, King Wu and the Duke of Zhou who institutionalized the heavenly principle and set up the norms of conductm for the world. Confucius said, "After the death of King Wen, doesn't the culture abide within me?" (*The Analects*, 9. 5). It is clear that Confucius regards King Wen as a sage and himself as a successor of King Wen, and therefore later generations regard Confucius as a sage.

Confucius maintains that the cause for the collapse of ceremony and propriety and the great disorder under heaven is the absence of heavenly principle and the abandonment of morality. Therefore, Confucius emphasizes,

"To subdue one's self and return to propriety is benevolence. " (*The Analects*, 12. 1) Virtue appears after benevolence, and the Dao (Way) appears after virtue. Obviously, Confucius takes a path from propriety to the Dao, i. e, from social norms to heavenly principle.

On the contrary, Laozi (Lao Tzu) takes a negative view toward history and he believes that the heavenly principle, in the temporal history, will necessarily degenerate into the so-called benevolence, righteousness, propriety and wisdom.

Laozi said:

"When the Great Dao (Way) ceased to be observed, benevolence and righteousness came into vogue. Then appeared wisdom and shrewdness, and there ensued great hypocrisy. When harmony no longer prevailed throughout the six kinships, filial sons found their manifestation; when the states and clans fell into disorder, loyal ministers appeared. " (*Dao De Jing* or *Tao Te Ching*, Chapter 18)

and —

"Thus it was that when the Dao was lost, its attributes appeared; when its attributes were lost, benevolence appeared; when benevolence was lost, righteousness appeared; and when righteousness was lost, the proprieties appeared.

Now propriety is the attenuated form of leal-heartedness and good faith, and is also the commencement of disorder. "(*Dao De Jing*, Chapter 38)

Therefore, Laozi holds that people should skip over benevolence, righteousness, propriety and wisdom and returnto the heavenly principle directly. Compared with Confucian deep reverence for history, Laozi shows an inclination for historical nihilism.

However, there is a logic advantage in Laozi's historical nihilism, i. e. , it can avoid the contradiction between temporality and eternity. Laozi has a deep insight into the destructive nature of time. As a temporal being, a man is doomed. If a man strives perseveringly for temporal gains, he will become bogged down in endless troubles. So the wisest choice is to throw away all the temporal creations and return to the eternity directly.

Laozi keeps himself aloof from the temporal world, and his basic attitude can be summarized in the following statement:

"Heaven and earth do not act from (the impulse of) any wish to be benevolent; they deal with all things as the dogs of grass are dealt with. The sages do not act from (any wish to be) benevolent; they deal with the people as the dogs of grass are dealt with. " (*Dao De Jing*, Chapter 5)

Confucius, however, is not that kind of sage that Laozi refers to. As he always cares about people and pays great attention to history, Confucius has made every effort to solve the contradictions between temporality and eternity, between history and heavenly principle, and between the heavenly Dao and virtue. But these are eternal contradictions and cannot be solved directly.

II. "Does Heaven Speak?" and Confucian Faith in Heavenly Principle

There is still a problem remained to be solved, i. e. , how to establish the faith in the heavenly principle after the construct being built up. In *The Analects*, Confucius takes the problem as a truism which doesn't need further explanation, just like the movement of Heaven-"Does Heaven speak?" whose context is as follows:

The Master said, "I would prefer not speaking. "

Tsze-kung said, "If you, Master, do not speak, what shall we, your disciples, have to record?"

The Master said, "Does Heaven speak? The four seasons pursue their courses, and all things are continually being produced, but does Heaven say anything?" (*The Analects*, 17. 19)

We can infer from the context that Tsze-kung had asked a question that is difficult for Confucius to answer, and that's why Confucius said, About"I would prefer not speaking. "

Which kind of question does Tsze-kung ask? Why does Confucius think it so difficult to answer?

We think that the question put forward by Tsze-kung must be an ultimate question which concerns the final foundation of Confucian moral doctrine, i. e. , the problem of heavenly principle, which Confucius refuses to answer, because he knows that it concerns the ethical faith and it is a truism for believers while a mystery for non-believers. The ethical world view calls for the eyes of the mind, with which people can see the heavenly principle.

III. "While You Do Not Know Life, How Can You Know About Death?" And Confucian Ethical World View

The reason why the construct of the heavenly principle and the faith in the heavenly principle are indispensable in ethics is that they are closely related to the construct of the ethical world view, without which the mortal human beings will be haunted by the temporal problems like "birth, aging, disease and death" and will be so worried that they cannot settle down and get on. With a great insight, Confucius purposely avoids the problems of "birth, aging, disease and death" and "extranrdinary things, feats of strength, disorder, and spiritual beings" -

Chi Lu asked about serving the spirits of the dead. The Master said, "While you are not able to serve men, how can you serve their spirits?" Chi Lu added, "I venture to ask about death?" He was answered, "While you do not know life, how can you know about death?" (*The Analects*, 11. 12)

and—

The subjects on which the Master did not talk, were-extraordinary things, feats of strength, disorder, and spiritual beings. (*The Analects*, 7. 21)

As for the remarks by Confucius on ghost and god as well as life and death, scholars usually explain that these remarks reflect a humanistic standpoint. However, we still have to ask:

What makes Confucius to take a humanistic standpoint?

Which kind of logic does Confucian humanism rely on?

The reason why Confucius set up the age of Yao, Shun and Yu as the Golden Age instead of the age of Yellow Emperor (Huang Di) or even earlier age is that Confucius is probably aware of the fact that history differs from nature. To Confucius, the epistemological quest for history will drive history to move back to the uncivilized nature in which human being is not different from animal. Therefore, later generations of Confucianism always emphasize the distinction between human being and animal. From a natural perspective, human being might be not different from animal. Mencius said, "When Shun was living amid the deep retired mountains, dwelling with the trees and rocks, and wandering among the deer and swine, the difference between him and the rude inhabitants of those remote hills appeared very small. But when he heard a single good word, or saw a single good action, he was like a stream or a river bursting its banks, and flowing out in an irresistible flood." (*Mencius*, 13. 16) Obviously, a human beings does not differ from animals in natural aspects, but he does differ from animals in moral aspects. In a sense, morality is the greatest creation of human kind. It overrides science and technology and any other forms of civilization. Just because of morality, a human being can finally get rid of his selfish animal instincts and begin to care about others.

Kant said at the conclusion of*The Critique of Practical Reason*: "Two Things fill the mind with ever new and increasing admiration and awe, the oftener and the more steadily we reflect on them: the starry heavens above and the moral law within."

People usually separate "the starry heavens above" and "the moral law within" They think that the former implies natural science and the latter morality. It is not the case. As a matter of fact, "the starry heavens above" means higher moral revelation because there will be no morality if there is no higher revelation.

To Confucius, Heaven is not only the natural heaven, but also the moral heaven. The natural heaven is always in the process of change while the moral heaven is eternal. If people catch a glimpse of the moral heaven, they can get rid of the natural life and death and settle down in this world. In other words, the moral heaven lays a foundation for Confucian humanism. In the moral world based on the ethical heavenly principle, what really matters is not the problems of "birth, aging, disease and death" and "extraordinary things, feats of strength, disorder, and spiritual beings", but rather "Treat with the reverence due to age the elders in your own family, so that the elders in the families of others shall be similarly treated; treat with the kindness due to youth the young in your own family, so that the young in the families of others shall be similarly treated. " (*Mencius*, 1. 7) Consequently, to conquer nature also serves the morality. Perhaps it can explain why Chinese pay much greater attention to human relations than to nature because Chinese established a fixed moral world view at the very early stage. According to this world view, human relations comes first, nature is relatively not so important.

IV. Visible Natural Heaven And Invisible Moral Heaven

People cannot distinguish moral heaven from natural heaven Although they are different. Even Confucius himself couldn't make a distinction between them, at least there is no such kind of distinction, so that many scholars equate natural heaven (cosmology) with moral heaven (ethics).

Why doesn't Confucius make a distinction between natural heaven and moral heaven? Maybe it is largely due to his worry about people's comprehension because most people believe "what they hear may be false", and only "what they see is true. " The moral heaven, however, is invisible and intangible. Believing it or not just depends on hearing, which is almost impossible for most people to accept.

After the emergence of enlightenment thought, science and technology prevail over morality. As a result, the problem of "visible vs. invisible" now becomes unavoidable because the moral heaven has been disenchanted by science. In the visible world of science, morality must defend its invisible world against the judgment of science. In modern times it becomes necessary to distinguish the visible from the invisible and the epistemological from the ethical because the natural heaven can be ruined without the support of the moral heaven. The reason that people are worried about the environment pollution, epidemic, natural disasters etc. is that we have forgotten the invisible moral world.

Just because of this, it is necessary for us to expound Confucian moral world, to analyze his construct of the heavenly principle and the faith in the heavenly principle, and to distinguish the visible world from the invisible world. In this way, we can hopefully rejuvenate traditional Chinese morality from which we may derive the typical Chinese wisdom to deal with contemporary moral crisis.

The Forum on New Interpretation of Classics:
the English version If *Lunyu*

Wisdom and Modern Connotation

Philosophy and Contemporary Value of the Analect: Speech at King's College, London

Tong Yun-kai

(The Confucian Academy)

Ladies and Gentlemen,

Let's first have a review on Confucianism's impact on Britain. Mr. Reginald Fleming Johnston, a British teacher of China's last emperor Puyi and a "master lecturer" of Confucian University founded by Mr. Chan Wun-cheung, reckoned that China has the best religion represented by Confucianism and what the western Christian missionaries do in China is unnecessary—"The political and religious culture of China is based on Confucianism... no foreign religions (no matter how elegant they are) can be comparable to Confucianism in China.

Mr. Johnston was extremely unhappy that some Chinese abandoned their own traditional culture, saying, "if China is attaching less and less importance and even abandons the mainstay she has relied on for thousands of years in her long revolutionary process, and if she westernizes all her ideal, philosophy of life, moral values and social system, it is certain that she will become wealthy, advanced and strong, or even become a super power in the world, but so will she also abandon her much more excellent qualities, the source of her happiness. All that she can be proud of will be gone and never return, and what takes the place will be tens of thousands of local village police stations!" James Legge (1815-1897), a British missionary, has translated ten books of "The Thirteen Classics" into English and was a professor of sinology in the Oxford University.

Bertrand Russell (1872-1970) is a thinker of worldwide influence in the Twentieth Century. He came to China in 1920 to be a professor in the Peking University. He said: "Chinese have found and been practicing for several centuries a life-style which will bring happiness to the whole world if accepted globally. However, we Europeans do not have such life-style. Our life-style demands struggle, plunder, endless changes, discontent and destruction. " Arnold Joseph Toynbee (1889-1975) is the most renowned philosopher and historian of Britain in the Twentieth Century. In his writing "Forecast 21st Century—the Dialogue between Tonybee and Dai sake Ikeda", he points out the centre of unification of the future world will not be the military but a continuous crystallization and expansion of the axes of geography and culture, and China, as an embodiment of Confucian culture in the eastern Asia, will be such centre in future. China can take the main leading role in the unification process of mankind. *Joseph Needham (1900 – 1995), a Fellow of the Royal Society of Britain points out in his book "Science and Technology History of China",* management work for such great number of prefectures and counties requires great development of bureaucratic politics. Therefore, such demand for administrative officials creates the conditions for Confucianism's dominance in the Chinese society. …. That is also the reason why Confucius became the "Crownless Emperor" of China. Macmillan *Publishers,* one of the biggest publishers in Britain, purchased the copyright in Britain of the book "Confucius from the Heart: Ancient Wisdom for Today's World" by Yu Dan published by Chung Hwa Book Company at the record-high price of 100,000£ for overseas copyrights of Chinese books. This makes it clear that Confucian thought has very great vitality in contemporary Britain.

The Confucian Academy has been making great effort for eighty years to promote Confucianism and Confucian teachings. Ever since I assumed the

office of President of The Confucian Academy, I have published more than
800 pieces of speeches and essays to promote Confucianism throughout China
and around the world, achieving common understanding with important
politicians of various countries and Confucian scholars, making great success
in the promotion of Confucianism. This can prove that Confucian thought is
applicable to all things in the world and is ever-lasting.

I. The Moral Concept in *"The Analect"*

With her many years of practice and research, the Confucian Academy
has found the correct solution for the education problem of strengthening
education for young people—the only way to nurture the moral quality of
young people is to restore the traditional virtues of Confucian thought. This
solution has long been upheld by Dr. Sun Yat-sen, who advocated for
"restoring the intrinsic morals of Chinese". Yet, such foresight and sagacity
were not met with extensive feedback at that time. In the so-called "Neo-
cultural Movement", some people upheld the opposite and put forward the
idea of destruction of the traditional morals and cultivation of new morals. The
outcome was that the traditional morals were destroyed but hardly any new
morals were cultivated. We should know that only on a foundation of
traditional morals and with adaptation to the change of an era can new morals
be produced. With traditional morals cancelled, new morals are just like
water with no source and will dry out for certain.

In the contemporary world, scientism is upheld and at the same time,
comes into existence a wrong tendency—derogation of humanism. In
Confucianism there is a very valuable concept—attaching equal importance to
benevolence and wisdom; integrating benevolence and wisdom. Confucius
said: "Of neighbourhoods benevolence is the most beautiful. How can the man
be considered wise who, when he has the choice, does not settle in
benevolence?" (*Verse 1, Chapter IV*).

Both Confucius and Mencius unify moral values with "benevolence" as
the core and rational knowledge. Benevolence and wisdom are

interdependent. Confucius also said: "The benevolent man is attracted to benevolence because he feels at home in it. The wise man is attracted to benevolence because he finds it to his advantage. " (*Verse 2, Chapter IV*). People of wisdom can act wisely, taking actions both advantageous to achieving benevolence and also upholding the value of benevolence at the same time. Confucius also sees wisdom as an important condition for the practice of benevolence. Confucian also said: "He cannot even be said to be wise. How can he be said to be benevolent?" (Verse 19, Chapter V). Of course, what Confucius means by wisdom is mainly moral rationality and moral knowledge, but it also implies the knowledge of objective law of nature at the same time. "Unification of benevolence and wisdom" is the core of Confucian humanism.

In the modern society, both science and democracy need to be planted in mankind's good moral quality first before they can grow in the correct direction with its use out of kind motives. Similarly, without the outward influence of science and democracy, it will be impossible for inner moral quality to produce a good effect on the world and it will become merely mystery and hollow words. Unifying benevolence and wisdom is certainly the inevitable direction of social development of advancement.

II. Political concept of "The Analect"

When asked by a ruler about ruling his country, Confucius said: "Let the ruler be a ruler, the subject a subject, the father a father, the son a son. " (*Verse 11, Chapter XII*). Confucius advocates that a ruler has to fulfill a ruler's duty up to the moral standard of a ruler and a subject has to fulfill his duty as a subject up to the moral standard of a subject. Mencius once told a ruler: "If a ruler loves his subjects as his body, the subjects will love their ruler as their body too; if a ruler regard his subjects as worthless, the subjects will regard him as common people; if a ruler regards his subjects as trifles, they will look upon him as an enemy. "The interactivity between a ruler and his subjects is on an equal basis. Only when a ruler and the officials rule the country in a proper way will the subjects accept his ruling happily.

Confucianism reckons that what the ruler and officials do plays an exemplary role for subjects. If they act properly, then the subjects will be influenced and act properly for kindness too. Confucius said: "If a man is correct in his own person, then there will be obedience without orders being given; but if he is not correct in his own person, there will not be obedience even though orders are given. " (*Verse 6, Chapter XIII*) He also said: "Government is being correct. If you give a lead in being correct, who would dare to be incorrect?" (*Verse 17, Chapter XII*). Mencius said: "It is better to be good at teaching well than ruling well. A ruler being good at ruling makes people fear him but being; good at teaching makes people love him. Being good at ruling brings the ruler people's wealth while being good at teaching brings the ruler the ardent support of people. The ruler and officials should listen to and base their ruling on people's opinion. That means, the ruler should respect and love his subjects. The ruler and officials also shoulder the responsibility to educate people and guide them to kindness.

Summarizing the above-mentioned, it can be concluded that the ruler should respect the common people's views and also the mind and view of Heaven. Yet, "What does the Heaven say?"The Heaven cannot communicate directly with the ruler and officials while people's mind and views are interlinked with the Heaven's. Thus, through understanding people's mind and views we can communicate with and know the Heaven's mind and view. The Heaven's decision on whether to support or dethrone a ruler is based on whether the ruler's ruling is beneficial to the people.

Confucianism's people-oriented principle is the best ruling policy for the time of monarchy. On the basis of Confucian people-oriented principle and making reference to the experiences and achievements of the western democracy, a good democratic political system can be constructed in the modern society.

III. Religious Concept of "The Analect"

Confucius's educational teachings are profound and comprehensive, among which the religious and moral ones are the most valuable. Confucius established Confucianism in accordance with the religious political and ideology of his time.

Confucianism is a religion with mankind as its core. It is a humane religion as well as a divine religion. It is an integration of the three zones of Heaven, Earth and Man, inspiring mankind's kindness nature to integrate with Heaven and Earth. The Chinese term "religion" embeds a tradition of passing on and inheritage, and respect for ancestors as well as a quality of promotion of teachings of their ancestral sages.

Confucius reckons that Heaven is the supreme power and it is omnipotent and omniscient, rational and fair, being strict and fair in *meting* out rewards and punishments. As Heaven is perceptive of the minutest detail of mankind's behaviour, there will be punishments for evil deeds and rewards for good deeds.

Confucian thought, ever since Confucius' founding of Confucianism during the 2000 plus years from the Spring and Autumn Period to today, has been flowing in the blood of and embedded deeply in the mind of every Chinese.

Concepts of filial piety, brotherhood, loyalty, fidelity, benevolence, love and peace are embedded in every Chinese family. To be frank, Confucianism has been the state religion of China ever since ancient time. I do believe that Chineseall over the world are Confucian disciples. Confucianism comes first among the Three Religions of Confucianism, Buddhism and Taoism. The United Nations has long affirmed that Confucianism is one of the thirteen religions. Confucianism is also one of the six major religions in Hong Kong alongside with Christianity, Catholicism, Islam, Taoism and Buddhism. The Confucian Academy, ever since its establishment by Dr. Chan Wun-cheung in 1930, has been the core organization of promotion of

Confucianism all over the world. There is a saying "If Confucius had not been born, the world would have still been in a long dark night. " Without Confucius' establishment of the system of benevolence, righteousness, the rite and fidelity there could hardly have been the ethical and moral foundation of Chinese. Without Confucianism as its pillar, how could such glorious civilization of such great nation have been standing firm for so many thousands of years?

IV. Educational Concept of "The Analects"

Confucius is the greatest educationist of China and even all mankind. As early as 2,000 years ago, he worked out an integrated curriculum, providing modern educationists and psychologists with a theoretical foundation. Confucius taught about 2,000 students and among whom, 72 were people of virtue. He advocated the principle of education for all people, and established a curriculum of four subjects, which are namely, virtue, language, politics and literature, teaching the six arts of the rite, music, archery, driving, calligraphy and arithmetic, developing the nurture of students' six capacities, which are moral, intellectual, physical, social, aesthetic and spiritual capacities. Howard Gardner, a psychologist in the Harvard University, put forward the Theory of Multiple Intelligences in 1983, but he did not know that Confucius had already talked about the "pluralistic" nature of mankind's wisdom and knowledge, which could be inspired from studying poetry and classics as well as the rite and music. His principle of full understanding, abiding by virtue and benevolence, etc. more or less equals to the "knowledge, skill, value and attitude" of modern education. Analyzing their individual characteristics, Confucius was able to tell the good, bad, strong and weak points of each of his students and adopt tailored methodologies and curriculums for teaching each of them, so as to achieve the best educational outcome. In modern terms, this is "not even one student be abandoned".

Nowadays, it is advocated that teachers should have passion for "teaching and learning", a concept Confucius put forward 2000 *odd* years ago—"I never feel bored with learning or find teaching tiresome"; "Even when I spurred my self on in my studies as though I were lagging behind, my fear was that I might not make it in time. " (*Verse 17, Chapter VIII*) . Confucius took cultivating oneself and rational understanding as the motivation for learning-"Men of antiquity studied to improve themselves; men today study to impress others. " (*Verse 14 Chapter XXIV*). Lev Semenovich Vygtsky, a contemporary educational psychologist, put forward the theory of "Marginal Zone of Learning Development", which can be traced back to Confucius' teachings "A man is worthy of being a teacher who gets to know what is new by keeping fresh in his mind what he is already familiar with. " (*Verse 11, Chapter II*) , "Is it not a pleasure, having learned something, to try it out at due intervals?" (*Verse 1, Chapter I*) and "What should I make my specialty? Driving? Or archery? I think I should prefer driving. " (*Verse 2, Chapter IX*). The "inborn" and "nurtured" concepts of modern educational philosophy can also be traced back to Confucius' teaching "Men are close to one another by nature. They drift apart through behaviour that is constantly repeated. " (*Verse 2, Chapter XVII*). Today's popular critical learning methodology and attitude can also be traced back to "There were four things the Master (Confucius) refused to have anything to do with: he refused to entertain conjectures or insist on certainty; he refused to be inflexible or to be egotistical. " (*Verse 4, Chapter IX*) , "If one learns from others but does not think, one will be bewildered. If, on the other hand, one thinks but does not learn from others, one will be imperiled. " (*Verse 15, Chapter II*) and "Do I possess knowledge? No, I do not. A rustic put a question to me and my mind was a complete blank. I kept hammering at the two sides of the question until I got everything out of it. " (*Verse 8, Chapter IX*) . As for the so-called "exploratory learning", Confucius also said: "He was quick and eager to learn: he was not ashamed to seek the advice of those who were beneath him in station" (*Verse 15, Chapter V*) , "Inquire earnestly and reflect on what is at hand" (*Verse 19, Chapter VI*) and "There are presumably men who innovate without possessing knowledge, but that is not a fault I have. I use my ears widely and follow what is good in what I have heard; I use my eyes widely and retain what I have seen in my mind. This constitutes a lower level of knowledge. " (*Verse 28, Chapter VII*). The concepts of "peer support" and "mutual lesson observation" can also be traced back to "Even when walking in the company of two other men, I am bound to be able to learn from them. The good points of the one I copy; the bad points of the other I correct in myself. " (*Verse 22, Chapter VII*). Confucius also talked about the proper learning attitude and methodology—"The gentleman seeks neither a full belly nor a comfortable home. He is quick in action but cautious in speech. He goes to men possessed of the Way to have himself put right. Such a man can be described as eager to learn" (*Verse 14, Chapter I*), "The man whose belly is full all day and who does not put his mind to some use is sure to meet with difficulties" (*Verse 22, Chapter XVII*) and "To say you know when you know, and to say you do not when you do not, that is knowledge. " (*Verse 17, Chapter II*).

Confucius advocated "life-long learning" very early—"He is the sort of man who forgets to eat when he works himself into a frenzy over some problem, who is so full of joy that he forgets his worries and who does not notice the onset of old age" (*Verse 19, Chapter VII*). He also upheld "pleasant learning"—"To be fond of it is better than merely to know it, and to find joy in it is better than merely to be fond of it. " (*Verse 20, Chapter VI*). Confucius has long started cultivating students' self-learning ability, saying "I never enlighten anyone who has not been driven to distraction by trying to understand a difficulty or who has not got into a frenzy trying to put his ideas into words. " (*Verse 8, Chapter VII*), and supplemented it with "When I have pointed out one corner of a square to anyone and he does not come back with the other three, I will not point it out to him a second time. " (*Verse 8, Chapter VII*). Being "pointed one corner of a square" is learning from one's teacher and being able to "come back with the other three" is self-learning.

V. The Analect and Global Financial Economy

In 2008, a global financial tsunami rarely seen in human history started from the United States, bringing great disasters to the global economy. Its destructive power was far more terrible and brutal than the financial storm in 1997. It has rung the alarm: we should put an end to all of it—a market mechanism with profit-making as its core value, a lust for gain as its drive, a development mode with environmental destruction and invasion of nature as its developmental goal and a virtual economic strategy with financial derivatives as its characteristic.

In the earlier time, the large-scale fraud case of Bernard Madoff, former chairman of the renowned National Association of Securities Dealers Automated Quotations in the United States caused a great stir around the world. Even many big banks and investment companies fell victim to his snare and suffered losses of almost 65 billion U. S. dollars. He took advantage of others' trust in him to attain enormous amounts of ill-gotten wealth from his victims, including even Jews, his fellow countrymen. Such behaviour is shameful indeed! There was also the later case of a magnate of the financial industry, Robert Stanford of Texas of the United States, in which investors were cheated to purchase certificates of deposits involving an amount of 8 billion U. S. dollars. Moral integrity shows in times of poverty. Today is the time for many people to choose to be a Small Man or a Gentleman.

Besides, the amount of money involved in swindling in Britain amounted to 60 million pounds just inthe first half of the year 2009. The number of cases was 160 odd, the highest in the recent decades. Britain's Ponzi Scheme involving 80 million pounds was exposed the earlier days as the biggest fraud in British history. The victims amounted to 600 odd, including quite a number of celebrities, among whom many even committed suicides due to bankruptcy. The swindlers made use of human greed to attract high-income people behind a fa ?　ade of high returns and even famous actresses and people of great wealth got hooked. There was later also the shocking news of

N. Levene defrauding 2. 5 billion U. S. dollars from financial transactions and absconding.

Since the financial tsunami, there has been news that some wealthy people around the world committed suicide under the pressure of large debt. The destructive power of the financial tsunami is really terrifying. Although the United States was once a country of very advanced economic management theories and at the same time, a country upholding democracy and the rule of law with a perfect legal system in various aspects, it was their speculation, misleading, swindling and irresponsibility that led to the serious financial tsunami. This makes one point very clear: the rule of law and knowledge by themselves cannot be a guarantee for the normal operation of a society. What is also necessary is the Confucian principle of "Unification of benevolence and wisdom". Only with both the foundation of the rule of law with the moral power of Confucianism can ensure a healthy state for a society.

The symptom of cub-prime mortgage crisis and the global financial tsunami is "economy" but the cause is "moral". From the Confucian point of view, moral is the key to successful treatment of this illness.

The core essence of Confucian culture is moral. Adoption of the Confucian principle "thorough knowledge of Heaven, Earth and Man" as the basic for reforming the global economic order and establishing again the core value of mankind, replacing the western commercial principle "profit-making comes first" with the Confucian principle "integration of righteousness and profit-making" and replacing the authorative expansion and invasion of market under rational economics, racism and nationalism with the Confucian merchants' principle of mutual benefit. Only on the basis of Confucian merchant culture can a peaceful and benign win-win commercial norm and order be established and can our society development be sustainable.

As the saying goes, what comes fast goes fast. I believe the losses in the financial tsunami have to be compensated with profits made for half a century, which is really distressing.

From the analysis mentioned above, it can seen that there would have been no financial tsunami had all people in the world abided by Confucian moral principles and even though it did occur, they could have got out of the predicament brought by it. In the fight against the financial crisis, it is necessary to promote the Confucian principles of "The benevolent love all people", "Balance of righteousness and profit", "be honest and trustworthy", "upholding virtue", "harmony is valuable" and the Doctrine of the Mean.

There are various types of Confucian disciples in the society—Confucian scholars, Confucian religionists, Confucian officials, Confucian military officials, Confucian merchants and Confucian doctors. Being in different social strata, they all abide by Confucian teachings and try their best to fulfill their roles happily and respectfully and at the same time, they are all working together trying their best to further promote and honour Confucian culture.

I   strongly believe that Confucianism has six major functions:

1. To promote world peace;

2. To enhance the moral quality of all mankind;

3. To continue and prosper together with the various pluralistic cultures in the world;

4. To serve as the spiritual axis for the 56 nationalities and 1.3 billion countrymen of China;

5. To enhance the unification of China;

6. To attain an equal status as other religions and cultures in the world.

The Confucian Academy has submitted a proposal to the Government of Hong Kong Special Administrative Region to have Confucius' Birthday (the Twenty-seventh Day of the Eighth Month of the Chinese Calendar) declared a public holiday. We sincerely wish for spiritual support from you all. If you support our proposal, please give a clap to show your endorsement.

Wishing you all good health and every success!

Thank you very much.

The Wisdom of Administration in *The Analects of Confucius*

Li Honglei

(The Department of Philosophy, Sun Yat-sen University

The Confucian School's thoughts mainly originate from the Classic works and decrees before the Zhou Dynasty, which record many experiences and lessons of governing state by the three ancient sages, Yao, Shun, and Yu, and by the three dynasties of Xia, Shang and Zhou. Therefore these thoughts have, from the beginning, directed relationships be them, and activities of, administrators, and once successively served Confucius himself as a local or state official who managed various affairs, important or trivial. Many of Confucius's disciples also held the various official positions like dukes and princes at that time. So it was not surprising that there were so many records about "the stories of governing state", "the advice of governing state", and "the execution of governing state" in a classic like *The Analects of Confucius*. Generally speaking, the fundamental spirits of the wisdom of administration in *The Analects of Confucius* include the five aspects as follows: "regarding humanity as the foundation", "taking the virtues primarily", "laying stress on the righteousness", "taking harmony as the most precious thing", and "taking the Mean as the guidance". These notions are still significant and enlightening in today's administrative activities.

I. The Wisdom of Administration: Regarding Humanity as Foundation

The central concept of Confucian philosophy is"benevolence"(仁 Ren). According to the book, *The First Comprehensive Chinese Dictionary*, (《说文解字》 Shuo Wen Jie Zi). "'Ren' means the intimate relationship which is established by two persons". Viewed from the structural perspective of Chinese characters, "Ren" is a complex character which means the combination of "two persons". This indicates that the philosophy of Confucianism is actually to take persons and person's relations as the starting point of its theory, as well as the starting point of its theory of administration and philosophy.

In the Confucian Classics, *The Book of Rites—Mean*, it is recorded that, when Lord Lu aigong asked Confucius for his advice of governing a state, Confucius answered "to govern state depends on the persons, to get people's support by the conducts, to cultivate conducts by the principle (道 Dao), and to obtain Dao through benevolence. " Here, the "person" is defined as the carrier of administration (including the subject and object of administration, namely the manager and the managed) . Also, in the Confucian Classic, *The Book of History—Gaoyao's Tactics*, there was a record that once Gaoyao and Yu talked about the governing of state affairs in front of Shun Emperor. They put forward three principles about " the governing of the state": (1) "to cultivate one's moral character", which requires a monarch to train his soul hard and strictly and to make efforts to sublime himself; (2) "to appoint the officials", namely, being good at discovering and appointing the officials; and (3) "to comfort the people", which means to give more kindness and benefits to the people and to make them live peacefully. Confucius, in *The Analects of Confucius*, inherited and developed those thought. He raised three tasks for the leaders: "to cultivate oneself so as to be polite", "to cultivate oneself so as to comfort officials", and "to cultivate oneself so as to make the people live peacefully"[1]. These

---

[1]　*Analects: Xianwen.*

express the Confucian spirit of administrative principle such as " to take humanity as foundation ", viewed from perspectives of a manager's self-administration as well as from that of the administration of the managed at different levels and then to the administration of the people all over the world.

In the thought of Confucianism, the relationship between the self-cultivation and the governing of a state cannot be separated, and conversely, the self-administration cannot be separated from the state governing. Confucianism regards the manager's self-administration as the starting point of all activities of administration. The Confucian Classic, *The Great Learning*, puts forward a concise formula which integrates the self-cultivation with the state governing, namely, "eight items": "to study the phenomena of nature, to acquire knowledge, to be sincere, to set the ideas rightly, to cultivate one's conduct, to regulate the family, to rule over the state, and to assuage the popular indignation". It means in detail that a person who wants to develop his virtues must rule his state well at first; in order to rule over the state well, he must first regulate his family; in order to regulate well his family, he must firstly cultivate his virtues and conducts; in order to cultivate his virtues and conducts, he must set his ideas firstly and rightly; in order to set his ideas rightly, he must be sincere; in order to be sincere, he must acquire knowledge and to acquire knowledge, he must study the natural phenomena. Among these eight items, "the cultivation of one's virtues and conducts is the core and of the most important. The cultivation-administration, including the cultivation of virtue and conduct, is the foundation of studying the natural phenomena, acquiring knowledge, being sincere and setting the ideas rightly, because the latter four are only the methods to cultivate virtues and conducts which are subordinated to the purpose of virtues and conducts. Departing from this purpose, all methods would deviate from their directions and lose their significance. The cultivation of virtues and conducts is also the base of regulating the family, ruling over the state and assuaging popular indignation. Although these three are the ideals of cultivation of virtues and conducts, to realize these ideals, it is necessary to start from the cultivation of virtues and conducts. Ruling over the people, the country, and the world is identified with "the ruling over oneself", which is the extension and expansion of the cultivation of virtues and conducts. Based on his personal cultivation of virtues and conducts, an administrative worker should extend it to deal with the relations well between the administrative stratum and then further to deal with the relationships well between the managers and the managed.

Confucius's so-called "to comfort the people" at that time meant the administration by the officials at all levels. It aims at ensuring that all administrative workers have proper places and play well their roles. This would involve the "appointment of the officials". According to Confucian Classic, *Dadai Book of Rites-Emperor Wenwang's Appointing His Officials*, includes two aspects, namely, "to discover the officials" and "to appoint the officials".

Insofar as "to discover the officials" is concerned, *Emperor Wenwang Appointing Officials* raises a method with "six signs" appraisal. "Six signs" means to check the officials' moral characters according to the expects an follows (including on-the-job officials and official candidates): (1) "to check sincerity", namely to check the virtues, character, and sentiment of the officials; (2) "to examine one's aspiration", namely to examine the aspiration of the officials through their remarks; (3) "to look at one's internality", namely to observe the internal temperament of the officials through their tones and tunes when they speak; (4) "to observe the complexion", namely to inspect the makings of the officials through watching the expressions of the officials; (5) "to inspect the concealment", namely to inspect the secret essence of the officials through the appearance information; and (6) "to estimate one's virtue characters", namely to evaluate the virtue character of the officials according to the above five expressions of the officials in general.

Again, insofar as "to appoint the officials" is concerned, *Emperor Wenwang's Appointing Officials* puts forward a viewpoint with "nine appointments". "Nine appointments" means to appoint the officials nine leading positions, according to their different characters and merits. For example, a person who is, benevolent and wise can be appointed as to be state's officials at different levels; a kind, honest, and reasonable person can be appointed to be the leaders at grass-root units; a person with upright, loyal, and faithful characters can be appointed to serve as the discipline supervision of the officials; a prudent, just, and perspicacious person can be appointed to hold the position like a judge; a fair and honest person can be appointed to be an official for the financial; a person who is cautious, honest, and impartial can be appointed to be an official who is in charge of the distribution and awards granting; a person good at business and making profit can be appointed to be a leader for agriculture and handicraft industry; a person adapting to communication and to deal well with the relations with the other people can be appointed as a diplomatic official; and a bold, power, fortitude, and decisive person can be appointed to be a military head. In a word, the appointment of the officials must be made in accordance with the different capacities and abilities of the candidates, in order to make them serve their proper positions and hold due responsibilities.

"To comfort populace" is to comfort people", this is the thought of "regarding humanity as the foundation" which is embodied in the governing activities of the state of Confucianism. Confucianism believes that populace is the foundation of the state, and "regarding humanity as the foundation" is the starting and summing point in all governing activities of state. Mencius raised once such a viewpoint as "people are noble and monarch inferior". He believed that under the background of then turbulent days, people who could acquire the popular support would rule the country. Therefore, Administrative stratum should pay great attention to the gain or loss of the populace and the support or opposition of people. Mencius pointed out that Jie of Xia Dynasty and Zhou of Shang Dynasty lost their empires because they lost the populace, and they lost populace because they lost the support of the people. The best method to gain the empire is to acquire the popular support the best method to acquire the popular support is to win the support of the people, and the best method to win the support of the people is to satisfy the needs of people. Xun Zi takes the metaphor of "boat and water" to reflect the relationship between a monarch and his subjects. He said: "monarch is like a boat and his subjects like the water; the water can bear the boat and can swallow it too". ①He linked the attitude of monarch towards his subjects with the long period of stability of the empire; in such a way that he, from even more practical perspective, reminded the state ruler of "comforting the people". The thought of "comforting officials", "comforting persons" and "comforting people" raised by Confucianism is centrally expressed to be the wisdom of the administrative workers. From the angle of modern administration, so-called "comforting persons" is to satisfy the needs of the managed. American psychologist A. H. Maslow induced the need of human bings into five levels, namely the need of physiology, safety, affiliation, respect, and self-realization. How to meet these needs is an important test of the administrative ability of a leader. From the time of Confucius till today, human society has passed more than 20 centuries. Time is progressing and society has changed, the conception of administrative activities become more and more complicated, but the administrative target "to comfort people" by Confucianism is still not out of date and its universality has been verified by history.

II. The Leadership Wisdom with Virtue as First

"Rule by virtue" is the most prominent sign that distinguishes the administrative thought of Confucianism from the administrative thought of other schools. In The Analects of Confucius, Confucius puts forward: "to govern a state by virtue is like the Polaris in the position to which all the stars turn" ② Relying on the leaders' models and then educating subordinates and

---

① Xunzi: Wangzhi.
② Analects: Weizheng.

populace by virtues—these are basic notions of leadership "to govern a state by virtue" stressed by Confucianism.

"To rule by virtue" advocated by Confucianism requires leaders to observe social virtues and regulations and to set examples to attract the subordinates and populace to follow them so as to form one heart and one mind to realize the administrative target. Therefore, this is a style of leadership stressed on the guidance of virtue. Confucius believed that the fundamental sign to judge whether a leader is qualified or not is his virtue. It is not worth talking if a leader is conceited and stingy and had inferior virtue though his leading ability can compare with Lord Zhou. Here, we can see that the "to govern a state by virtue" stressed by Confucianism itself contains requirements of leaders to do their jobs as the examples.

So Confucianism believed that a leader is an example of the led, and his remarks and behaviors have demonstrative significance. A leader should pay attention to his own virtue cultivation and play a role of setting examples to be followed by his subordinates so as to bring the whole organization to raise virtue standard. Thereby the highest leader of the organization does not need to rack his brain to consider and handle the detail affairs in administration, and as a result he can concentrate his energy to enact and implement the virtue standards, and the organization would be able to be managed well. It seems to Confucianism that as a highest leader of an organization, what he should grasp is a standard of virtue, what he should do is to properly appoint and use his talents, and what he should cultivate is to train his virtue. Advocated by monarch and harmonized by ministers, and pioneered by monarch and followed by ministers, the advocated and pioneered here do not mean the affairs in detail, but mean the value orientation and spiritual guidance. Confucianism believed that so long as a leader could grasp well the value orientation and the value education of his subordinates, he would be able to manage a hundred by one.

Why can a leader get good administration results through "worship of virtue"? This is actually the relation of "good virtue making orders to be executed" which is repeatedly verified by Confucianism. Confucius said, "to stand straightly and no order is needed for action; to stand not straightly and observance is not made though order is given"①. Xun Zi made a hepapher that monarch is like a time-testing pole and the populace is like the shadow; if the pole is straight, the shadow is straight, too; a monarch is like a dish that holds water, his populace is like the water in the dish; if the dish is round, the shape of the water in the dish is round, too.

The theory of Confucianism is not essenttal a theory of governing a state. It stressed on rule by virtue. Confucianism considers that only talents of sage or above can serve as a leader or a manager of a state. Among these characters, the most important one is "virtue", and then the "talent". A real manager must possess both of them. Confucianism holds that in administrative activities, "virtue" is the most important personality. A real person of authority comes from his charisma of personality. Confucianism strongly emphasizes the influence of personality and requires a leader to cultivate his virtue and raise his virtue standard in order to use his influence to fulfill the task of administration. It seemed to Confucius that the so-called "to govern a state" means the rectification. This is to say a leader should rectify his virtue and conduct firstly; if a leader can firstly rectify his virtue and conduct, who dares not to rectify himself? If a leader firstly rectifies his virtue and conduct, populace would be willing to obey his orders. The virtue and conduct of a leader is like wind and the virtue and conduct of his servant is like grass; when the wind blows the grass, the grass would shake due to the way of the wind. For the same reason, how a leader is to do, the populace would follow him to do the same; how can a leader ask the populace to do what he is not willing to do?

Peter F. Drucker, a "social ecologist" in America, when writing the preface for his book *The Effective Executive* in 1985, pointed out: "what a book on the general administration talks is about how to manage others, but

---

① *Analects: Zilu.*

what this book talks is about how to effectively manage himself; a man who has the ability to manage well others is not a good manager, only those who have the ability to manage themselves can become good managers. In fact, people cannot expect those who cannot manage well themselves to manage well their organizations or mechanisms. Essentially speaking, administration is to set examples. Those who do not know to make their work effectively are in fact to set wrong examples. " [1]Rectifying oneself and others, and standing straightly in order to execute—these are the true meaning of administration known late by western Administrativists. And this, due to advocating by Confucianism and carrying out by managers, has already become a general knowledge in Chinese traditional administration.

III. The Wisdom for Business with Righteousness

The values of Confucianism can be summed up as" the combination of righteousness with interest". "Righteousness" here means the spiritual values (virtue value) and "interest" means the material value (including economic value). The relationship between righteousness and interest is the relationship between spiritual value and material value. Confucianism attempted to solve the conflict between "righteousness" and "interest" and to unify and merger the spiritual value with the material value.

In *The Analects of Confucius*, Confucius once said "A superior man knows righteousness and an inferior person knows interest. " [2]This said to, in fact, raised different requirements for managers and the managed. In those days of Confucius, "superior man" and "inferior person", besides the moral meaning, have the meaning of social stratum, namely indicate the managing stratum and the managed stratum at that time. Confucius, on the basis of admission of the social rulers' material interest, raised even higher virtue requirements towards the rulers; at the same time he stressed that only if the

---

①   P. F. Drucker , *The Effective Executive*, New York: Haper & Row , 1985.

②   *Analects: Liren.*

basic material requirements of the ruled were met, can they be guided by spirit.

"A superior man knows righteousness and an inferior person knows interest. " is later regarded by the people as the values of Confucius's righteousness and interest, and is explained as "superior man with noble virtue speaks of righteousness and inferior persons without virtue speaks of interest", actually this is a misunderstanding. In fact, this words in *The Analects of Confucius* is only to embody Confucius's different requirements and guidance towards the ruler and the ruled, and is not the values of righteousness and interest of Confucius himself. I consider that only another sentence quoted from Confucius by *Zuo's Commentary*, "using rites to implement righteousness, using righteousness to make interest, and using interest to pacify the people"[1]. That can entirely express Confucius's values of righteousness and interest, and is also the key for us to understand the meaning of the sentence. Here, "using rites to implement righteousness" before "using righteousness to make interest" is the expansion of that "superior man knows righteousness" which stresses on meeting the material interest of the managed; and the middle "using righteousness to make interest" is just the connecting point of the above and the below, namely the manager and the managed, the requirements of morals and the need of materials.

The proposition of "using righteousness to make interest" is in the key and core position in the theory of Confucius's as well as the Confucian administration philosophy. That is to say that according to the administration value theory of Confucianism, the thought of "using righteousness to make interest" should be carried out in the whole process of administrative activities. The administrative activities with so-called "using righteousness to make interest" is a process in which spiritual value establishes material value, at the same time restricts it, too. This process includes various links such as

---

[1]   *Zuozhuan: chenggong' ernian.*

"thinking righteousness when interest is gained" in value recognition, and " interest should be taken by righteousness " in behavior standard, "righteousness before interest " in practical effect and combination of righteousness with interest" in value judgment.

Confucius pointed out: "thinking righteousness when interest is gained, accepting order when danger appears, and don't forget for a long time ones words"①—It seemed to Confucius that here the " accomplishment of a person", namely a person with perfect virtue, should have both wisdom and courage and should be both versatile and have few desires as well. Beside these, he must also know rites, music, literature and arts. However, the most fundamental requirement he should have is "thinking righteousness when interest is gained".

Insofar as " interest should be taken by righteousness " is concerned, Confucius pointed out: "wealth and rank are desires of people, a man who should not get but got them would not enjoy them; poorness and lowliness are disgusting to people, a man who should not get but got them would not discard them. "② This was the earliest source of the so-called "monarch loved wealth but gained it with virtue".

Insofar as "righteousness before interest" is concerned, Xun Zi, another representative of Confucian school, puts out: "righteousness before interest is glory, but interest before righteousness is shame; glory is always unobstructed but the shame is always limited; the unobstructed always controls people but the limited is always controlled by others—this is the difference between the glory and the shame. " ③The meaning of this phrase is that people who value righteousness firstly and then make interest can get honor, and people who made interest at first and then speaking righteousness would get shame; people who got honor were always understandable but people who got shame

---

① *Analects: Xianwen.*

② *Analects: Liren.*

③ *Xunzi: Rongru.*

were always embarrassed; understandable people always controlled others but shame embarrassed people were always controlled by others. This was the fundamental difference between honor and shame.

Insofar as"combination of righteousness with interest" is concerned, the prevailing viewpoint is that in value judgment, Confucianism holds that "valued righteousness is above interest". I also used to accept this viewpoint in the past, but through my study, I found that Confucius, Mencius, Xun Zi, and other philosophers before Qin Dynasty indeed "valued righteousness", but they did not "lighten interest". When Mencius met King Liang Huiwang, he started with "why speaking interest" and ended with "why speaking interest". His real attempt is not to deny interest but stress that the ruler should take lead to speak righteousness so as to gain more interest. Confucius "rarely spoke interest" but advocated that "wealth and rank were desires of people" ① he admitted the reasonableness of interest seeking and required the ruler to gain "the interest needed by the people" ② and to seek wealth for the people. Therefore, generally speaking the basic value and position of Confucianism before Qin Dynasty should be " valuing righteousness but not lightening interest" and its value judgment should be "combination of righteousness and interest".

In the aspect of the"stressing on righteousness", there were large amount of expositions by Confucian philosophers before Qin Dynasty. Confucius pointed out " superior man valued righteousness as 'shang' (above everything) ". ③"Shang" here means "worship" and "nobility". "Shang Yi" means "stress on righteousness". Mencius said "fish was a desire to me, and bear's paw was a desire to me too; if both can not be gained concurrently, I would take bear's paw and discard the fish; I wanted to live and to be righteous too, if I can not get both of them concurrently, I would devote my

---

① Analects: Liren.
② Analects: Yaoyue
③ Analects: yanghuo

life to keep righteousness "① Life is the most important interest to mankind and righteousness is the highest value of life, both of them are the needs of human, but when there is a contradiction between them, Mencius stands for sacrificing life to keep the righteousness. Here "righteousness" is valued to be more important than life; other material interests can not even compare with this; this is, of conne, the meaning of "stressing on righteousness".

Confucian philosophers before Qin Dynasty also clearly knewthe relativity and compatibility between righteousness and interest. Xun Zi thought that "both righteousness and interest are needed by people" ②Here he clearly points out that both righteousness and interest are indispensable to persons, and wise sages like Yao and Shun also couldn't reject the material needs of people; and fatuous directors like Jie and Zhou also couldn't forbid the spiritual pursuance of the people; if a director would value righteousness, righteousness would restrain interest; if a director would value interest, interest would control righteousness; if righteousness would restrain interest; all would be at peace; if interest would control righteousness, the world would be in tumult. All of these were important warnings to the rulers.

IV. The Wisdom for Organization with Harmony

"Harmony is noble" is put forward firstly by *You Ruo*, a disciple of Confucius. He said that "in performance of rites, harmony should be regarded as nobleness, this is the best tradition which applies to all things; but that man only knows ' the nobleness of harmony' won't do, and that to violate rites speaks ' harmony' absolutely won't do" ③ Here, the nobleness of harmony in the administrative activities is affirmed to say that in rulers' governing state, harmonious atmosphere in organization can be created and things can be properly handled. Harmony in administration involves the administrative

---

① *Mencius : Gaozi*, Part 1.

② *Xunzi: Dalue.*

③ *Analects: Xue' er*

standard—sticking to principles and involves relation handling principles—harmony but existing difference.

"To take harmony as nobleness ", here, " nobleness " means preciousness, which contains the meaning of nobleness judgment. The so-called "nobleness of harmony" is meant that harmony is the most valuable under the Heaven and the best status in the world. Why does harmony possess such a high value? Confucius here affirmed the role played by harmony from the perspective of state-ruling. He considered that the stability of a country does not depend on how much wealth there is, but on whether the distribution is fair; and nor does it depend on how big a population there is but on whether the people's minds are set rightly. "There were no poverty if equality could be realized, and it were not alone if harmony could be realized, and a state would not decline if the people were at peace. "[1] That is to say, if the distribution is fair, people would not feel poor, a harmoneous organization would not comfort just a few people, and a stable and peaceful state has no danger. Mencius put forward a viewpoint that "the time isn't as important as the terrain, but the terrain isn't as important as unity with the people. " He cited an instance that a small town with only three kilometers in side and seven kilometers around which could be said very small, but the enemy, after several attacks, could not conquer it—this proved that "the time isn't as important as the terrain"; he cited another instance that there is another town with high city-wall, deep city-moat, good weapons and enough food which could be said very firm, but when the enemy came, all town guards escaped—this proved that "the terrain isn't as important as unity with the people. " [2]Harmony within an organization depends on whether the people support it or not. It seemed to Mencius that speaking of a country, the so-called "close border", "dangerous mountain ranges" and "sharp weapons"—all of these are only external things, and only the support or opposition of the

---

[1]   *Analects: Jishi.*

[2]   *Mencius : Gongsunchou*, Part 2.

people is the key to the victory or failure of a war, and the survival or downfall of a country. And if a ruler wants to get supports from the people, he must implement a correct way of ruling the country—"A just cause enjoyed abundant support while unjust cause found little support". Adhering to the correct way of ruling country, the leader and the people would be able to be single-minded and ever-victorious.

Xun Zi raised the concept of "group" which, from the structure, expounded the harmony within the organization. It seemed to Xun Zi that people are the noblest animals. The strength of people is not as big as cows, people don't run as fast as horses but cows and horses are driven by people. Why? The reason is that human beings can get well with each other. "Why can human beings get well with each other? Mencius said that this is because of duty and rights. How can duty and rights be carried out? Mencius said that this is because of righteousness. Therefore, if righteousness is implemented by duty and rights, harmony is obtained; harmony makes people single-minded, which mean more strength, which means power and power means something by which to win victory. " [1]Here, it involves three aspects: Firstly, to grade administration; secondly, the members' coordination; and thirdly, organized integration. According to Xun Zi's viewpoint, "harmony is one and one means power". If the relation within the organization has been coordinated, and the members in the organization can be as one heart and one mind and united as one, then, as a result, the strength of the organization would become stronger. Aristotle, a philosopher of ancient Greece, once put forward a famous proposition, which says that "the whole is greater than the sum of parts". Modern organizational theory also points out that the essential role of human organization is to converge and amplify manpower resources. Exposition of Xun Zi here is a mere coincidence with them.

Here, the "harmony" praised highly by Confucianism is definitely not the same as "holding harmony for the sake of harmony", but is to admit

---

[1]   *Xunzi: Wangzhi.*

difference and to seek good co-existing and coordinating status. Confucius, from the angle of the difference between the monarch and his subjects, pointed out the differences between "harmony" and "Tong" (integrity). He said that "a superior man holds harmony but allows differences and the inferior people stand for integrity but not harmony. " [1]"Harmony" here means something that consists of many different or opposed factors, and these opposed factors at the same time are mutually supplemented and coordinated, and formed new status and produced new things; and "Tong" (integrity) here means no different factors, no different voices and no different opinions but mere addition of integrity things, which can not produce new status and things.

Ancient Classic *Guo Yu* (国语) and *Zuo's Commentary* (左传) once made some expositions about the difference between " harmony" and "integrity". *Guo Yu* points out that "harmony can produce things but integrity has no succession. " Metal, wood, water, fire, and soil (five elements), matching each other, could produce different things on the earth; sour, sweet, bitter, hot and salt (five flavors), mutually mixing, could produce tastes that suited people's tastes; different tunes, mixing together, could produce pleasing music. "Harmony" is the law that can produce all things on the earth and "integrity" is only addition of things and has no mutual supplement and action of opposed things and therefore could not produce new things. *Zuo Commentary* records a paragraph said by Qi Prime Minister Yan Ying to Marquis Qi which gave exposition of the connotation of "harmony but not integrity" in detail. He points out that the key of "harmony" is regulation. Yan Ying also points out that the principles of harmony are like various ingredients, such as sauce, vinegar, salt, plum, etc. If there was too little, you put more, if there was too much, you reduced some, and only in such a way could you feel that the food tasted good and have a happy mood.

This was like a chef cooking food and a musician playing music; if there

---

[1]   *Analects: Zilu*

were no ingredients and only water, the chef could not process good soup; and if the musician only played one tune, the music was not beautiful.

It seemed to Confucianism, that "harmony but not integrity" should become a fundamental principle to handle the relation between the higher and the lower. In the process of administration, if the higher thought that something was right but there existed something incorrect, the lower should point out the wrong or imperfect part; if the higher level thought something is wrong but there contains something right, the lower should point out the right to eliminate the wrong. The ideal status of the higher and the lower is harmonious but not trended to; the lower should seek truth from facts and uphold truth; and genuinely assisted the higher in work but not blindly follow the higher level's opinions so as to achieve "harmony but not integrity".

V. The Wisdom for Coordination with Application of Mean

To realize harmony of organization, it is necessary, on the one hand, to keep the difference amongorganization members and encourage the organization members to hold up their own opinions and to practice harmony but not blindly follow others, and on the other hand, to keep certain tolerance and to control contradictions or disputes within the reasonable scope. Traditional Chinese culture stresses on harmony and coordination, but at the same time respects and encourages personal opinions, values and ideals. Confucian Classic *The Doctrine of the Mean* points out: "what keeps a superior man strong and brave is harmony, but not drifting with the current. " It considered that being good at getting well with others but not drifting with current is the first condition for a monarch to become a staunch man. If "harmony" had no "rites" to restrict it, some excessive or inferior actions would occur, and harmony and coordination would not be realized; only "harmony but not drifting with current" can maintain the real coordinating relations between the people. "Harmony but not drifting with current" affirms the mettle of "harmony" with reservation and grace with strength.

"Harmony" with reservation and "harmony agreeable to reservation" requires certain tolerance in administration. This, in the Confucianism's wisdom of administration, is prominently expressed as the thinking mode of the "Mean".

The thought of the Mean originates from the thought of the "Mean" worship and harmonious worship of the ancient times. Rao stressed that ruling of society must "allow to use Mean, and not excessively to pursue a certain aspect. Shun was just the person who could correctly master this principle, so Rao passed the throne to Shun. Shang Dynasty Ruler Pan Geng required the public to "think and work together with one heart" and Lord Zhou advocated implementation of "virtues of the Mean". In *The Analects of Confucius*, Confucius said, "The Mean, as a virtue, is the highest, but it has been a long time that common people lack of this virtue. " ① He considered that there generally existed "going too far or not going far enough" in the then society and lacked consciousness of relying on the principle of the Mean to do things, therefore he advocated the Mean to be a principle for people to conduct themselves and to do things.

The Mean, as a thinking mode, is just as what Confucius says: "deduction of two ends". He said that "do I have knowledge? certainly, I have no knowledge; a country folk asked me, I knew nothing about his question. I only asked the question in the way of deduction of the two ends; in such a way I entirely made clear the problem" ②The Doctrine of the Mean, as a kind of behavior standard, is just what Confucius advocated "neither going too far nor not going far enough".

Zi Gong asked, "Shi and Shang, who was virtuous? Confucius answered: that Shi has mistakes and is not as good as Shang. Zi Gong said: But teacher was better than him. Confucius said: Going too far is as bad as not going far enough. " ③"Deduction of two ends" and "I had mistakes and was not as good

---

①   *Analects: Yongye.*

②   *Analects: Zihan.*

③   *Analects: Xianjin.*

as Shang" were the basic connotations of Confucius's "Doctrine of the Mean".

"Deduction of two ends" meant that a matter had two ends and "I had mistakes and was not as good as Shang" meant gonging too far and not going far enough—in short, no matter it's things or people, they certainly had "end". Because of the influence of this thinking, people often regarded the middle as "neither going too far nor not going far enough". Actually this kind of understanding did not conform to the original meaning of Confucianism.

In fact, so-called "Mean" of Confucianism had neither "two ends" nor "the middle". Each sticking to one end is a peephole view and exclusively sticking to the middle is one-side action, both of which are vigorously opposed by Confucianism. Judging from this, to achieve the "Mean", it is necessary to have "expediency". Concerning the relation between the two, Chen Chun of Southern Song Dynasty had a good saying: "expediency meant taking action according to circumstances; ' monarch's words and actions should conform to the doctrine of Mean'; conforming to the doctrine of Mean was expediency; the conventions of heaven and earth was the truths of ancient and today; the universal truth in modern or ancient time was expediency; what was the difference between expediency and the Mean? someone asked: understanding of the Mean can make expediency and can know expediency and the Mean, some one answered; the Mean, of course, meant going neither too far nor not far enough; and expediency meant to take the reasonable result in estimation of things, which is going neither too far nor going not far enough. " ①The "Mean" is the objective truth and expediency is action adopted by the subject; the essence of the both is going neither too far nor not far enough, so they are both exterior and interior.

Sticking to truth and reaching expediency in administration requires administrative people not only to adhere to fairness, but also to dare to break common convention. Mencius said, "Tang used ' Mean ' as principle to

---

① *Beixiziyi: Jingquan.*

manage state affairs and appointed saints without sticking to one pattern. " ①
Zheng Xuan explained: "pattern is convention", and Jiao Xun said: "there is
no convention but virtuous in talent appointment" which means allowing
expediency when sticking to truth". So-called "appointing saints without
sticking to one pattern" is the example cited by Mencius: "Shun is appointed
from field, Fu Yue was appointed from architecture, Jiao Ge was appointed
from selling fish and salt, Guan yuwu was set free from jail and appointed as
official, Sun Shuao was appointed to the Court from his seclusion, and Bai
Lixi is appointed as Prime Minister from the marketplace. "② Of these state's
famous historical governing talents, one was a peasant, one is an original
bricklayer, one is a fish and salt dealer and one is at first a criminal…they
totally have no fixed growing mode, but the managers, "by extension and no
fixed pattern", appointed talents and ruled state well. The word "by
extension" here contained the truth of the Mean in sticking to truth but
maintaining expediency which suited to any administrative activities.

From the view of it, the administrative thought of Confucianism is wide
and profound, and contains abundant contents. Comparing with the western
science of administration, the administrative wisdom of Confucianism that
stresses on humanism and personal development has unique value in modern
activities of administration.

---

① *Mencius : Lilou, ,* Part 2.

② *Mencius : Gaozi,* Part 2.

The Analects of Confucius and Rebuilding of Modern People's Spirit

Gu Zhi-ming
(Nankong Political Institute)

[**Abstract**]   It has become a global issue to loss the spiritual home in modern days, the ideas and comments of Confucius in ancient China are still golden sayings which give import ant enlightenment to us nowadays: the values of life, happiness and glory are essentially attitudes towards life, cultivation and transcendence of life, rather than abundant material conditions. We should make a great effort to fulfill self-cultivation and nurture relationship within family members and friends in a creative way. To be a self-respecting and moral person no matter poor or rich can help modern people to get away from difficulties and enter the realm of clear and bright.

[**Key words**] the Analects of Confucius; modern people; rebuilding of spiritual home

As we can see a world through a classic literature, the Analects of Confucius exhibit a clear and bright world of human's spirit. Looking around the world, the loss of spiritual home has become a global problem. Modern people seem to have everything, but find themselves difficult to rebuild their spiritual home. By reading the classic of ancient China, you will find its ideas and comments are still golden rnles which have become important guidelines of real lives for us to rebuilt our spiritual home.

Self-Cultivation, The Golden Key To Open The Modern People's Spiritual Door

All the difficulties of modern people's existence give prominence to many modernistic problems. Over-extended of technology and economic rationality as well as the increasing capital "objective authority" have been making people more and more material, some people are getting used to value themselves in a market-oriented way, to chasing fame and fortune, They separate spirit from material, purpose from means. There the modern people's morality, emotion and even the entire inner world have been seriously underestimated and even become "desertification". Modern people has become busier and richer than anytime before, however, they feel more lost, confused and disturbed. Daniel Bell, who is popular for his advocating the theory of post- industrial society, remind people of this world again and again to be highly on guard against the powerful "inhumanization incline" in modern society. ① In this case, besides institutional solutions of modernistic problems, self-cultivation of individuals, to which the Analects of Confucius have provided wealthy resources, becomes especially important.

Self-cultivation is especially emphasized in the *Analects* by Confucius. It begins with that benevolence is the basic rule of human beings and comes first in the Analects by Confucius. Confucius said, "A young man should be a good son at home and an obedient young man abroad, sparing of speech but trustworthy in what he says, and should love the multitude at large but cultivate the friendship of his fellow men. If, after all these activities, he has any energy to spare, let him use it to making himself cultivated. "② Confucius also said, " What can a man do with who is not benevolent? What can a man

---

① Daniel Bell. *The End of Ideology*. Translated by Zhang Guo-qing. Jiangsu People' Publishing House. 2001. p. 21.

② The Analects of Confucius: Book 1.

do with who is not benevolent?"① This shows that one can only making himself cultivated as well as learning rites and music on the basis of benevolence. Confucius also believes that only benevolent people can selflessly treat others and get people's praise. " It is the benevolent man alone who is capable of liking or disliking other men. "② What should we do to become benevolent? Yan Yuan asked about benevolence, Confucius said: "To return to the observance of the rites through overcoming the self constitutes benevolence. If for a single day a man could return to the observance of the rites through overcoming himself, then the whole Empire would consider benevolence to be his. "③ It is clear that we are not born to be benevolent, self cultivation and control is the only way for us to become a benevolent man. For this reason, Confucius also made external standard of benevolence: "Unbending strength, resoluteness, simplicity and slowness of speech are close to benevolence. "④ He also put forward five action principles to cultivate a benevolence: " They are respectfulness, tolerance, trustworthiness in word, quickness and generosity. "⑤ Confucius said that if a man is respectful he will not be treated with insolence, if he is tolerant he will win the multitude, if he is trustworthy in word his fellow men will entrust him with responsibility, if he is quick he will achieve results, if he is generous his fellow men will be willing to do his biding. Confucius believes that a man who can implement these five virtues will be regarded as benevolence.

It gives specially emphasis on the usualness, consciousness and all-sidedness of self-cultivation in the *Analects* of Confucius. "Every day I examine myself on three counts. In what I have undertaken on another's behalf, have I failed to do my best? In my dealings with my friends have I failed to be trustworthy in what I say? Have I failed to practise repeatedly

---

① The Analects of Confucius: Book 3.
② The Analects of Confucius: Book 4.
③ The Analects of Confucius: Book 12.
④ The Analects of Confucius: Book 13.
⑤ The Analects of Confucius: Book 17.

what has been passed on to me?"① That means to stress the need to reinforce self-cultivation consciously and continually. "He has not lived in vain who dies in the evening, having been told about the Way in the morning. "② It also emphasizes all-sidedness of self-cultivation in the *Analects* of Confucius. "I set my heart on the Way, base myself on virtue, lean upon benevolence for support and take my recreation in the arts (rites, music, shooting, driving, odes and maths). "③ It is the only way to be a good man. Confucius believes that self-cultivation is often constrained by various factors, so we need to improve our inner quality in many fields. "Be stimulated by the Odes, take your stand through the help of the rites and be perfected by music. "④ Confucius also warns that there are three things the gentleman should guard against and nine things the gentleman turns his thought to. The three things are "In youth when the blood and qi (It is the basic constituent of the universe. The refined qi fills the human body and, amongst other things, circulates with the blood.) are still unsettled he should guard against the attraction of feminine beauty. In the prime of life when the blood and qi have become unyeilding, he should guard against bellicosity. In old age when the blood and qi have declined, he should guard against acquisitiveness. "⑤ And the nine things are "to seeing clearly when he use his eyes, to hearing acutely when he uses his ears, to looking cordial when it comes to his countenance, to appearing respectful when it comes to his demeanour, to being conscientious when he speaks, to being reverent when he performs his duties, to seeking advice when he is in doubt, to the consequences when he is enraged, and to what is right at the sight of gain. "⑥ In conclusion, a man should guard against his own desire at anytime, have strict demands on

---

①   The Analects of Confucius: Book 1.

②   The Analects of Confucius: Book 4.

③   The Analects of Confucius: Book 7.

④   The Analects of Confucius: Book 8.

⑤   The Analects of Confucius: Book 16.

⑥   Ibid.

himself at everywhere, and be close to a benevolence and virtue regardless of any circumstances. For this reason, Confucius emphasized that self-cultivation needs to be enhanced in various ways.

It also provides methods of self-cultivation in the Analects of Confucius. Have firm faith and be fond of learning "① and " Being widely versed in culture but brought back to essentials by the rites. "②" When you meet someone better than yourself, turn your thoughts to becoming his equal. When you meet someone not as good as you are, look within and examine your own self. "③ In the Analects of Confucius, it emphasizes that we should seek a way out of the Vanity Fair in our daily life, and make sure that the relationship between wealth and status, morality and benefits, principle and desire is well-handled: "Wealth and high station are what men desire, but unless I got them in the right way I would not abide in them. Poverty and low station are what men dislike, but even if I did not get them in the right way I would not try to take myself away from them. "④ Furthermore, wealth and high station, poverty and low station are relative, and people at different levels comprehend them differently. Wealth mainly means material values, while high station mostly refers to spiritual welfare. Only a spiritual wealthy people can well raise his values, then be close to the real "high station". As today's people are increasingly moving towards materialism and impetuosity, these thoughts in the Analects of Confucius seem particularly valuable.

Cultivating Natural Affection And Friendship To Rebuild The Spiritual Home Of Modern People

In the life, every one has a problem of spiritual home, regardless he is the official in the high position, the rich man toting myriads of cash around

---

① The Analects by Confucius: Book 8.
② The Analects of Confucius: Book 12.
③ The Analects of Confucius: Book 4.
④ Ibid.

the waist, or the common person. Natural affection and friendship is the important part of the person's spiritual home. "Who says the little soul of grass waving, could repay for the warmth of the spring sunlight?" Natural affection is forever the sincerest and deepest emotion, which doesn't need to be dissimulated, but is willing to be paid. In addition to natural affection, friendship is another kind of very precious emotion, which isn't supported by blood relationship; but true friends are of one mind, share weal and woe, encourage and console each other. Natural affection on the left side and friendship on the right side accompanies life, could never be divided, is the warm bay which the person looks forward to, the important spiritual pillar of human being. Modern social individuals are inclined to keep off others or are utilitarian when associate with others. The busy work, the nervous rhythm, the fierce competition, and the independent existence usually make some people despise natural affection and downplay friendship.

Natural affection and friendship, which was highly valued and detailedly elaborated in the Analects of Confucius, still stimulates deep thought when it is readen today.

Confucius treated "benevolence" as the supreme moral ideal. When FanChi asked him what is "benevolence"? Confucius answered: "Love your fellow men. "[1] Loving people concretely includes both sides contents: one is "loving family members"—to deal with relations between the close relatives; another is "respecting elder"—to deal with interpersonal relations in the society. Confucius thought that only when a person had done well in both sides then he can be said to achieve "benevolence".

How to deal well with the relation between close relatives? In the Analects of Confucius, it emphasizes to pay attention to the principles of filial piety, which are thought to be the root of acting as a man. Zilu asked what was the filial piety? Confucius said: " Nowadays for a man to be filial means no more than he is able to provide his parents with food. Even

---

[1]   The Analects of Confucius: Book 12.

hounds and horses are, in some way, provided with food. If a man shows no reverence, where is the difference?"① So the key point of the filial piety is to respect parents. Confucius asserted: "Observe what a man has in mind to do when his father is living, and then observe what he does when his father is dead. If, for three years, he makes no changes to his father's ways, he can be said to be a good son. "② Confucius also said: "In serving your father and mother you ought to dissuade them from doing wrong in the gentlest way. If you see your advice being ignored, you should not become disobedient but should remain reverent. You should not complain even if you are distressed. "③ Confucius specially emphasized that "it's your duty to do everything in your power to wait upon your parents"; it isn't filial to worry your parents because of your corruption or stealing or illegality in the society. All the parents hope that their sons and daughters have good moral qualities cmes are stronger than their parents. Such high expectations are the starting point that the parents educate their sons and daughters. So, it is of course filial to provide a first-rate material condition for the parents, but it is not the root of the filial piety. It's really filial to behave and act as a man according to the parents' wills and instructions, and win honor for the parents.

How to deal well with social interpersonal relations? Confucius insisted a liberal mindset about this problem. "Is it not a joy to have like-minded friends come from afar?"④ At the same time, the Confucius specially emphasized "trustworthiness". The Confucius said: "I don't see how a man can be acceptable who is untrustworthy in word. When a pin is missing in the yoke-bar of a large cart or in the collar-bar of a small cart, how can the cart be expected to go?"⑤ The trustworthiness is very important in a person's life.

---

① The Analects of Confucius: Book 2.
② The Analects of Confucius: Book 1.
③ The Analects of Confucius: Book 4.
④ The Analects of Confucius: Book 1.
⑤ The Analects of Confucius: Book 4.

There are many elaborations concerning trustworthiness in the Analects of Confucius. Confucius said: "To be trustworthy in word is close to being moral in that it enables one's words to be repeated. "① He also said: "He stands to benefit who makes friends with three kinds of people. Equally, he stands to lose who makes friends with three other kinds of people. To make friends with the straight, the trustworthy in word and the well-informed is to benefit. To make friends with the ingratiating in action, the pleasant in appearance and the plausible in speech is to lose. "②

Today, the network links up all people very closely, and isolates them in the meantime; the expanding world makes people's home wherever one is, but some people lose "home", wander about everywhere boundlessly and absentmindedly; makes people all within the four seas call each other brothers, but some people have no relative, or refuse to have anything to do with all kin and friends; the Earth becomes a "village", but an apathetic iceberg has been built in the deep places of some villagers' hearts...A fresh news showed, two people living in the same city suburban area in a certain Western developed country took the same train to go into the city to go to work every day for 15 years, but hadn't spoken one word to each other. ③ This kind of self-close association and life style usually leads to many mental or spiritual problems easily.

It has become the main topics of contemporary philosophy and social science that how to "look for the missing spiritual home", make the spirit "return home", adorn the human existence with beauty, make the mind has some concernments and then live a hearty life in the world. Cultivating natural affection and friendship, and making great efforts to construct the spiritual home for modern people, are the profound apocalypse which is given us in the Analects of Confucius.

---

① The Analects of Confucius: Book 1.
② The Analects of Confucius: Book 16.
③ The People Court Paper. May 28. 2010.

Striving To Practise And Create To Promote The Spiritual Realm Of Modern Peoole

It is very noble to face any hardship in fulfillment of moral cultivation. In the Analects of Confucius, it claims: The gentleman "puts into effect his words before allowing them to follow the deed"[1], is "conscientious and trustworthy and in deed single-minded and reverent"[2]. It's you moral duty to advocate practical fulfillment, to practice what you preach, to preach after your practice, to be loyal and keep faith and to be worthy of being depended on and wary. Confucius thought, people like this will be welcome all over the world. The gentleman is "slow of speech but quick in action"[3]. That is, the gentleman is likely to be silent superficially, but be firm and resolute at heart, and so is equally esteemed highly by others. But there are persons who are good at "sweet words and flattery", indulge in exaggeration, "excel at talk rather than practice", Confucius thought that the such persons are really disgusting.

It should upgrade the moral realm in the personal practice of moral cultivation. Therefore, Confucius constructed the ideal personalities of gentleman. The world "gentleman" appeared more than one hundred times in the Analects of Confucius which have just more than twenty thousands. The "gentleman", as a concept of broad sense, is emphasizing the strength of personality, the ideal behavior style which Confucius pursued; it is lofty, but also attained by everyone who had done one's best in real life. Therefore, it brings forward the demands for gentle's personality as follows in the Analects of Confucius:

Firstly, to be kind at heart. The person who repairs his ego first to attain perfectness and affluence at heart, then displays leisurely and magnanimous

---

[1] The Analects of Confucius: Book 2.

[2] The Analects of Confucius: Book 15.

[3] The Analects of Confucius: Book 4.

presence, is a gentleman whose powers come from his personalities and heart. So, the gentleman should have a kind heart, and be virtuous. Confucius advocated: the gentleman should "love the multitude at large but cultivate the friendship of his fellow men"①, "help others to take their stand in that he himself wishes to take his stand, and get others there in that he himself wishes to get there"②, "help others to effect what is good", "be free from worries and fears", "be introspective and find nothing to reproach himself for"③, not to swindle and cheat others, put himself in another's position, not to do to others as you would not wish done to yourself, to behave on the up-and-up, to have a clear conscience, don't do ungrateful act at ordinary times, Don't be not afraid of ghost to knock on door at the midnight. Confucius emphasized again and again that the goodness is benevolence, honest, to behave righteously, friendly, lenient, not to haggle ever every ounce, to illuminate others, to warm oneself, to keep gentleness, peace and calm at heart, filled with sunshine in life and vigorous.

Secondly, to have the courage to take on heavy responsibilities. To be kind is the first demand on gentleman personality, the premise of becoming a gentleman; but it's not enough, one also need to brave to take the social responsibilities. Confucius said: "A Gentleman who is attached to a settled home is not worthy of being a Gentleman. "④ "A Gentleman must be strong and resolute, for his burden is heavy and the road is long. He takes benevolence as his burden. Is that not heavy? Only with death does the road come to an end. Is that not long? "⑤ It needs to have a vast outlook, to own a hard-bitten volition, to believe "the load is heavy while the way is long", to strive for ideality unremittingly, to spare no effort in the performance of one's duty to the end of one's days. Such a sense of responsibility evolved into the

① The Analects of Confucius: Book 1.
② The Analects of Confucius: Book 6.
③ The Analects of Confucius: Book 12.
④ The Analects of Confucius: Book 14.
⑤ The Analects of Confucius: Book 8.

concept that the gentleman should "regulate the family", "rule the state" and "govern the motherland", "each common person is responsible for the motherland's flourishing or eclipse", which belong to Chinese Confucian personality. Confucius said, the person who just likes above-mentioned is a true gentleman. Confucius emphasized that in order to take on the responsibility of developing the motherland, the gentleman should be rigidly self-disciplined, not to cover up his laws and mistakes. "The gentleman's errors are like an eclipse of the sun and the moon in that when he errs the whole world sees it and when he reforms the whole world looks up to it. "[1] At the same time, the gentleman should "be versed in what is moral" rather than "what is profitable"[2] persistently, "cherish benign rule" rather than "his native land" persistently, "cherish a respect for the law" rather than "generous treatment"[3] persistently. That is, the gentleman should attach importance to and reconstruct justice principles, moralities, law systems, rather than think a lot of and pursue benefits, immovable estate and boon excessively. The gentleman should be friendly, willing to hold intercourse with others, good at holding others together, but not obey the denominationalism, be "conscious of his own superiority without being contentious, and comes together with other gentlemen without forming cliques"[4]. Confucius thought, the true gentleman should "cultivate himself and thereby achieves reverence", "cultivate himself and thereby bring peace and security to his fellow men", "cultivate himself and thereby bring peace and security to the people"[5].

Finally, to be free and conscious. That is the highest level of the gentleman personality pursued in the Analects of Confucius. As Confucius thought, to be a gentleman is to be the greatest of yourself, to be good at ego

---

[1] The Analects of Confucius: Book 19.

[2] The Analects of Confucius: Book 4.

[3] Ibid.

[4] The Analects of Confucius: Book 15.

[5] The Analects of Confucius: Book 14.

orientation, to act personally, to practise every little bit, "to object to flattery
when he is poor and be opposed to self-importance when he is rich", to be
"big-hearted", to be leisurely and calmly, to be free from worries and fears,
to be composed by the ups and downs of life. "To cultivate the Way is to
cultivate one's heart. " Confucius especially paid attention to leading and
encouraging people to look at his own heart, attach importance to construction
of his own mind, strive to cultivate inward faith and ability of keeping calm.
"The Three Armies can be deprived of their commander, but there is no way
a common man can be deprived of his purpose. "① There are contradictions in
the process of carrying out the ambitions, "for gentlemen of purpose and men
of benevolence while it is inconceivable that they should seek to stay alive at
the expense of benevolence, it may happen that they have to accept death in
order to have benevolence accomplished"②, in the meantime, "not to murmur
against heaven and blame others"③, not been influenced by nonego, be
diligent, exertive and persevering to attain the free realm of "understanding
the Decree of Heaven", "attuning the ear", "following one's heart's desire
without overstepping the line"④. Confucius thought that if a person once
attained such a realm he would be worldly-wise and erudite, grasp the outside
world profoundly, respect others farthest, give audience to different kinds of
opinions open-mindedly, ponder in others' position, think and practise
without overstepping the line.

"In the highly modernized globalization age, we are developing More and
more quickly, but we have lost our orientation. " Modern people's lives
present vagarious phenomena: to understand the nature profoundly, while
cherish her superficially; to grasp outside world positively, while comprehend
human ourselves superficially; to pursue material wealth strugglingly, while
cultivate our spirits inadequately, under such a circumstance, It is difficult

① The Analects of Confucius: Book 9.
② The Analects of Confucius: Book 15.
③ The Analects of Confucius: Book 14.
④ The Analects of Confucius: Book 2.

for some people to find the right niches for themselves, so they have to "wander about everywhere boundlessly and trancedly". In the *Analects* of Confucius, It reveals the truth of life: the true happiness and honor is irrehent to the abundant material wealth, if consists in the transcending of life attitude, and cultivation and realm. To absorb positive spiritual nutrient in the *Analects* of Confucius is helpful for us to get rid of the puzzledom and enter the realm of brightress.